THE FIELDING SCHOLAR PRACTITIONER:

Voices from 45 years of Fielding Graduate University

Library of Congress Cataloging-in-Publication data
The Fielding Scholar Practitioner by Katrina S. Rogers (Ed.)
and Monique L. Snowden (Ed.)
1. Education systems – higher learning.

THE FIELDING SCHOLAR PRACTITIONER:

Voices from 45 years of Fielding Graduate University

Edited by
Katrina S. Rogers, PhD and Monique L. Snowden, PhD

Fielding University Press

Table of Contents

PART II: FIELDING'S ACADEMIC VISION: AN INDEPENDENT GRADUATE SCHOOL TAKES SHAPE

PART III: RESEARCH BY FIELDING SCHOLAR-PRACTITIONERS

FOREWORD
Michael B. Goldstein, JD, D.H.L (Hon.)

In my address to the Fielding community, upon being awarded the high honor of Doctor of Humane Letters, I observed that a Fielding graduate student goes through a very distinctive learning experience. Each Fielding student – I prefer to call them "learners" – essentially creates, within surprisingly wide boundaries, her or his own version of a sophisticated and rigorous graduate education. That is an exceptional opportunity that in significant measure is as important as the substantive learning experience, in itself a life changing experience. To a considerable measure, that is why Fielding is a unique institution. More to the point in writing the opening to this collection of essays by Fielding faculty and alumni, as well as important contributions to the body of human knowledge by Fielding graduates, this is the reason why I believe Fielding learners and graduates are so exceptional, and why Fielding Graduate University is such an important part of the global higher education community.

We like to say that being a Fielding learner is transformational. What does that mean? All graduate schools tell us that their curriculum emphasizes the mastery of a body of knowledge and the attainment of a set of advanced intellectual skills, such as critical thinking, cognitive complexity, research methodology, and scholarly writing. And many succeed admirably in this task, as of course does Fielding. It is, however, the rare institution that dares to try to create a framework for graduate education that involves one's heart as well as one's mind.

In *The Courage to Teach*, Parker Palmer notes that "to educate is to guide students on an inner journey toward more truthful ways of seeing and being in the world." That is truly a lofty goal. It is also the fountainhead of the Fielding learning philosophy: to guide the student to become an effective and creative learner on his or her own terms. A core strength of the distinguished faculty that work with Fielding learners is their unfailing commitment to this ideal. Teaching is the process of imparting knowledge. Learning is the vehicle by which knowledge can be transformed into positive social change in the service of creating a more just and humane world. Fielding faculty deeply understand both the commonality of, and difference between, those terms.

As a member of the Fielding Board of Trustees for a quarter of a century with the privilege of having served as Chair, I witnessed this process unfold over and over. During that long span of time I experienced challenges, leadership changes, the development of new programs and new ways of thinking about content, and of course I watched with considerable pride as each cohort of learners moved through the university. What was present at the creation of the then-Fielding Institute, and what has endured and continues to this day, is a unique and all-encompassing learning environment that combines the transmission of knowledge and skills, intellectual challenge, and the development of the learner as a humane as well as educated person.

When we talk about the 21st Century University, we tend to think in technological terms: the application of artificial intelligence, data analytics, and immersive learning technologies. But there is another definition, one that I believe accurately describes the Fielding Graduate University: a community where students become learners and where learners become effective and compassionate citizens of the world, committed not just to apply their knowledge to their vocations but their hearts to the cause of a just and humane world. The former cannot exclude the later, at least not if we are to survive as a species. Fielding is in fact a shining example of the 21st Century University, and the world is a better place for it.

As you read the stories told here by alumni and faculty, and consider the sampling of work done by Fielding learners, what I hope stands out for you—as it has for me—is their connectedness. Together they weave a complex tapestry that is the Fielding experience, in all its glory.

About the Author

Mike Goldstein is Senior Counsel and founder of the education practice at Cooley, LLP, a global law firm. He was formerly an Associate Vice Chancellor and Associate Professor of Urban Sciences at the University of Illinois at Chicago and Assistant City Administrator and Director of University Relations for the City of New York. He has been at the forefront of technological change in higher education and an advocate for intelligent regulation that advances the interests of learners by stimulating innovation.

DEDICATION

To our Fielding students—past, present, and future—whose reflective and reflexive lines of inquiry and research yield practice and scholarship that has, is, and will positively impact the lives of individuals, groups, organizations, and communities. As we now proclaim, "Change the World: Start with Yours."

President Katrina S. Rogers and Provost and Senior Vice President Monique L. Snowden
Santa Barbara, California

INTRODUCTION

Katrina S. Rogers, PhD
President, Fielding Graduate University

"Will your organization be part of my study?" they pressed. "I want to understand the different worldviews between moderate and radical conservation organizations and your organization would be my case study for the moderate mindset." Having been assigned this doctoral student researcher because I was the only one on staff with a PhD, I was both puzzled and intrigued. Puzzled as they did not fit the mold of my mental picture of a doctoral student—they already had a career, for example, and did not seem bound to the traditional academic career track. Intrigued as well as they were particularly well versed across different literatures, including theories of leadership, environmental policy, and organizational behavior. Admittedly, my first reaction was an internal sigh—so much to do, so little time—how could I possibly be a liaison for a doctoral student in any meaningful way? But the more they spoke, the more I realized several things: they had a close relationship with their dissertation committee and a clear sense of purpose based on their many years of experience in the sector. Honestly, the more I listened, the more curious I became.

Although I didn't realize the significance of this interaction at the time, I filed away the name of the institution, Fielding Graduate University. As our working relationship continued to unfold, I found myself increasingly drawn into this student's educational experience in an unusual doctoral program. Our conversations often reflected the philosophical foundations of their learning experience with Fielding. Several concepts stood out. The first was the idea of a graduate education focused on the "adult" learner, that is, a learner with a mature mindset that brings their full selves to the learning (Merriam, 2001). Malcolm Knowles, one of Fielding's first faculty members, brought the idea of andragogy to the institution, defined as the art and science of helping adults learn (Knowles, 1980, p. 43). Important to this concept is the notion of adulthood as a psychological state in which the learner develops a self-concept striving toward independence (Beeson, 2018). This independence is key to the faculty and students ability to co-create a robust learning environment. This is not about maturity in the sense of responsibility, but the adult learner is at a different psychological stage in terms of synthesis, knowledge and integration. Fielding faculty members understand that, which helps colleges like ours stand out (Rogers, 2018).

As this framework evolved within Fielding's doctoral programs and later with master's and certificates, faculty investigated and added key concepts to Knowles' initial conceptualization: the importance of self-direction, the role of mentoring, the centrality of the scholar-practitioner and the practitioner-scholar, and the possibilities of transformation.

Figure 1: Andragogy in Practice - Knowles' six assumptions about adult learners
(Adapted from Knowles, Holton, and Swanson, 2005)

As educators striving to create high quality learning environments for adult learners, Knowles elaborated on these assumptions. First, it is important that the learning environment take into consideration the learner's need to know the why, what, and how of the educational experience. Second, the self-concept of the learner as self-directing and autonomous needs to be evident in the operationalization of the curricula. Third, faculty can design curricula around the prior experience of the learner, and involve them as people with a variety of mental models and previous experience that they bring to their learning process. Four, Knowles suggested that adult learners are ready to learn from a developmental standpoint—that they are open to their own learning. Five, learners want practice based, problem centered learning environments that take into consideration broader institutional and societal contexts. Six, adult learners are internally motivated towards goal attainment and problem solving.

The Fielding student that included my institution in their doctoral research discussed how disorienting the first year of the program had been. For one thing, it was expected that they would create a learning plan that laid out their pathway ahead. As this student expressed, this was a new concept and one that was distressing because they expected to be told by faculty what to do and how to think about their work. Second, even the courses within a structured curricula, they observed, required self-direction and individual responsibility to complete.

As I eventually became part of Fielding initially as faculty and Associate Dean and later as Provost, then President, their story came back to me. I found that many Fielding faculty are intellectually congruent with Mezirow's ten phases for transformative learning. Phase 1 is the disorienting dilemma, which is often the shorthand for the entire theory. The full theory, however, is evident in Fielding's learning mindset.

Ten Phases of Transformative Learning

Phase 1 A disorienting dilemma
Phase 2 A self-examination with feelings of guilt or shame
Phase 3 A critical assessment of epistemic, sociocultural, or psychic assumptions
Phase 4 Recognition that one's discontent and the process of transformation are shared and that others have negotiated a similar change
Phase 5 Exploration of options for new roles, relationships, and actions
Phase 6 Planning of a course of action
Phase 7 Acquisition of knowledge and skills for implementing one's plans
Phase 8 Provisional trying of new roles
Phase 9 Building of competence and self-confidence in new roles and relationships
Phase 10 A reintegration into one's life on the basis of conditions dictated by one's perspective

Figure 2. Mezirow's (1978a, 1978b). Ten Phases of Transformative Learning (Adapted from Kitchenham, A., 2008

Creating an environment that supports disorientation, self-examination, critical assessment, and recognition followed by exploration, planning, and taking action requires an intentionality that the faculty at Fielding seek to create across their disciplines and knowledge bases. In the fourteen years I have been at Fielding, I have observed the many students who have moved through these phases and watched them blossom intellectually and personally as they develop competence, self-confidence (Phase 9) and finally, reintegration (Phase 10), all of which leads them to becoming effective scholar-practitioners.

Throughout this monograph, one can see all of these concepts supporting the adult learner and transformational learning expressed and shared across the university. In the first section, several alumni write about how their evolution from practitioner to scholar-practitioner inspired their life's work. Other alumni discuss their specific fields and research as they pertain to social change. The second section of this book is dedicated to a robust recounting as Fielding took shape as an independent graduate school. Faculty members explore learner centered education, the culture of scholarship and social justice, and adult transformative education. Our stories include the founding of some of our centers, new disciplines, new understandings of established disciplines, such as systemic learning about systems as well as reflections from long-time faculty members. The last section highlights students and faculty together for discussions on mentoring, personal transformations through research, and specific areas of research. Finally, Dr. Pam McLean, the long-time partner of our founder, Dr. Frederic Hudson, concludes with an afterword. All told, the tales we tell provide a small sampling of the rich, complex tapestry that is Fielding. Welcome!

References

Beeson, E. T. (2018). Andragogy. *The SAGE Encyclopedia of Educational Research, Measurement, and Evaluation*. Ed. B. Frey. https://dx-doi-org.fgul.idm.oclc.org/10.4135/9781506326139.n43.

Kitchenham, A. (2008). The evolution of John Mezirow's transformational learning theory. *Journal of Transformative Education.* Vol. 6, No, 2, April, 104-123.

Knowles, M. S., Holton, E. F.III, & Swanson, R. A. (2005). *Adult learner: The definitive classic in adult education and human resources development* (6th ed.). Burlington, MA: Elsevier.

Knowles, M. S. (1980). *The modern practice of adult education: From pedagogy to andragogy* (revised and updated). Englewood Cliffs, NJ: Cambridge Adult Education.

Mezirow, J. (1978a). *Education for perspective transformation: Women's re-entry programs in community colleges.* New York: Teacher's College, Columbia University.

Mezirow, J. (1978b). Perspective transformation. *Adult Education*, 28, 100-110.

Merriam, S. B. (2001). Andragogy and self-directed learning: Pillars of adult learning theory. *New Directions for Adult and Continuing Education*. No. 89, Spring.

Rogers, K. S. (2018). Staying top of mind for adult learners. *EvoLLLution*, November, https://evolllution.com/attracting-students/todays_learner/staying-top-of-mind-for-adult-learners/.

About the Author

Katrina S. Rogers, PhD, is President of Fielding Graduate University. As faculty, she has taught in her field of global environmental politics and policy, social movements, research, and theory. In the course of her career, Rogers has served in many roles, including executive, board member, and teacher. She led the European campus for Thunderbird School of Global Management in Geneva, Switzerland for a decade, working with international organizations such as the Red Cross, World Trade Organization, United Nations Development Program, and the European Union. She also developed externships for students at several companies, including Renault, Nestle, and EuroDisney (now Disneyland Paris). She holds doctorates in political science and history. In addition to many articles focused on organizational leadership in sustainability, Rogers currently serves on the Boards of Prescott College, the Master's in Sustainability Advisory Group for Northern Arizona University, the Toda Institute for Global Policy & Peace Research, First Nature Ranch, and the Public Dialogue Consortium. She has also worked in conservation as a leader with the Arboretum at Flagstaff and Grand Canyon Trust. She received both a Fulbright scholarship to Germany as well as a Presidential post-doctoral fellowship from the Humboldt Von Humboldt Foundation where she taught environmental politics and history at the University of Konstanz.

PART I

THE FIELDING IMPACT: ALUMNI VOICES

CHAPTER 1

JOINING FIELDING'S SCHOLAR-PRACTITIONER COMMUNITY: HOW MY PHD DEGREE LAUNCHED MY CAREER AS AN ART THERAPIST

Maxine Borowsky Junge, PhD

Professor Emerita, Loyola Marymount

In 1986 I was 44 years old, Associate Professor of Clinical Art Therapy and Marital and Family Therapy, and Chair of the Department at Loyola Marymount University in Los Angeles, when they told me I would never be promoted to full professor without a PhD. (No one seemed to care what kind, only that I had one.) I had always loved learning, and every time I got bored I considered going back to school, but a valued mentor, Dr. Barbara Solomon, told me "Don't go to school unless you know why you're going." Good advice. Now I knew why I was going.

I looked around the L.A. area at university mental health programs of various stripes and found them wanting, very wanting. Running out of possibilities, I decided I could keep my mouth shut long enough to get a PhD at USC, where I had earned a MSW 20 years before. I made an appointment with the dean of the School of Social Work who, after telling me they would like me to go there, said I would need to go to junior college for two semesters to take algebra so I could pass the GRE. I said "I'm too old for that!" I pushed, but the rule held and I said "Then I'm not coming here." And I didn't.

Some years before, I had heard about Fielding from an L.A. psychologist who had been on Fielding's initial regional accreditation site team. She said "Something interesting is going on there." So I decided to make a trip to Fielding's Santa Barbara headquarters to have a look. Staff and faculty I met were smart, funny, and full of life and the well-structured study guides I read were written in the female pronoun. Like the site visitor before me, I said "Something interesting is going on there." I applied.

While I was driving home on the Harbor Freeway after my entrance interview with Judy Stevens-Long at Cal State L.A., my car was clipped by a truck, sending it into an uncontrollable spin. I went careening across the lanes of traffic, watching approaching cars come at me and expecting to die, and finally crashing into the center divider. The car was totaled; I was unhurt. An omen? About Fielding? I decided it was a good omen that I was still alive!

For a long time I had been saddened at how few people at all, much less academics, were interested in any form of *action* toward change instead of merely studying, researching, and talking and talking and talking. Academics studied and researched. And then they studied and researched some more. Then they talked. I grew frustrated. One said to me "What's the use of doing it, if it hasn't been done before?" "That's exactly why I want to do it," I said. Many of them had never been out working in "real life" at all.

At Fielding I found doers, what they called "scholar-practitioners." The Human and Organizational Development (HOD) program was led by Don Bushnell and Anna DiStefano then. I discovered that the school, program, and faculty had a social justice and action bent and that they really meant it. They asked the tough questions and were willing to go deeply into the dark complex thickets of change. Wow! Another student and I, collaborated with two faculty members to diversify the HOD faculty. We searched out interesting, accomplished people of color and helped them through the unique, personal, and rigorous hiring process. Peter Park was our first. I had found him through a Loyola Marymount pastor that I knew and went to visit him at his apartment to convince him to apply at Fielding.

It's a cliché to say I found a home at Fielding, but I did. I found a sense of place and comfort I'd never known before, nor found since. There is something to be said about fitting in that is deeply satisfying. I loved the intense questioning and arguments that went on. It was safe to open my mouth for once and say what I really thought, as half-formed as my ideas might have been. Hard-wired as a social activist person, sick of all the right words in academia that actually meant very little, I found a true intellectual and practical commitment to change and inclusion at Fielding, a motivation I could admire, respect and, with integrity, be part of.

I had been a visual artist since childhood, a painter, critic, and art historian, and art became part of many of my Fielding projects and papers—such as "Paintings and Drawings in the Spirit of Different Personality Theorists", "Feminine Imagery and a Young Woman's Search for Identity", "The Perception of Doors, A Sociodynamic Investigation of Doors in 20th Century Painting." All of these projects started at Fielding; afterwards they were accepted in peer-reviewed journal articles and later appeared in a book, my favorite of all of them. My art was appreciated and supported more than it had ever been at art school or in MFA work, where the male-dominated philosophy and environment sought to critique and destroy the competition and to ignore women altogether.

I was lucky to have Will McWhinney as my mentor at Fielding. Will taught me confidence in my own far-ranging style and challenged me to expand it into the unknown. The word around Fielding was that Will could be abrupt and scary. It was rumored he had written "bullshit, bullshit, bullshit" on one student's paper. With me he was a constant, gentle guide, and also a pushy one, eager to dump me into the abyss to find the riches there, while he offered me support to climb my way out again. I consider my dissertation, a phenomenological study of visual artists and writers ("Creative realities, the search for meanings") the best work I have ever done. In it I created an important theory of creativity.

Since graduating from Fielding, I have published 10 books. (The eleventh, *An Art Psychotherapist Considers Mass Murders, Crereativity, Violence and Mental Illness*, is in process for 2019.) Many of them began as projects at Fielding and all are in its spirit. In 2012 I published *Graphic Facilitation and Art Therapy, imagery and metaphor in organizational development* with a magical Foreword by Charlie Seashore. I believe it was one of his last pieces before his death. Among many things, Charlie taught me the healing pleasures of humor.

With my first book, *A History of Art Therapy in the United States* (1994), I was able to make an important contribution to the profession of art therapy, the first inclusive history of art therapy ever. Sixteen years later, in 2010, *The Modern History of Art Therapy in the United States* was published. It is used as a text in graduate programs across the country.

My other books have primarily been about creativity and art therapy, but in 2016 a very different kind of book, reflective of my social action bent, was published, *Voices from the Barrio: Con Safos: Reflections of Life in the Barrio.* This was the story of the first ever independent Chicano literary magazine. In the late 1960s and 1970s during the movement for Chicano civil rights and school walkouts, I ran an arts and education program "Operation Adventure" in East Los Angeles (before I ever heard the words "Fielding" or "art therapy"), where I met and worked with the writers and artists who put together *Con Safos.* I published a poem in the journal "Upon submitting proposals for federally funded summer programs." My last book, in 2017, *Dear Myra, Dear Max,* was an epistolary about aging with Myra Levick.

After Fielding, I continued teaching at Loyola Marymount University, then Goddard College (Vermont) and Antioch University in Seattle. I teach, supervise, hold many kinds of groups, and mentor students and mental health practitioners in my living room on Whidbey Island, Washington, with the fire roaring and the ferries making their way across Puget Sound outside my window. I have continued to draw and paint, and won "Best of Show" at the Island County Fair for my Mass Murders Triptych, which was exhibited along with the usual paintings of cows, horses, and dogs.

Education should be transformative. Mostly it isn't. At Fielding it was. Although I am not the kind of alumna who comes to reunions, Fielding remains for me a touchstone of how it should be done and how it *could* be done.

By the way, I earned that promotion to full professor at Loyola Marymount and am now Professor Emerita.

References

Junge, M. (2008). *Mourning, memory and life itself, essays by an art therapist*. Springfield, IL: Charles C Thomas.

About the Author

Max is Professor Emerita at Loyola Marymount University in Los Angeles, where she was Chair of the Marital & Family Therapy/Clinical Art Therapy Department. She has also taught art therapy, psychology, and organization development at Immaculate Heart College (Hollywood), Goddard College (Vermont), and Antioch University (Seattle). An art psychotherapy clinician and consultant, she is considered a pioneer in the art therapy profession. Born and raised in Los Angeles during the Hollywood Blacklist period, Max is a lifelong visual artist. From Whidbey Island, Washington, where she has lived for 18 years, she has published nine books. The latest one, containing 15 years of her mass murders artwork, is *Mass Murders, Violence and Mental Illness* (in process, summer 2019).

CHAPTER 2

ON BECOMING AN AXIOLOGICAL HERMENEUT

Clifford G. Hurst
Westminster College

When introducing myself to college classes or to workshop participants I sometimes describe myself as an *axiological hermeneut.* This gets a mixed reaction of laughter, blank stares, and raised eyebrows. That is what my Fielding experience has done to me. I've become an axiological hermeneut.

Those of you who have studied with faculty colleague Katrina Rogers know that a basic definition of hermeneutics is that it is the art of interpretation. A hermeneut is one who practices the discipline of hermeneutics. A hermeneut will argue that what matters is not so much what process philosophers call the *situation* or what phenomenologists call *lived-experiences* that count for meaning as it is the person's interpretation of those experiences or situations.

Axiology refers to the study of human values. Formal axiology is a particular theory of the evaluative thought structures underlying people's values. I am a student and scholar of formal axiology. Hence, being an axiological hermeneut means that I seek to understand how people make meaning of their lives through the lens of the structure of their values.

A Career Change

My Fielding experience allowed me to make a late-in-life career change. I now find meaning in my work and I hope that, in ways small or large, I am making a difference for good in the world. I am an associate professor of management in the Bill and Vieve Gore School of Business at Westminster College in Salt Lake City. Westminster is a small, private, not-for-profit liberal arts college. I teach entrepreneurship and social entrepreneurship at the MBA and undergraduate levels.

I entered Fielding's HOD doctoral program in September of 2006 at the age of 53, having spent the previous 18 years running my own OD consulting practice. My goal at that time was to become a more theoretically grounded consultant. In my consulting practice I was using an assessment tool known as the Hartman Value Profile (HVP). It is based on the theory of formal axiology, which had first been articulated by the philosopher Robert S. Hartman (1967, 2006). It is a powerful tool, but I knew very little of its psychological and philosophical underpinnings. I wanted to know more. A strong impulse behind my desire to earn a doctorate was to become more knowledgeable about formal axiology. Pursuing this showed me the power of Fielding's adult learning model. Few of the faculty members were familiar with Hartman's work; none were experts in it, but that did not stop them from guiding me in my study of it. I remain especially grateful for the encouragement in this pursuit that I received from faculty colleague Miguel Guilarte, whom I eventually asked to chair my dissertation committee.

By the time I was midway through my studies at Fielding, I had become captivated by a vision of a new career as an academic. I set my sights on becoming a professor as soon as I earned my PhD. I began my academic job search shortly after my pilot study was concluded and was hired by Westminster in the same month that my Final Oral Review for my dissertation was completed. That was in March of 2012. I began teaching at Westminster in August of that year and am now in my seventh year as a full-time professor. Looking back on my time as a doctoral student, the road to my current profession seems straighter in hindsight than it ever did during my five-and-a-half years at Fielding.

Of course, an earned doctorate was a prerequisite for becoming a professor, but the encouragement to publish that I received from my faculty during my years as a doctoral student, coupled with the modeling of what it means to be a teacher of adults, aided greatly in the launch of my new career.

Westminster prides itself on being a teaching college, as opposed to a research university. I am proud of the time I spend in the classroom and proud of the influence that, I believe, I am having upon my students. Two years ago, I developed the curriculum for a new inter-disciplinary undergraduate minor in entrepreneurship, which is proving to be quite popular. I am particularly proud of my part in establishing a social impact incubator at our campus. It was undoubtedly Fielding's emphasis on social justice that allowed me to appreciate the power of using startup business principles to do good in the world.

In addition to Westminster's emphasis on teaching, our business school expects of our faculty a certain standard of scholarly output, primarily in the form of publications in peer-reviewed academic journals. Fielding prepared me well for both roles.

The Beginning

Having applied to Fielding without a master's degree, I was required to demonstrate evidence of scholarly writing. Faculty colleague Dottie Agger-Gupta advised me to take one of my previously published trade journal articles and revise it as if I were submitting it to an academic journal. I followed her advice. Consequently, I was accepted into the New Student Orientation (NSO) that began in September of 2006. Having spent so much time writing that paper as part of my application, I began to wonder what else I could do with it. After attending writing workshops offered by HOD faculty and colleague Judy Stevens-Long at two National Sessions and inviting her to rake my manuscript over the coals a few times, I decided to submit it for publication. It was accepted after minor revisions (Hurst, 2008). This gave me an idea. What if I could use the in-depth portions of some of my KAs as opportunities for subsequent publication? Here again, Miguel Guilarte encouraged me to do this. He guided me through my Knowledge Area (KA) in Human Development, the in-depth portion of which became a manuscript that was eventually published in the

Journal of Formal Axiology: Theory and Practice (Hurst, 2009). It was a comparison of the Hartman Value Profile with the more widely known Rokeach Value Survey. What I learned in that KA continues to inform my research in value theory today.

A second study guided by Miguel also resulted in an article in the same journal. This was my treatise on "The Non-Mathematical Logic of a Science of Values" (Hurst, 2011). I consider this article to be my most significant contribution to the refinement of the theory of formal axiology to date. A more recent paper entitled, "The Intentions of Axiological Interpreters" (Hurst, 2014), reveals my indebtedness to Katrina Rogers and what she taught me about philosophical hermeneutics during an advanced doctoral seminar on that subject.

For their encouragement of my nascent publication efforts, I remain grateful to Miguel Guilarte, Katrina Rogers, and Judy Stevens-Long, and also to Keith Melville, who demonstrated through his teaching and in his own writing that it is possible to write in a way that is both scholarly and readable.

As soon as I began applying to become a professor, I learned how much emphasis hiring committees place upon publications in peer-reviewed journals. Without the three papers I had published as a doctoral student I doubt that I would have been hired to a permanent teaching position at a four-year college or university. The subject of my dissertation aided in my job search as well. And it allowed me to envision a future research stream that is gradually coming to fruition.

Most Recent Publication

Since my appointment as a professor, I have published several additional articles and reviews in the *Journal of Formal Axiology*. Eager to expand my writings about formal axiology and the HVP into more of the mainstream of management literature, I was delighted when my article entitled, "An Axiological Measure of Entrepreneurial Cognition" was accepted this past fall by the *International Journal of Entrepreneurial*

Behavior and Research (Hurst, 2018). This latest paper is a direct outgrowth of a stream of research I had begun with my dissertation.

What's Next?

Having spent much of the past 10 years studying the deep-seated evaluative thought patterns of entrepreneurs, I am now turning my attention to a study of how undergraduate college students think. I seek to answer the question: "Do we, as educators, impart any lasting, meaningful, and positive impact upon students' developing cognitive patterns?" Given that Fielding, too, prides itself on providing its students with a transformative education, I would also like to partner with Fielding to extend this study to doctoral students and attempt to measure how their deep-seated cognitive patterns change or fail to change over the course of their graduate studies.

Shortly after graduating from Fielding, I was invited to serve on the board of the Robert S. Hartman Institute of Formal and Applied Axiology (RSHI), a 501(c) 3 not-for-profit organization. I currently serve as the Vice President of Research and as editor of the *Journal of Formal Axiology: Theory and Practice*.

During the summer of 2018, I received a Gore Summer Research Grant from Westminster College that allowed me to take two undergraduate students to the University of Tennessee where, for 10 days, we dug into the Hartman Archives at the Special Collections Library there. Hartman had been a visiting professor of philosophy at Tennessee when he died, unexpectedly and too young, at the age of 63. Although Hartman was a prolific writer, only one book of his was ever published in English in his lifetime. Throughout his career, he had kept copious records of his lecture notes, essays, speeches, and numerous drafts of various journal and book manuscripts. More than 100,000 pages of unpublished papers, mostly in the form of typewritten carbon copies, are stored in those archives. Since Hartman's death in 1973, the Institute has published two of his book-length manuscripts, but much of what Hartman wrote remains unread and unpublished. I am currently developing a proposal to the Board of the

Institute that we undertake to systematically transcribe, edit, and publish a much larger selection of Hartman's work. The world today needs Hartman's ideas.

Hartman's Body of Work

The more I study Hartman's body of work, the more admiration I have for the depth and breadth of his thought. Hartman did much more than just develop a value theory. In 1947, he founded the Council of Profit Sharing Industries (Hustwit, n.d). During our time at the Archives, we discovered a manuscript written circa 1958 entitled: "The Partnership Between Capital and Labor," which lays out Hartman's belief in this new form of capitalism based on partnership. I intend to transcribe, edit, and publish the introductory portions of that manuscript soon.

Hartman was a founding member of an organization of concerned scientists against nuclear proliferation and wrote extensively about the threat of nuclear annihilation and how, through developing a science of value, we may be able to avoid a nuclear war. It is for this work that he was nominated for the Nobel Peace Prize in 1973. His warnings from that era are even more important to us who are living today.

Hartman was also an early member of the Association of Humanistic Psychology, founded by his close friend Abraham Maslow, and other thought leaders who are well known to Fielding people, including Virginia Satir, Carl Rogers, Gordon Allport, and Rollo May (AAHP.org). During our archival research, my students and I uncovered additional writings by Hartman about humanistic psychology and its relation to philosophy.

Summary

In summation, I applied to Fielding in part to begin to understand more fully the theory of formal axiology. I've learned a great deal about it since then and I continue to learn. Today I am leading the effort to bring more of Hartman's work to the light of day. I serve as editor of the only peer-reviewed journal dedicated to the refinement, expansion, and application of that theory. I did not enroll at Fielding intending to become a professor, but now that I am one, I realize that Fielding led me to my true calling. I am increasingly becoming able to bring formal axiology into my classrooms, in hopes of stimulating a new generation of value theorists who can—through this knowledge—make this world a better place. The world needs a new generation of axiological hermeneuts.

References

Hartman, R. S. (1967). *The structure of value: Foundations of scientific axiology*. Eugene, OR: Wipf & Stock.

Hartman, R. S. (2006). *The Hartman Value Profile (HVP) manual of interpretation*, 2nd Ed. Knoxville, TN: Robert S. Hartman Institute.

Hurst, C. G. (2008). Sustainable telemarketing? A new theory of consumer behavior. *Direct Marketing: An International Journal, 2*(2), 111-124.

Hurst, C. G. (2009). A meaningful score: Hartman v. Rokeach. *Journal of Formal Axiology: Theory and Practice, 2*, 79-96.

Hurst, C. G. (2011). The non-mathematical logic of a science of values. *Journal of Formal Axiology: Theory and Practice, 4*, 1-12.

Hurst, C. G. (2014). The intentions of axiological interpreters. *Journal of Formal Axiology Theory and Practice, 7*, 1-10.

Hurst, C. G. (2018). An axiological measure of entrepreneurial cognition. *International Journal of Entrepreneurial Behavior and Research.* Advance online publication. DOI: 10.1108/IJEBR-05-2018-0337.

Hustwit, W. P. (n.d.) The father of profit-sharing. *Wooster Magazine*. Retrieved from: http://www.axiometrics.net/Wooster.htm.

About the Author

Clifford (Cliff) Hurst is an associate professor of management at Westminster College in Salt Lake City, Utah. He teaches entrepreneurship and social entrepreneurship at the undergraduate and MBA levels. Cliff earned his PhD from Fielding in 2012 and was hired as a professor immediately thereafter. He has lived with his wife, Dayna, in Salt Lake City for the past seven years. He developed the curriculum for Westminster's new undergraduate minor in entrepreneurship and was instrumental in founding the college's social impact incubator. He serves on the Board of Directors of the Robert S. Hartman Institute for Formal and Applied Axiology and as editor of the annual peer-reviewed *Journal of Formal Axiology: Theory and Practice*. He is currently editing a series of monographs on the previously unpublished writings by Hartman, which will be published by the Institute.

CHAPTER 3

MY TRANSFORMATIONAL JOURNEY FROM PRACTITIONER TO A SCHOLAR-PRACTITIONER

Gary Wagenheim, PhD
Adjunct Professor of Management
Beedie School of Business, Simon Fraser University

Introduction

My Fielding learning experience transformed me, from practitioner to scholar-practitioner. As Robert Quinn (1996) wrote, "Deep change is different than incremental change in that it requires new ways of thinking and behaving. It is change that is major in scope, discontinuous with the past and generally irreversible."

In the classroom, I changed as a teacher. In the office, I changed as a consultant. I have a greater breadth and depth of content knowledge, a keen awareness of my ontological and epistemological approaches, and a deeper level of understanding of client and learner needs. I discovered that becoming a scholar-practitioner is more than merely choosing a culture of inquiry for research or a model for consulting; it is integrating inquiry as a lifelong practice. My journey to becoming a reflective scholar-practitioner was about transforming my consciousness, changing my mindset, illuminating my self-awareness, being knowledgeable and informed by theory, and changing from being a consumer of knowledge to a producer and purveyor of knowledge.

My Graduate Education

My career was not a predictable path nor a straight line. I started a clothing store at the age of 24 with no money and no experience in retail. That store was successful, so I expanded to a chain of stores and eventually sold it to employees when I was 37. As I was winding down my business, I studied for my MBA because I was unsure of what to do next and thought I would figure it out in school. In the last year of the MBA program, I did figure it out, as I started a consulting firm and taught part-time at two community colleges and a liberal arts college. I loved both teaching and consulting. Upon graduation, I searched for a faculty position, mainly at community colleges and a few universities. To my surprise, I was hired at a Big Ten University. Fortunately, they were searching for a scholar-practitioner and I fit the bill, at least the practitioner part. I was hired as an assistant professor on a tenure track without a PhD, and rose to the rank of full professor, still without a PhD.

While I had been in the field of higher education for a long time, the demands of teaching, scholarship, and service at a major university paradoxically left little time for advancing my own education. The sound of the tenure clock ticking led me to choose the path of tenure over education, and led to the postponement of studying for a PhD. Much like going for my MBA as I was exiting business, I went to Fielding for my PhD after resigning my position at Purdue and moving to Vancouver, Canada to marry. I went for both graduate degrees for the same reason. I was interested in learning and deep personal change; I was not interested in instrumental learning or credentialing. I aspired to know more, to be more, and to do more with my life in teaching and consulting. I wanted to make contributions to the field and transfer that knowledge to students and clients.

As a lifelong independent learner, my approach closely follows Kolb's (1984) experiential learning model. I am an active experimenter who jumps into a learning experience cold, reflects on the outcomes, seeks additional information and theories to inform my learning, and then applies that new knowledge to solve a problem. I then follow a cycle of practice, reflect, and modify until I develop the skill to the best of my ability.

In Fielding's andragogy (Knowles, 1980) my experience, independence, and action-oriented learning style were acknowledged and supported. Rather than change my learning style to fit Fielding, Fielding encouraged me to use my natural learning style. In this way, Fielding's student-centered model perfectly filled my learning needs.

As a mid-career professional with a busy international consulting schedule, Fielding's flexible distributed education model afforded me the opportunity to study while I continued working. In addition, the student-directed approach allowed me to study the specific topics I taught, topics where Fielding faculty had expertise, while developing myself as a scholar and practitioner.

My Transformation

So how did this transformation evolve? It was a combination of exploring the subject matter combined with reflecting on my personal development that enriched my learning and deepened my change. My exploration of knowledge expanded, which led to more reading, more thinking, and more writing, resulting in more questions than answers. Of course, this created a certain emotional tension and frustration that ultimately blossomed into my maturation as a scholar. I eventually realized that asking that the right questions was more important than having the right answers. It was the process of getting lost in the knowledge that facilitated the development of my inquiry.

Fielding's faculty capably served as guides, always leading with questions, occasionally adding content, focusing me on the process of self-learning. Also, the Fielding learning model of knowledge areas addressed both ends of the theory-practice continuum. Studying at three distinct yet connected levels—overview, in-depth, and applied— for each knowledge area yielded the deep learning I craved.

The faculty encouraged me to survey the width of a field in an *overview*, which meant reading numerous books and countless journal articles on a given topic, all the way back to the classics, then picking a specific element of the field *in-depth* that I wanted to explore in a robust and deep way and, lastly, to do an *applied* level where I was required to use my knowledge in practice in my teaching or consulting. I came to understand how theories and fields develop, to understand the tenets upon which that knowledge is built, and to see the benefits, controversies, and flaws in the knowledge. I began to engage actively in the discourse and to think about how to make contributions to my chosen field.

In addition, learning contracts for each knowledge area contained doctoral competencies—that is, critical thinking, scholarly writing, and a scholar-practitioner mindset—that I wanted to develop along with knowledge of the field. In this way, faculty members assessed my work on a given topic while providing feedback on the doctoral competencies I was working to develop. I also did a self-assessment in each knowledge area, which simultaneously honed my reflective practice skills.

How I Am Different as a Scholar-Practitioner

Fielding encouraged me to adopt an interdisciplinary perspective combining theories of personality, social psychology, human development, learning, motivation, and leadership that formed the foundation for enriching my work. It was not always obvious how to combine these fields to produce an integrative way of knowing; however, in the struggle I found more learning. At first, I simply sought to use and understand these perspectives separately; however, it was as I slowly learned to integrate them that I clearly saw different views and discovered better solutions. This eventually led to an inquiring learning cycle of framing, naming, and reframing of problems that produced better knowledge and effectiveness in my teaching and consulting.

I explored the broad spectrum of theories, gained more depth by focusing on specific topics of interest, and, most of all, applied my new knowledge in my consulting, writing, and teaching. The learning model at Fielding facilitated this learning development.

So while I was integrating knowledge from interdisciplinary perspectives in my PhD, I was doing it in my lifelong personal development journey, too. I have always sought to integrate my life in ways that allow me grow as a person and contribute to the community through education, business, and volunteerism. I love being with and helping people. I really view ambiguity and change as opportunities for learning. Certain personal core values—independence, hard work, flexibility, and honesty—allow me to see many possibilities and few roadblocks in life. I try to balance my life so that what I do for play I also do for work, creating a professional life and personal life that are truly integrated. I am coaching and teaching when talking with friends in a coffee shop in much the same way I am with students in a class. Now this was true before Fielding, but what is different is how I manifest my transformation into scholar-practitioner in the same endeavors after Fielding.

I was reading books on leadership before I ever dreamed of matriculating into an MBA program; counseling employees long before I discovered the discipline of organizational behavior; and training employees before I knew the meaning of the word pedagogy. I was doing all of this intuitively, doing it because it was my temperament. I was not knowledgeable about what I was doing. What I learned in my PhD program at Fielding were the theories to better inform and improve my work. Kurt Lewin's (1951) maxim captures it best: "There is nothing so practical as a good theory." Theory really does inform my professional practice; it provides vocabulary, explanation, and frameworks for action. Theory is the scholar I now bring to my practitioner.

My own personal growth combined with subject matter knowledge learned at Fielding directly informs my work in creating innovative pedagogy to teach in MBA and executive education leadership programs. I transfer theory to practice and practice to theory in my research and contribute to the field of leadership through journal articles, conference presentations, teaching, and consulting. I use my Fielding education whether I am teaching students in an MBA class in Vancouver, facilitating a team of executives at a retreat in Helsinki, coaching skiing on the slopes of Whistler, writing an article for an academic journal, or participating in a Fielding Board of Trustees meeting in Santa Barbara.

As an educator teaching in graduate programs and an organizational development consultant working with senior managers of international organizations, I constantly utilize my Fielding education to inform my practice. Graduate students and senior managers, as discriminating consumers of knowledge, expect lessons grounded in theory and often ask for references or divergent theories. Their expectations of a graduate education are considerably higher than what they find in best-selling business books or trade magazines, which often rely on anecdotal rather than theoretical data. These students are critical evaluators of information and want to know not only the theory that supports the lesson, but the research behind the theory.

The Fielding learning model facilitated incorporating pertinent theorists into my research and eventually into my teaching and consulting practice. One of the key aspects of my teaching and consulting is helping students and managers understand the connection between theory and practice, as a generative way of increasing both their knowledge (knowing) and effectiveness (doing). Theories are useful because they help provide explanations for our actions, create vocabularies for discussion, frame our issues, and serve as catalysts for reflection.

I based my Fielding learning practice on constructing an understanding of theories from multiple perspectives that informed and influenced the field of human and organizational development, and that can be incorporated into my teaching practice. My maturation as a learner moved along the continuum from dualism to relativism, from single perspective to multiple perspectives, from one truth to many truths, which is to say I became a more effective teacher and consultant by becoming a more effective learner at Fielding.

The real magic of the Fielding education model was helping me navigate my own development as a scholar-practitioner. I really do see the world differently, ask different questions, and generate different and, I hope, better solutions. For me, becoming a scholar-practitioner is more than merely choosing a culture of inquiry that seems interesting or effective for research purposes; it is integrating my life with inquiry as a lifelong practice. The Fielding experience allows me to fully immerse myself more in my life in ways that produce harmony and integration.

Fielding helped me cross the learning chasm from passive patron of existing knowledge to active creator of new knowledge, which marks the definitive migration from practitioner to scholar-practitioner. Transforming from practitioner to scholar-practitioner fundamentally changed my life, shifted my worldview, and forged a perpetual curiosity for acquiring knowledge that motivates me to cultivate a spirit of inquiry as a way of being—all of which is to say that Fielding transformed me to a higher level of consciousness.

Every step in the Fielding education model, from application to graduation, values human development as the core tenet. An interesting double-loop learning concept (Argyris, 1993) forms the basis of the Fielding model, so while students study *about* human and organizational development they are engaged in a model *of* human and organizational development. Stated another way, Fielding practices what it preaches in educating and developing scholar-practitioners. There is congruence between espoused and actual learning in the Fielding education model, and my transformation is yet another example in a long line of alums with the same transformative experience.

References

Argyris, C. (1993). *Knowledge for action: A guide to overcoming barriers to organizational change.* San Francisco: Jossey-Bass Publishers.

Knowles, M. S. (1980). *The modern practice of adult education: From pedagogy to andragogy.* Englewood Cliffs, NJ: Cambridge.

Kolb, D. A. (1984). *Experiential learning: Experience as the source of learning and development.* Englewood Cliffs, NJ: Prentice Hall.

Lewin, K. (1951). Problems of research in social psychology. In D. Cartwright (Ed.), *Field theory in social science: Selected theoretical papers* (pp. 155-169). New York: Harper & Row.

Quinn, R. E. (1996). *Deep change: Discovering the leader within*. San Francisco: Jossey-Bass.

About the Author

Gary Wagenheim, PhD is adjunct professor of management at the Beedie School of Business at Simon Fraser University and Aalto University Executive Education and former professor of organizational leadership in the School of Technology at Purdue University. His research, teaching, and consulting interests are reflective practice, organizational change, leadership, and organizational behavior. He has published one book and 25 academic journal articles in *The Management Teaching Review*, *The Journal of Management Education*, *The International Journal of Teaching and Learning in Higher Education*, and *Reflective Practice: International and Multidisciplinary Perspectives*. He owns the Wagenheim Advisory Group, which provides training and development programs. He currently serves as vice chair of the board of trustees of Fielding Graduate University and is a member of the advisory board of the Department of Technology Leadership and Innovation in the Polytechnic Institute at Purdue University. Gary received a PhD in Human and Organizational Systems from Fielding Graduate University.

CHAPTER 4

THE CURRENCY OF VOICE

Carrie A. L. Arnold, PhD, PCC
Principal Coach and Consultant
The Willow Group

In a recent conversation with a client organization, I asked the director of organization development to share a little bit about a female client with me. He responded by saying she is highly regarded, with a well-respected voice. His answer was genuine, quick, and unrehearsed, as the main topic of our conversation was less about the female leader and more about the organization dynamics I needed to understand. What a remarkable compliment! It is one most, if not all, women in leadership aspire to hear.

Rebecca Solnit (2017), an American writer and contributing editor at *Harper's Magazine*, recently quipped, "The right to speak is a form of wealth that is being redistributed." In the past, simply holding a leadership role was the only form of currency needed; this is no longer true. It is those with a valuable voice that carry the highest degree of exchange, and it is wealth that can be lost or gained depending on the effort made to be heard. As counterintuitive as it seems, occupying a leadership position does not automatically bring the right to speak. When the elements of race, gender, sexual orientation, national origin, religion, or other personal characteristics are considered, this figurative wealth can be reallocated to groups that hold a higher degree of privilege or status.

As a woman wrestles to gain access to authority, status, and leadership, she cannot lose sight of the need to protect her most valuable asset—her voice.

When I began my doctoral journey at Fielding Graduate University in 2014, I wanted to study the linguistic moves made by leaders that inspire followers. I sought to understand their metaphors, cadence, story, and use of speech acts. I had seen and heard multiple examples of language that did not work. Leaders can overuse the same patterns or catchphrases until they become a behind-the-scenes mockery. I also saw cases of leaders who used language choices that became adopted, quoted, and leveraged. Followers mimicked, not out of disrespect, but out of passionate acceptance. Something was said that counted and, despite how basic the rhetoric, it resonated in ways that spread. Words matter, and I wanted to make sense of the relationship between them and the leader.

Unfortunately, just as trying to wear a pair of shoes that do not quite fit every part of the foot appropriately, something kept rubbing me wrong regarding my topic of interest. I realized I could "dissertation" my way through the speech patterns, leader linguistics, and powerful metaphors of individual executives but never make a difference with those who do not speak with a level of purpose and effectiveness. I first needed to understand what kept leaders so muted, muffled from all the same language choices and rhetoric, so silenced. Thankfully, I had supportive faculty and students at Fielding that were patient with me as I grappled with the needed research question.

This shift, or the flipping of the topic, gave me a chance to refocus on a nuanced angle that has not been given much attention within scholarly leadership conversations. There is a growing body of research on *employee* voice and silence, but there is little to none on the idea that leadership could and does feel silenced. I decided to explore this subtle distinction, and I set out to better understand the female leader and her passage from feeling silenced to feeling heard. I finished my PhD on the silenced female leader in 2016 and realized I was far from finished. My sample size was enough to earn a doctorate in Human Development, but I was not satisfied that I had enough to understand the phenomenon of female leader silencing entirely. In my Fellow role with the Institute for Social Innovation, I tripled the sample size of women, and I continue to study and collect stories as I speak on this crucial topic.

With the support of Fielding, here are a few things I learned about the silenced:

First, it was easy to find women interested in being part of the research. More hands raised than I had time or ability to interview. It was not a challenge to find participants. The difficulty was finding female leaders who could talk about their recovery. Far too many women in leadership currently feel silenced. Finding those who could speak to the journey to valuable voice became not just difficult, but a finding in and of itself.

Second, when women in leadership feel silenced, they often feel sick. It became clear to me after dozens of interviews that the experience of silencing impacts women like a virus. They feel compromised cognitively, emotionally, spiritually, physically and, of course, their leadership is not at its best when they do not think they have the agency to speak.

Third, silencing in leadership is rarely about sex. It is essential to make a distinction between "breaking the silence" specific to sexual harassment and assault as opposed to the leader silencing that is pertinent to my research. Women and men are breaking silence around the "casting couch" experience they had to endure at a younger age with high-ranking privileged people. This phenomenon is often true of younger women who are entering into professional roles. My research was less about harassment or assault, and more about the damage women in leadership experience when they feel psychologically silenced.

Here the silencers do not have a consistent profile. Female leaders can feel silenced by board members, peers, bosses, direct reports, customers, and a variety of different stakeholder groups. Sometimes the silencers are specific, with names and profiles provided. At other times, the silencers are systems that do not work for one-half of the population. Equal numbers of men and women hold middle management positions. Unfortunately, women often plateau at this level and are not promoted to higher levels of leadership for which they are capable. Systems that favor men are institutional, tangled, and difficult to shift.

Fourth, there is also a finding that women silence themselves to maintain a relationship with their organization. Often they are the primary wage earners in the family and carry a strong sense of responsibility that may keep them from the confidence to make job changes when they begin to feel suppressed. Staying and suffering is an adverse finding in the research.

Last, the ways in which women in leadership feel silenced varies. We often wish we could categorize all of the negative issues to identify and then eradicate them from reoccurring. However, like any form of microaggression, these issues are individualized. What feels egregiously silencing to one female leader may feel like a slight paper cut to another. Eye rolls, disinvites, raised voices, name-calling, talking over, public shaming, discrediting, lack of eye contact, ignoring, excluding, or any variety of marginalizing behavior can have varying degrees of impact. The most important finding was not how the silencing occurs. Instead, it is important to note that women silence other women just as often as men silence women. Many participants in my research argued that feeling silenced by a female is often more painful and acute than anything experienced by men.

The research that explored the silencing was dark. The stories were hard to hear, hold, and put in print. After a period, I had to wonder if I would ever quite capture the light, as it seemed so fleeting. I needed to hear how women improved. Did they recover? Who helped? What helped? How long did it take?

With encouragement from my Fielding dissertation committee to go deeper, here is what I learned about voice recovery.

It takes time. For those that did recover, on average women explained the healing process as lasting up to two years. Once they reached true recovery of voice, they were still susceptible to feeling silenced, but they had a "never again" attitude and were able to regain voice faster with setbacks.

Second, women said that men were not always part of the problem, but they were, more often than not, part of the solution. Having healthy, respectful, and good male champions makes an enormous difference for women experiencing silencing. Knowing they had a man in their corner who would support them was crucial to healing.

Third, women healed when they found care and community. I have learned the hard way that many women have an allergy to the term "self-care." When self-care is the solution, women automatically think of healthy eating, exercise, and weight management. No one refutes that these are all important and necessary for good living. However, this is not the type of care that creates healing when one is silenced. When women are with others who listen and share equally, this is care. Too many times, women who feel silenced are the designated listeners in their leadership or social circles. They need time to speak and be heard.

When women can be with other generous women who share a leadership context, this is care. Leadership is a lonely role, and so few women find themselves in senior positions. Peer groups and community are often hard to access. Executive women need to discover or create communities of practice with other executives. Not every female friend will be able to understand the other's experience in leadership.

Last, when women begin to speak up on behalf of other silenced women, this is care. Healing from silencing can happen when women ensure that they do not become silencers themselves. Giving voice to those who are stifled or suppressed is often the antidote to enable female leaders to stay in healthy places of valuable voice.

Thus, self-care is not the word I use now when I talk about recovering from feeling silenced. Instead, I go back to the compliment I wrote about in my first paragraph. Women need to examine their ability to have self-regard—to regard themselves as having agency, authority, and influence. When we view something highly, we compliment, listen, spend time, enjoy, and appreciate. Women who find and cultivate self-regard are more likely to recover from silencing experiences. Then, as they heal, they need to nurture and support their own sense of valuable voice.

Finally, as a Fellow and Fielding alumna, I have learned that voice alone is never enough!

Anyone can make an utterance, expression, or declaration. We all use speech, but we do not all use it with a degree of effectiveness. As female leaders move away from their silencing experiences and embrace the voice that is inherent in their leadership roles, they need to balance purpose with efficacy. They need to understand what is heard and how. They need to know when to leverage declarative language that is assertive and action-oriented with language that is effective and contextual, filled with metaphor or story. Just finding their authentic voice is rarely sufficient. They need to discover what is authentic and then be able to pivot and access all the degrees and shades of rhetoric, discourse, and language that needs to be heard from the platform of their leadership role.

Understanding silencing and voice is a journey that is taking me back into some of my original interest in leadership linguistics. How do leaders speak in ways that are heard? What makes people engage and follow versus disconnect and barely comply? In this day, where leadership is so riddled with complexity and ambiguity, how are we leveraging our ability to speak? How do our words create transformation in ourselves and others? Fielding Graduate University not only helped me find my voice, but has also prepared me for this lifelong work and research that does not end with a graduation ceremony. As women find voice with currency, they pave the path for everyone to find a voice, which is essential in our collective pursuit of a just and sustainable world.

References

Solnit, R. (2017). Silence and powerlessness go hand in hand—women's voices must be heard. *The Guardian*. Retrieved from https://www.theguardian.com/commentisfree/2017/mar/08/silence-powerlessness-womens-voices-rebecca-solnit

About the Author

Carrie Arnold received her PhD in Human Development from Fielding Graduate University in January 2017. She is a Fellow with the Institute for Social Innovation and continues to conduct post-doc research on voice and silencing. Previously, she trained as a leadership coach at Georgetown University through their Center for Continuing and Professional Education. She is certified by the International Coach Federation (ICF) and is a Professional Certified Coach and a Board Certified Coach. Since 2011, she has owned and operated her own consulting business, The Willow Group. As a leadership coach, she has served within the federal government, in all levels of education, health care, and in the private sector, working with over 200 individual and group clients. Prior to that, she had 20 years' experience working in health care, human resources, training, and organizational development. She has worked for multi-hospital systems in leadership positions and has taught at the university level.

CHAPTER 5

MAINTAINING THE GARDEN: EPISODES IN SUSTAINABILITY AND ORGANIZATION DEVELOPMENT

Julie Smendzuik-O'Brien, PhD, MPA
Institute for Social Innovation Fellow (ISI)
Fielding Graduate University

Laced throughout the learning plan I drafted at the beginning of my doctoral journey at Fielding Graduate University was the image of a garden in which my scholarship and learning would grow. Before enrolling at Fielding, the garden as metaphor for both creation and stewardship had been with me through formation in my religious faith, while coaxing the growth of reluctant vegetables with my father, and during my study of hunger in the world—an introduction to global systems of politics, economics, foreign aid, development in its many forms, and the dilemmas wrought by the Green Revolution.

In this essay, I discuss three experiences with the garden and its changes, characterized as past, present, and future, to show a few of the impacts my PhD studies have had. The past experience was a small research project conducted in 2008 that resulted in changes for sustainability. The second is my current experience on the board of the Organization Development and Change (ODC) Division of the Academy of Management, on which I have served since 2013. The third is an exposition of where I have been taking my research and practice since completing my doctorate in 2017, specifically with efforts related to a major watershed in my region of the United States with my faith congregation to better understand issues of climate change and sustainability, and with internal organization development practitioners who are working with sustainability changes.

For the *praxis* or *applied* dimension of my social change knowledge area, I investigated a climate protection agreement entered into by mayors throughout the United States (see https://www.usmayors.org/mayors-climate-protection-center). The originator of this mayors' agreement, the mayor of Seattle, Washington, had a problem with cruise ships that would leave their engines running while moored in the city's harbor. Because the engines were fueled with diesel, serious air-quality issues arose for Seattle. The mayor and other city leaders decided to invite the cruise ships to use the city's electrical grid to maintain power rather than emit black diesel smoke, which was also not only affecting human health but was also melting the snow pack in the nearby mountain range, a major source of water for the city. This resolved the air-quality issues of the city and prompted the mayor to consider whether other U.S. cities could make some difference in climate change by taking initiatives in their own areas. No leadership was coming from Washington, DC due to the reluctance of the George W. Bush administration to sign the international Kyoto Protocol for various reasons (see, for example, Hovi, Sprinz, & Bang, 2010).

With this background, I became curious whether cities in my home state of Minnesota were involved in this climate protection effort. On a list of engaged cities, I found to my satisfaction that the state's two major cities, Minneapolis and St. Paul, had signed the agreement. Upon further investigation, I found that these two cities had been involved in climate-related activities for cities sponsored by the United Nations for a number of years. Because I lived in one of the suburbs, however, I decided to check on their involvement as well. I found that eight of the suburbs of Minneapolis-St. Paul had signed the mayor's protection agreement, and I wondered how they were implementing it. I decided to research the motivations for signing and ask about activities related to climate protection in suburbia. Because this was going to be a research project involving human subjects, I had to gain approval of my survey instrument and my research approach from the Institutional Review Board (IRB) at the university. Upon receiving approval from the IRB, I proceeded to contact the eight suburban cities and to interview city staff members about the two areas noted—motivation to sign the agreement, and actions that the cities were taking. One of my findings was that my own suburb was not a part of this nationwide effort. So after I submitted my paper to my Fielding faculty assessor, I decided to contact my home suburb to share my results with the city planner.

The planner and I arranged for me to present my research to the city council. It was a very long council meeting; I was at the end of the agenda and began my presentation at about 11 p.m. My results were challenged by one council member who thought that research meant conducting an experiment rather than the social science research that I recommended. Ultimately my mayor signed on to the mayors' climate protection agreement. In 2014 Maplewood was recognized for its sustainability efforts (City of Maplewood Minnesota, 2014, September), and in July 2018 the city was awarded the Green Step Cities/Step 5 Award by the Minnesota League of Cities (https://maplewoodmn.gov/1003/GreenStep-Cities). The city planner told me on more than one occasion that my research was the spark that prompted the city to take action. The time from when I first presented my research to when the city received awards, however, was six and 10 years, respectively. These are indicators of how long change may take.

The second example of using my doctorate to good effect is my current involvement with the Organization Development and Change Division of the Academy of Management, a scholarly professional organization with over 20,000 members worldwide whose work has influenced the field of management for decades. The ODC Division has about 2,000 members. In 2013 my name was submitted by a fellow Fielding student to serve as a student representative on the board of the ODC Division. I was honored to have my name submitted, and further honored to be accepted as the student representative that year. The membership of the ODC Division was aging, and a recent self-study by the division showed a need for improvements in recruitment and other areas. I was excited by the potential to contribute.

One of the major changes was the need to create bylaws for the division, and to identify more clearly the roles of both elected and appointed board members of the division. A new position created in the bylaws was for an appointed membership engagement coordinator. Because no other board members were interested, I volunteered to serve as the membership coordinator for the division. This was an opportunity to help facilitate organizational change for a significant professional association within my discipline of organization development and change. In the years since that appointment, I have analyzed membership data, created newsletters, worked with board members to engage members at the annual meeting each August, offered workshops for students to explain how the Academy functions, and have been the advocate for division members in both the scholarship and practice of the field of organization development and change. My work has been acknowledged and endorsed by fellow board members. I have been reappointed three times to additional two-year terms, and will serve in this capacity until July 2020.

The benefit for me first as a doctoral student and now as a PhD graduate is the opportunity to see the workings of a scholarly organization firsthand and to actively participate in shaping its programs. I have learned intimate details of how the annual international conference is staged and have successfully submitted designs for five professional development workshops, served as a paper-session chair, chaired a symposium on the education of scholar-practitioners in organization development and change, and have frequently served as a reviewer of papers submitted for the program. I have had less personal success with submission of scholarly papers, but I persist.

For the future, three areas of endeavor are emerging. In January 2018, I was elected to the board of the North Woods and Waters of the St. Croix Heritage Area (NWW) regional watershed program. The St. Croix River, designated a Wild and Scenic River by both federal and state agencies, is situated between Minnesota and Wisconsin in the upper Midwestern part of the United States (see https://www.rivers.gov/rivers/st-croix.php).

I joined an ongoing effort to create a heritage area for the St. Croix Watershed and to seek federal designation under the US Department of the Interior's National Park Service. Designated heritage areas are regions of the United States that contributed significantly to the development of the country. Local citizens began an effort to designate the St. Croix River Watershed one of these heritage areas because of the importance of trade waterways, kinship and treaty relationships with Native Americans, significant lumber contributions to the built environment, the variety of European immigrants who came to the area, and the relationships between immigrants and Native peoples.

In the late eighteenth and early nineteenth centuries (1787-1803) this part of Minnesota and Wisconsin was in the vast, unsettled Northwest Territory of the United States. It was for many years off the "beaten path," that is, not on the more frequently used trails to the West, so relationships between native peoples and European immigrants were more cordial than elsewhere in the country. Swedish and French immigrants worked side by side with native peoples to fell the forests, build homes, and trade for needed items. The area is important to U.S. heritage not only because of this peaceful relationship between immigrants and native peoples but also because of the profound economic impact of lumber from the area. After the great Chicago fire in 1871, lumber from this part of Wisconsin and Minnesota was sent to Illinois to rebuild that major Midwestern city. So extensive was the logging for this and other projects that land in the St. Croix River watershed was essentially denuded, and the area experienced severe natural resource issues such as erosion and fires. This led the people of the region to establish conservation measures to restore forests and today, in 2018, the region boasts a sustainable forest industry. Other benefits of the conservation effort include recreation and tourism.

The region was the also the birthplace of the first Earth Day in 1970, due to the cooperation of national legislators from the area, Senator Gaylord Nelson of Wisconsin and Senator Walter Mondale of Minnesota. While it is not a national holiday, citizens throughout the United States often acknowledge the day with celebrations and activities about the value of our earthly home and our planet's natural resources. For much of my career I worked in agriculture and natural resources management, and I wrote my dissertation in part about sustainability issues not only in the United States but also globally. By applying my experience as well as the skills learned through my doctoral program I believe I can contribute to the sustainability of my part of the United States. I have an opportunity on this board to offer my expertise in research and practice to foster social change and ongoing civic engagement to enable residents of the area to support designation of the heritage area and to then benefit from possible economic developments, pride of history and place, and increased protection of natural resources.

Another arena in which I hope to make some difference regarding sustainability issues is within the Catholic community. About 600 institutions in the U.S. Catholic community have signed on to a Catholic Climate Covenant in response to the serious reports of climate change and potential impacts on people, property, and the planet. Many have signed this Catholic climate agreement, but as yet the leader in my local church community, the archdiocese in which I live, has not yet signed it. I hope to be among those trying to persuade the bishop to engage in this important global issue.

Last of my emerging activities, I am honored to have been named an ISI Fellow of the Institute for Social Innovation at Fielding. My project is to develop and advance a model for internal organization development practitioners related to sustainability changes within their organizations. I am a member of the Minnesota Organization Development Network's program committee, where I am committed to advancing that idea. I have been invited to participate in national conversations occurring in 2018 and 2019 about the future of the profession of Organization Development and Change, where I plan to promote this idea as well.

As I reflected on what I might highlight in this essay, I realized that some things have persisted for me from my post-baccalaureate days through my doctorate at Fielding. Important to me are the roles of faith and belief in the potential for good stewardship of the earth and its resources. Another is my ability to learn from my experience and to apply past successful efforts to new efforts for organizational and social change. Last is the recognition that through my work at Fielding Graduate University in this PhD program and in writing my dissertation, I have found a more distinctive voice. I plan to use that voice to do what I can to address climate change, to encourage the belief of my fellow humans about the beauty and importance of maintaining our earth and, with humility and persistence, to make a genuine difference that will benefit many.

This institute: https://www.ncronline.org/news/environment/nearly-600-institutions-back-catholic-climate-declaration has been deemed by leaders in our field as a major milestone in its development.

References

City of Maplewood Minnesota. (2014, September). Maplewood recognized for environmental sustainability efforts. *Maplewood Living*, 1. https://issuu.com/maplewoodmn/docs/2014/63.

Hovi, J., Sprinz, D. F., & Bang, G. (2010). Why the United States did not become a party to the Kyoto protocol: German, Norwegian, and US perspectives. *European Journal of International Relations, 18*(1), 129-150. Doi: 10.1177/1354066110380964.

About the Author

Julie Smendzuik-O'Brien, PhD is an accomplished scholar-practitioner who served more than 25 years in professional, mid-level, and senior-level management positions in the agriculture, natural resources, and higher education state agencies of Minnesota. An innovator, she created two internal organization development consulting programs, and directed many other change efforts in policy development, organizational improvement, and strategic planning. She was a founding member of a nonprofit focused on the sustainability of the U.S. food and farm system that has continued for over 30 years; it now educates immigrant organic farmers. She serves on the boards of the Organization Development and Change Division of the Academy of Management and the North Woods and Waters of the St. Croix Heritage Area, an 8,000 square mile watershed between Minnesota and Wisconsin. When not fretting about world problems, she enjoys reading, gardening, outdoor activities with family, and word games on her Android phone. She holds a bachelor's degree in religious studies, master's degrees in public administration and human development, and happily finished her doctorate at Fielding Graduate University in 2017.

CHAPTER 6

HOW FIELDING HAS SHAPED MY PROFESSIONAL LIFE

Timothy K. Stanton, PhD
Senior Engaged Scholar
Ravensong Associates

In 1977 I accepted an appointment to the directorship of the Field Study Office in the College of Human Ecology at Cornell University. In this role I provided academic leadership and administration of a small, interdisciplinary undergraduate program that engaged students in intensive service-learning in New York City, across North America, and in the local Ithaca, New York area. There were four of us on the faculty. We were "extradepartmental," located under the college dean outside of and, in some ways competitive with, the college's academic departments.

When I took this job, I had a master's degree in education from San Francisco State University. My only higher education experience was as a part-time adjunct behavioral sciences instructor in a community college district. My main occupation then was organizing young people to engage in civic and community activities aimed at providing needed human services and desired social change. The four of us faculty members in the office quickly developed our programs into nationally recognized innovations in academically accredited, service-based experiential learning. It seemed that the more successful we were in attracting and serving students and our community partners and gaining national recognition, the more we were attacked by our more conventional, department-based colleagues for whom experiential learning was both "too touchy-feely" and "lacking in subject matter." The department chairs were continually after the dean to close us down and divide our budget among them.

One day the dean invited the four of us into his office and said, "I have a problem. You need to get your proper credentials." At the time only two of us had terminal degrees. One had a PhD in community development; the other had an EdD in education. The other "two of us" were me and the fourth colleague. The dean said, "I will help you do this as much as I can in terms of time off and some modest financial support. You need to get going right away, as I can't hold off the critics of your work much longer."

At about the same time a postcard arrived unsolicited in my mailbox announcing first-time accreditation for the Fielding Institute. I had not heard of Fielding, but I found the information about it on the card—a graduate school for mid-career professionals with an interdisciplinary curriculum in human development—immediately attractive. Until Fielding entered my consciousness the only feasible alternative route to a PhD I could see was Cornell's employee degree program. This was not attractive to me, because there were no degrees offered outside my college that deeply interested me and could potentially motivate me to pursue and complete doctoral study. The degrees offered within my college, while interesting and potentially motivating, did not appear feasible politically. How was I going to study and be assessed by colleagues with whom I was simultaneously fighting for budget and academic respectability?

Attracted by its interdisciplinary curriculum and its andragogical approach to graduate study, I applied to Fielding and, fortunately, was invited to attend what was then an ACW—Admissions Contracting Workshop—in Santa Barbara. What I found there was an amazingly diverse, friendly, supportive cohort of like-minded students; intellectually exciting, supportive faculty members, or rather mentors, some of whose work I was familiar with and used in my Cornell teaching; and Don Bushnell, who became my main advisor, mentor, and guide to "over the wall" recreation at La Casa de Maria in Montecito. I immediately signed up and began my studies, joining a New York City cluster group advised and hosted by faculty colleague Jeremy Shapiro.

Perhaps most compelling to me about Fielding, and what became most valuable about it, was the encouragement I received from faculty and advisors to craft my knowledge area, contracting in such a way that my work-work was my Fielding work. This was important financially, as I needed to maintain my full-time employment. In addition, it enabled me to pursue my studies in ways that exposed me to new theories and knowledge and to apply this learning to papers I was writing for publication, assignments and examination exercises I could use in my courses, and personal exploration of areas of interest I had yet to contend with at that point in my life. My discovery of this approach to graduate education, or rather its discovery of me via the mail at just the right moment in my professional life, was one of the most important gifts I've received. It enabled me to deepen and advance my work at Cornell and later at Stanford University, where I spent 30 years directing and teaching in both undergraduate and graduate programs on the main campus, in the medical school, and in Cape Town, South Africa. For this discovery of or by Fielding and my experience of the university and its marvelous community, I am eternally grateful.

How specifically has Fielding shaped my professional life? It guided me in the exploration of fields (e.g., systems theories) in which I had great interest but lack of in-depth knowledge, knowledge I could share with my students and apply to my understanding of my world, as well as the social policy problems with which I was engaged and in which I engaged my students. It exemplified an approach to and process of enabling self-directed, critical learning to which I aspired in my own teaching. It exposed me to professional work in fields related to mine of which I was ignorant.

For example, in 1984, about midway through my Fielding studies, I took sabbatical leave from Cornell to focus on my Fielding work in the San Francisco Bay Area. Faculty colleague Don Bushnell suggested that I undertake a part-time internship during that year with Pacific Gas & Electric Company's Organization Planning and Development Department. This turned out to be one of the most intense, challenging, and rewarding experiential learning experiences I have had. I acquired skills and knowledge that tempted me to leave higher education and join the OD field. Ultimately it made me both a stronger university administrator and a much better teacher.

I joined the Bay Area cluster when I came back to San Francisco from Cornell and continued with them until completion. A highlight was our work with faculty colleague Frank Friedlander to craft an "overview" seminar for ourselves in the systems theory knowledge area. It was a deeply collaborative effort, with each person taking a theoretical area to research and present during our two-day seminar. Those days were hugely enriching and exciting, both intellectually and personally. I remember returning home after we concluded thinking "that's what education should be about!"

Don and faculty colleague Malcolm Knowles encouraged me to craft a dissertation that could be integrated with my Stanford-based work with a national organization, Campus Compact, which was promoting civic engagement and service learning. It became a year-long follow-up study of faculty members who had participated in a week-long, national service-learning curriculum development institute I and others offered at Stanford for the Compact. My study was most interesting and rewarding in that it enabled me to observe first-hand and analyze the experiences of these faculty members on their campuses as they attempted to design and offer courses in what were then hostile environments for the kind of teaching we were promoting. It led to my researching and writing the first and only history of my field's first 30 years via an oral history focused on its early "pioneers" (Stanton, Giles, & Cruz, 1999), and numerous additional publications.

My dissertation and, actually, most of my Fielding experience deepened and cemented my commitment to what was then a nascent, embattled field. It was a building block in my leadership abilities, dedicated to further developing this field, installing service-learning pedagogy in the core academic mission of Stanford and at numerous other North American and international higher education institutions. In my post-Stanford retirement life I have established a small, international consulting firm that continues to work these issues with universities around the world, drawing on much of what I learned and developed at Fielding, including my time at PG&E.

I could go on, but will close with one quick anecdote. At Stanford I often had PhD students working with me on various projects. Occasionally we would compare notes on our experiences of pursuing our degrees and dissertations. Without exception these students would almost salivate at the opportunities I had: to direct my own studies with supportive advising and integrate them with my Stanford work; to create my own courses with fellow students in my San Francisco cluster group; to experience the kind of nurturing, mentoring, and recognition I received from my dissertation committee members and external examiner. Stanford at the time may have had a broader reputation and higher status in the academic world, but these students were convinced that I was getting a better and more humane education, with which I had to agree. Thank you, Fielding, and congratulations on your 45th birthday!

References

Stanton, T., Giles, D., & Cruz, N. (1999). *Service learning: A movement's pioneers reflect on its origins, practice, and future*. San Francisco: Jossey-Bass.

About the Author

Tim Stanton is Senior Engaged Scholar for Ravensong Associates, through which he consults in global service-learning design, development, and research in the US, Africa, and Asia. He is Director Emeritus of Stanford University's Bing Overseas Studies Program, Cape Town, where he established and coordinated the Community-Based Partnership Research Programme. He co-founded and directed the Scholarly Concentration in Community Health at Stanford Medical School, and served as Associate Director and Director of Stanford's Haas Center for Public Service, teaching in African studies, American studies, education, medicine, public policy, and urban studies. As Campus Compact Engaged Scholar, Tim helped organize and coordinate the Research Universities Civic Engagement Network. He has served as adjunct lecturer in education for Queens University and as the Roberta Buffett Visiting Professor in International Studies at Northwestern University. He has published numerous articles and two books and was named "Distinguished Scholar" by the National Society for Experiential Education.

CHAPTER 7

SECURING THE 2016 SUMMER OLYMPICS AND PARALYMPICS IN RIO

Gregory E. Walsh, EdD
Utica College

I recall heading to Santa Barbara for my new student orientation at Fielding Graduate University feeling very inadequate to be entering a doctoral program. My master's degree work was over a decade old at the time, and that work had focused on research using 20th Century methods. The World Wide Web was just awakening, and online access required hooking up a landline phone receiver to the computer . . . and waiting. I was also inexperienced at scholarly technical research writing but, as the years passed and I advanced through my program, my skills developed. During that time, I would also learn the important lesson that not all research had to be conducted in a lab or require a questionnaire—a lesson that contributed to my traveling to Brazil to study police and military practices in 2016.

On 9/11/2001, I was a New York State police lieutenant overseeing a homicide investigation. On September 12, 2001, I unexpectedly found myself a new member of a nationwide anti-terrorism team, and within days I was heading a newly formed counter-terrorism unit in my region of the state. Within months I was a member of the U.S. Attorney's Anti-Terrorism Task Force and was chairing a counter-terrorism conglomerate consisting of over 60 law enforcement agencies. Within a year I would be enrolled at the then-Fielding Graduate Institute for the purpose of obtaining my doctorate in Educational Leadership and Change. Having been exposed to an immersion in terrorism-related training, I specifically chose Fielding due to its flexibility in allowing students to focus on an area of interest while completing their coursework, and at every opportunity I took that path.

For example, when studying leadership for one of my first courses, I focused on the Taliban's initiative to assume control of Afghanistan starting the late 1990s. Fielding's faculty allowed me to merge my practitioner work with my academic research, which not only made my coursework more personally and professionally meaningful, but my newly gained knowledge from researching and writing on such subjects also made me more effective in leading counter-terrorism investigators. In turn, I was selected by New York State administrators to provide leadership training to police chiefs and commanders around the state, a challenging assignment that provided me with outstanding experience for my future career as a college professor. To say that the Fielding Effect was in play throughout this professional development would be understating its impact.

Shortly after joining Utica College's faculty in 2008, I immediately registered for the course on terrorism, and began modifying it from its historical focus to a Why-terrorism-yesterday-and-today-matters-tomorrow theme, wanting it to be more practical for students. I was fortunate to have two major mass-gathering sporting events take place each semester—the World Series in the fall and the Super Bowl in the spring. I assigned the class to serve as my anti-terrorism unit for these events, tasked with identifying potential threats to and vulnerabilities of the venue, prioritizing them, and then determining the most effective target-hardening security measures that could be put in place, given time and budget constraints. The Olympics have coincided with some semesters, and I then use the games as our mass-gathering sporting event to assess. It was from these exercises that I found a new research interest: studying the security and anti-terrorism initiatives of Brazilian security officials for the 2016 Summer Olympics and Paralympics in Rio de Janeiro.

Heading to Rio

Mass gathering anti-terrorism planners are paid to be paranoid so that the public does not have to be. After eighteen months of studying every possible way that things could go wrong in Rio for security personnel, and with the support of a fall, 2016 sabbatical from Utica College, I boarded a plane to Brazil to further support my research by actively observing security initiatives first-hand. My primary areas of focus would include public transportation, Olympic Park, where a majority of the athletic competitions were held, and the Athlete's Village, where most of the athletes were housed.

Public Transportation

By far, public transportation was my greatest concern in terms of vulnerability to a terrorist attack in Rio during the games, as it is nearly impossible for a bus or subway line to be fully secured while still maintaining schedules and public tolerance. As a consequence, I spent the greatest percentage of my pre-event research examining public transportation routes in Rio, with an emphasis on designated routes to competitions. I planned to be a passenger on as many of the bus and subway lines as I could during my stay to watch for security routines and vulnerabilities.

People come and go quickly on public transportation, very often carrying bags and packages more than adequate in size to hold materials capable of causing significant harm and/or damage. Even if everyone getting on a bus was thoroughly screened before being allowed on, every single traffic light or standstill in traffic—ever-present in Rio—represented an opportunity for anyone from the street or a following vehicle to easily and quickly attack the bus, and that is for only one bus. Add to that a whole city of bus lines moving every which way, and then a subway line, and the security challenges become obvious. What security planners are left with, then, is shoring up the most populated areas (the designated stops) with stationary forces, supplemented by roving random patrols to add to the unknown deterrent factor.

I was pleased to see that Brazil's police leaders had the stationary security presence at designated line stops and platforms along the games' routes, but they stopped there. Not once did I see a uniformed official riding on a bus or train, and I traveled on both a lot. Also, venturing just one stop off of or beyond a designated route to the competition indicated no trace of uniformed security personnel even at the designated stops or platforms. I searched for them, but they just were not there. Undercover? Perhaps, but that defeats the very important overt deterrent purpose, creating a potentially dangerous security gap, which I found surprising and risky.

One person intent on hurting as many people as they can as quickly as they can has the opportunity to do a lot of damage. Quick response to a threat or attack on public transportation is critical, but Brazil's security leadership did not appear to address this. Even a small bomb detonated on an unoccupied subway car resulting in no injuries could have had a devastating impact on the city's transportation system and plans during the games.

Athletes' Village

The vulnerability of having thousands of athletes from most of the countries in the world in one place for an extended period of time is an obvious concern for security planners in an era of increased international terrorism. I anticipated the Athletes' Village in Rio to be well secured, and it was. Brazil's security presence at and around the Athletes' Village was strong. From military vehicles and personnel along the pedestrian approach to the venue, to multiple layers of varying height fencing/barriers surrounding its perimeter, to airport-style screening of all entrants, security was impressive. Inside the village, roving patrols were always visible. I felt safe, and I was comfortable that the athletes were as safe as reasonably possible. As an example of the security in the athletes' residential area, knowing that I wanted to observe security measures inside the village, I was required to go through several vetting steps. First, I needed to be sponsored by a United States team, which then had my credentials verified by the U.S. Department of Homeland Security. Then, upon passing through security to enter the village in Rio, I had to report to a secondary station to surrender my passport in exchange for a visitor's day pass. It was very uncomfortable handing my passport over to a stranger in another country, but a researcher has to do what a researcher has to do, right?

Olympic Park

Olympic Park served as the home to many of the sporting competitions in Rio. I did not anticipate seeing a lax security effort at the Park, and there was not. Getting inside the park was equivalent to going through airport security in the United States, complete with conveyor-belt style baggage scanners and all entrants having to pass through a metal detector. I watched security personnel closely to see if they were truly vetting entrants and conducting secondary searches to resolve alerts, or if they were merely acting as a deterrent and passing people through. I never observed an omission on their part, and was impressed by their professionalism.

Inside the park, though, uniformed personnel were nonexistent during my visits, and I was looking hard for them. Granted, an argument can be made that everyone in the park had been passed through security and, therefore, the park was secure, but unexpected emergencies happen, requiring a quick response from emergency personnel. Also, terrorist organizations had had years of advanced warning that Rio was hosting the games, which provided them with plenty of time to plan ways to circumvent security, such as having a group member(s) apply for a job in the park during the games. Even if never needed, having uniformed officials patrolling the vast park on foot was a missed opportunity for Brazil and Rio police to show goodwill, and for local citizens, national citizens, and international visitors to see and interact with police officers in a friendly environment. Just as the United States is going through a difficult time with police/urban and minority relations, so too is Brazil (Amnesty International, 2016). Law enforcement leaders cannot afford to miss opportunities for their officers to be seen smiling and interacting with the public.

Final Thoughts on Rio

The Olympics and Paralympics are the two biggest international sporting events in the world, and to say that contemplating ways to secure them is ominous would fall far short of target, even if things were bright in the host country in the years and months leading up the games. In Brazil, things were not going well in 2016. Corruption investigations were underway at every level of government—investigations of the President, of the governor of the State of Rio de Janeiro, and of the mayor of the City of the Rio de Janeiro (Chade, 2016; Langlois, 2017; Romero, 2016). Each were accused of skimming finances earmarked for the games' preparations, which may have very well played a role in the security omissions I have reported on in this paper. Even the vice president of the International Olympic Committee described early preparations as he toured the city as, "the worst I have experienced" (Barnes, 2014). Still, in spite of many calls for an unprecedented last-minute move of the games to other countries, Brazil pulled it off.

There is not much that isn't beautiful about Rio. Turn one way and you look out over the Pacific Ocean and incredible beach scenes, with large rock structures jutting out high into the air. Turn another way, and you watch coastal mountains climb into rain forests. Even Rio's *favelas*, which are Brazil's version of a shantytown or slum, are amazing to look at due to each structure seeming to have its own unique coloring and/or shape, often perched precariously on the side of a mountain. People have plenty of reasons to travel to Rio regardless of an Olympic competition, but any international traveler who was in the city during the games, who paid attention to the many security warnings and alerts for tourists, has only themselves to blame if they didn't enjoy an incredible experience.

Conclusion

My doctoral work at Fielding Graduate University provided outstanding preparation and training for my current position as an associate professor of criminal justice. After my Rio security research, I began discussing my findings at conferences and colleges around the country, which I continue to do today. I have enjoyed this experience so much that I have contacted the United States Olympic Committee to see if I could become a volunteer member on their support team at the 2020 Summer Olympics in Tokyo. I also intend to request support from my college to continue my Olympic security research in Japan, which would allow me to start making comparisons of how two different countries, from two different parts of the world, and with very different financial and safety records, went about securing the games they hosted.

I remember hearing my dissertation chair, Dr. Nicola Smith, and my research faculty member and New England cohort advisor, Dr. Sue Gordon, telling me repeatedly, as I worked through draft after draft of my chapters, that I could try to tell the world everything that I know at another time, but at that moment I needed to finish my dissertation. This became a line that I would repeat to countless times with my own graduate students at Utica College years later. Armed now, though, with research and technical writing skills from my course work, comprehensive exams, and dissertation, as well as the mentoring and support from so many at Fielding, I am following through and trying to provide new knowledge through my ongoing research efforts into security and anti-terrorism initiatives around the world. It has been 15 years since I first met Fielding's faculty, staff, and students at my new student orientation in Santa Barbara. Although I haven't seen most of these people in a long time, I find myself smiling at the thought that I will have another reason to visit Fielding in 10 years. Beyond its being the 25th anniversary of my joining the Fielding family, the opening ceremony for the 2028 Summer Olympics and Paralympics is scheduled to be held in Los Angeles on July 21st, only a 90-mile drive down Interstate 101 from the Fielding campus. I hope to see you there!

References

Amnesty International. (2016).
https://www.amnesty.org/download/Documents/AMR1954672016ENGLISH.pdf

Barnes, T. (2014). Preparations for Rio Olympics "the Worst" committee officials say.
https://www.nytimes.com/2014/04/30/world/americas/preparations-for-rio-olympics-the-worst-committee-official-says.html

Chade, J. (2016). *Stadium deals, corruption and bribery: the questions at the heart of Brazil's Olympic and World Cup 'miracle'.*
https://www.theguardian.com/sport/2017/apr/23/brazil-olympic-world-cup-corruption-bribery

Langlois, J. (2017). *Former Rio de Janeiro governor sentenced to 14 years in prison for corruption and money laundering.*
http://www.latimes.com/world/brazil/la-fg-brazil-governor-20170613-story.html

Romero, S. (2016). *Dilma Rousseff is ousted as Brazil's President in impeachment vote.*
https://www.nytimes.com/2016/09/01/world/americas/brazil-dilma-rousseff-impeached-removed-president.html

About the Author

Gregory Walsh received his EdD in Educational Leadership and Change from Fielding Graduate University in 2011. He is an associate professor of criminal justice at Utica College in Utica, New York, where he teaches courses on terrorism, policing, and emergency management. Prior to joining Utica College, he served in the New York State Police for 25 years, retiring as captain of the Bureau of Criminal Investigation in the central region of the state. Walsh focuses his research and presentations on police leadership topics, as well as mass gathering security and anti-terrorism planning. He resides in Syracuse, New York with his wife of 33 years, Jill, and they have three children. When Walsh can gather one or more of those children, they enjoy traveling to watch Jill race internationally as a member of the United States Para-cycling team.

CHAPTER 8

SPRINGBOARD TO GROWTH AS A SCHOLAR-PRACTITIONER

Josette Luvmour, PhD

At fifty-four years young, compassion, presence, gratitude, and service emerged in the process of earning my doctorate at Fielding Graduate University, and other aspects of wisdom have continued to emerge in my practice ever since. Already known in my field of experiential programs for families and youth, I felt compelled to expand my knowledge and standing in the academic community, regardless of the publication of *Natural Learning Rhythms* (Luvmour & Luvmour 1993).

The dissolution of many assumptions about the nature of reality triggered new openings. The affirming encounters at Fielding helped to create a new internal architecture that challenged my thinking, stimulated dialectical confrontations, and led to my transformation into a scholar-practitioner. Specifically, I learned how to stop the past from defining the future by stepping into the fray, engaging the dialectic, and emerging with new perspectives, new meaning-making, and an expanded sense of self. Motivated by my personal values of empowering families and seeing children as a part of social justice, I gained respected membership in the learning community, developed increased knowledge about the influence of social and cultural contexts, and expanded my responsibility as a change-maker.

There are many commonalities between my post-doctorate growth and those of the participants in my initial doctoral study. Entering the graduate process to address my own disorienting dilemmas led to new learning, transforming the past by making new meaning; this changed both my cognitive and emotional development. I now access greater aspects of well-being (including self-acceptance, courage, becoming more open-minded, connection with others, and feeling more competent and confident as a scholar-practitioner), as well as many qualities of wisdom, not least of which is using my knowledge, skills, and expertise for the benefit of others. Through collaboration with colleagues and relationships of open engagement, I continue to make satisfying contributions in my field (e.g., as a teacher of other teachers, in publications, creating training programs for youth mentors and service providers, and mentoring several master's thesis projects).

Postdoctoral Contributions in my Field of Human Development

My doctoral study demonstrated that positive adult development can occur when the adult is in a conscientious relationship with the child. What's more, wisdom often emerges when adults take action to nurture the child's developmental needs. Parenting can be a transformational experience that changes the adult in positive ways. Parents who have knowledge of *Natural Learning Relationships* child development have more realistic expectations and are more likely to behave in developmentally appropriate ways with their children. This research project demonstrated how adult and child grow together.

Based on the adults' lived experiences, the question "what's in it for me?" is answered. In fact, five dimensions of adult development occur when intentional effort is made to nurture children's development: cognitive development of perspective changes; differentiation from former ways of knowing, and new meaning-making of the self and the world; emotional development of trust, empathy, and affective complexity; exercise of personal agency to make intentional effort; the emergence of well-being; and the emergence of wisdom.

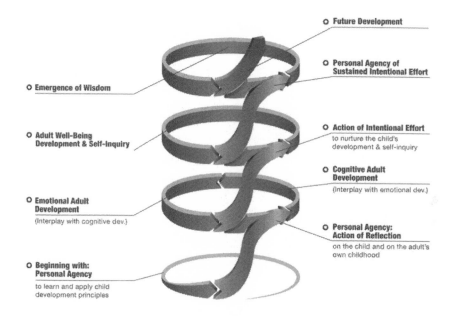

Figure 1. The spiral effect of adult development as an adult nurtures a child's
developmental imperatives (excerpt, 2017, p. 43).
(Note: the spiral is not intended to imply a hierarchy.)

As an agent of change in my field, my postdoctoral work continues to transform relationships with children in all the communities I collaborate with: parents; teachers; school communities; educational organizations; counselors; and therapists.   In addition, I have collaborated on the founding of two nonprofit organizations that are dedicated to awakening the greatness in humanity. I have published eBooks (2018), transformed my dissertation into a trade book (2017), and published journal articles (2011). Maintaining a national and international presence through public speaking engagements, and conference presentations (several as the keynote speaker) has also been rewarding.

Before Fielding, I worked with my husband and partner to develop a map of the evolution of consciousness throughout childhood called *Natural Learning Relationships*. The way we know our existence (epistemology) is through our whole being (ontological). It is how we come to know who we are as whole beings—knowing at each stage of childhood and at each stage of life. In this view, *knowledge is emergent*, needing context and relationship to come into being. Thus, natural learning relationships are an ontological epistemology that elucidates the awareness that the subject (who lives in time) and the object (timeless origin) are always one whole (i.e., not separable). Much like adult development, the direction is toward expressions of wisdom in an integrated whole person.

Along with my growth as a scholar-practitioner, the developmental understanding of natural learning relationships has also evolved and matured while in use by teachers, in classroom curriculum creation, teacher training, social and human services, adult education, nonprofit and school partnerships, youth at-risk prevention, Rites of Passage youth programs, college course materials, graduate student curricula, professional training programs for teachers and staff, and parenting support groups.

Research on Natural Learning Relationships
It has become clear to me through my research that there is a nexus between holistic human development and education. I have continued my research post-graduation.

One particular research project was on parents who attended evening classes once a month from September through June—a total of 10 classes. My research findings revealed that parents benefited with increased (1) knowledge and understanding of Natural Learning Relationships and its use in the family; (2) confidence in communication with their children; (3) confidence in parenting skills; and (4) an increased sense of connection. One mother said,

> The approach of Natural Learning Relationships child development gives me something more concrete to work with as a parent. I can go back to the basics: What stage is my child in? What nourishment does he need? What are his developmental limitations? (Karen-Jo A.)

Another important postdoctoral research project I designed involved teacher training. Teachers voluntarily enrolled in my training program, attending classes three times each month for four months, approximately 50 hours of class time followed by a practicum project. The research findings from this project revealed that the participants who completed the program benefited with: (1) increased understanding and classroom use of Natural Learning Relationships; (2) greater confidence in communication with colleagues; (3) competence in self-reflection and professional growth; (4) greater ability to meet students' developmental needs; and (5) an increased sense of connection with the school community. Teachers also benefited from having a clear and common language to utilize when describing their learning, and when they interacted with students and parents in the school community.

With confidence, I identify as a scholar-practitioner who works in the area of relationships with children. Who is the child? What are the social implications of creating developmentally appropriate environments? What are the benefits to adults who nurture children's developmental imperatives? My academic background offered the grounding to span boundaries as an empathetic and effective practitioner. I continue to make contributions in my field by providing programs that elevate the awareness of children's developmental needs and the benefits to the adults that provide them. Over the years, my career has grown and transformed from that of a frontline school administrator to service provider and consultant who supports professionals, schools, and families. In my position as consultant I also support adults who are facing conflicts in their professional careers and/or parenting practices that often impede their success.

My life as a scholar-practitioner has confirmed that knowledge of the Natural Learning Relationships of children gives professionals and parents the ability to understand the child's worldview and, consequently, to understand the child's needs. The usefulness of knowledge about child development is undeniably important and can be found in education, counseling, and therapy practices; family law; teacher training; in building positive relationships in classroom cultures; and for parents and families. The developmental growth between adult and child is a state of consciousness involving full engagement and awareness, as we attend to the inside of our being as well as the child's being. When we do this dance, well-being flourishes in both child and professional.

My transformation came about in many ways through the years; foremost is the multiple ways that relating to children has precipitated change in how I see myself and the world. Our wholeness emerges in relationship.

Through my doctoral work, professional applications, and program creation, along with my spiritual practice and relationships with family and colleagues, I discover again and again that we are not the *contents* of our consciousness, but pure awareness. Awareness is not thought. We perceive the manifestations of our consciousness but we are not those manifestations. One way I know this is that I can make change with intentional effort. Sometimes just taking a moment or two to let the dust settle and tune in to how I am feeling physically, emotionally, and mentally after a particularly challenging meeting, a difficult consultation, or a hard day is essential to being fully present. Making a conscious choice to remain aware and present with what is happening both inside and around me in the moment (simultaneously) allows me to respond in a way that promotes well-being in any child, parent, family, or professional that I engage.

All in all, we grow together. I feel all the feelings, including the emotions of suffering, love, and compassion that give meaning and purpose to life. Every day is a new opportunity.

References

Luvmour, J., & Luvmour, B. (in press). *Everyone Wins: Cooperative games & activities,* Revised and updated 3rd edition. Gabriola Island, <u>BC</u>: New Society Publishers. Forthcoming 2019.

Luvmour, J., & Luvmour, B. (2018). eBook Series (Vol. 1-5):

Brain Development and the Natural Learning Relationships of Children, (Vol. 5). Portland, OR: Luvmour Consulting, LLC.

A *Compendium of writings: The work and ideas of Luvmour & Luvmour* 2010-2016, (2018). (Vol. 4). Portland, OR: Luvmour Consulting, LLC.

Freedom in Education: Talks at the Brockwood Park Krishnamurti School 30th Anniversary (2018). (Vol. 3). Portland, OR: Luvmour Consulting, LLC.

Effective Boundaries with children: Creating and maintaining healthy boundaries with all age children (2018). (Vol. 2). Portland, OR: Luvmour Consulting, LLC.

Natural Learning Relationships: An introduction to whole-child development (Vol. 1). Portland, OR: Luvmour Consulting, LLC.

Luvmour, J. (2017). *Grow Together: Parenting as a path to well-being, wisdom, and joy.* North Charleston, South Carolina: Create Space Publishing.

Luvmour, J. (2011). Developing together: Parents meeting children's developmental imperatives. *Journal of Adult Development, 18*(4), 164-171.

Luvmour, J. (2011). Education and the Consciousness of the Developing Child. *Encounter: Education for Meaning and Social Justice, 24*(4), 15-23.

Luvmour, J. (2011). Nurturing children's well-being: A developmental response to trends of over-diagnosis and over-medication. *Journal of Humanistic Psychology, 51*(3), 350-368.

Luvmour, J., & Loomis, M. (2009). Nurturing the child's well-being: Key markers to support well-being in physiological and psycho-emotional development. *Naturopathic Doctor News & Review, 5*(9), 1-4.

Luvmour, J., & Luvmour, B. (1993). *Natural Learning Rhythms: How and when children learn.* Berkeley, CA: Celestial Arts.

About the Author

As an educator, writer, developmental consultant, and public speaker, **Josette Luvmour** specializes in the fields of human development, the natural learning relationships of children, the consciousness of the developing child, transformational learning, nurturing well-being in family relationships, how adult and child grow together, relationship-based and holistic education, and teacher professional development. Josette and her husband started several relationship-based education schools, a holistic learning center for families and children, and many whole-family immersion programs in both California and Oregon. She is also a teacher of other teachers (undergrad and graduate master's students), many of whom have gone on to start their own schools in the U.S. and Canada using natural learning relationships child development and holistic approaches in their teaching practice. She is co-founder of two nonprofit organizations dedicated to awakening the greatness in humanity, and principal producer of the popular podcast series, *Meetings with Remarkable Educators*. Josette has authored five eBooks and six print books, including *Grow Together, Parenting as a path to well-being, wisdom, and joy*, as well as articles that focus on relationships with children. *Grow Together* has earned the Mom's Choice Award.

CHAPTER 9

ALUMNI VOICES: FIELDING AS A LEARNING COMMITMENT, FIELDING AND OUR PARNTERSHIP TOGETHER

Susan Mazer, PhD, and Dallas Smith, "Trailing Spouse"

Learning is lifelong for any musician who plays professionally.
In fact, every performance is a final exam.

After finishing my last degree at Stanford University in 1969, I left academia, discouraged by the egocentric nature of graduate education and graduate faculties. My understanding became that if you truly wanted to do something unique, something that did not piggy-back on the work of a professor, it was not going to be supported. Thus, as a harpist no longer interested in another degree in performance or one in the specialties at the time (early music, computer music, Mozart), I had to leave.

The following 25 years were spent performing full time as a jazz harpist. Success and skill were the great outcomes of my playing every night, having unlimited freedom in repertoire, and also being able to move my harp into the larger world of electroacoustic instruments. Then, life happened and I found myself wanting more for myself and a more purposeful place for my music. Still, I did not want to become a music therapist or really change into any other existing professional role that was similar to what I was doing.

When I began working in healthcare, inspired by a harp student of mine and an organization in San Jose, California, that had hired me to develop workshops for nurses, I embraced new ideas, new knowledge, and science. I was not very comfortable in the New Age world, as I found that some of the promises made were not grounded in research or just did not fit my own experience as a performer and scholar.

Fast forward to 2006. At this point, my husband and I had a successful company and our product, the C.A.R.E. Channel, aired in almost every state in the U.S. and in over 800 hospitals. Still, I craved going back to an experience of deepening my knowledge of the human condition and how the context in which we live each day informs who we are.

Fielding came to my attention because of an associate whose wife was getting her PhD there. I looked online and also realized that a close friend, Dr. Jerry Nims, was on the faculty in psychology. Thus, I did my research and applied. Little did I know that Fielding was not merely a graduate university filled with requirements and deadlines, but it was far more invested in transformational learning that would, in turn, improve life across the globe. I was 59 years old, no longer willing to be an obedient student sitting in a classroom listening to someone tell me much that I could not remember nor find of value. Nope. I did not want exams or the most traditional ways most educational experiences seem to unfold.

Here is the list of my discoveries during my five years at Fielding:

1. Understanding the underpinnings of what we call "universal truths" results in realizing that we as humans construct our worlds according to layers of beliefs.
2. The scientific method and science itself are a construction originally motivated by a desire to move away from religious doctrine and towards an objective set of natural laws which must be discovered.
3. Philosophy is the bridge between religion and science.
4. Social change happens in extraordinary ways, usually driven by destructive innovation or changes in economic norms.
4. I have the power in my dialogue and critical thinking regarding my work to cause dynamic shifts in practice.
5. Changing a paradigm is harder than changing a norm, a belief, or an expectation.

6. Scholarship is of little use if it is not put to use! Scholar-practitioners raise the bar of academic scholarship to one of real-world relevance.

7. My thinking changed in so many ways, discovered again and again each day as I asked questions about what I do, why it matters, and what my hospitals are telling me.

I am ever grateful for my Fielding Experience, for the community that is still central to my life-world. Being a Fielding alumna (MA, PhD) is itself an accountability: to go out into the world and to do what is being called for to improve the human condition. Today, I remain a pro-fessional musician, a published author, a teacher, and a thought-leader in healthcare environments and the patient experience. I finished in 2011. I am now 72. Each day I start with a beginner's mind. I am grateful.

And now for the "trailing spouse's voice": I am writing this essay to express my appreciation for being able to support my wife's doctoral studies as well as being able to attend and participate in many Fielding Graduate University gatherings. Fielding students are accomplished, articulate professionals, which makes the social environment at Fielding gatherings very stimulating. I took the liberty of attending as many sessions as possible during these gatherings. I attended numerous sessions with my wife, Susan, as well as choosing different sessions according to my particular inclinations. Most people probably just assumed that I was a fellow graduate student, and I participated fully in discussions within various sessions I attended.

In the course of my Fielding experiences, it was particularly rewarding to befriend several faculty members and students. In David Blake Willis I found a friend with many shared travel experiences and mutual interests. Having lived in Scandinavia myself, I connected with Fred Steier around the Scandinavian experience. I had good conversations about music with Professors Jeremy Shapiro and Valerie Bentz. There were other singular encounters with amazing individuals, such as Charlie Seashore.

Fielding Graduate University is an outstanding institution within

American educational culture. I consider my experiences there to be personally enriching in the best traditions of a liberal arts education. I find that the subjects discussed at Fielding's Winter and Summer sessions applicable across academic communities. Indeed, the interaction between faculty and students representing different nationalities, cultures, professions, and academic backgrounds is an important experience for all those lucky enough to attend. I offer my sincerest thanks to all those who have co-created and who have led and continue to lead Fielding Graduate University!

About the Authors

Susan E. Mazer, a co-founder of Healing HealthCare Systems, holds a PhD (HOD) from Fielding, where she also holds a Master of Arts degree. She was previously awarded a graduate fellowship to Stanford University where she completed her master of arts in musicology. Dr. Mazer is also a fellow of the Institute of Social Innovation. Prior to her work in health care, she had a full-time career as a jazz harpist, performing with Dallas Smith, and such notables as Ahmad Jamal, Frank Sinatra, and Julio Iglesias. Dr. Mazer is known for her expertise on the issue of hospital noise, her accredited educational programs, and presentations at conferences. In addition, she is considered an expert in the field of privacy and HIPAA. Dr. Mazer writes about the patient experience in her blog on the Healing HealthCare Systems website and was a contributing blogger to the *Huffington Post*. Drs. Mazer and Smith's music has been featured on NPR, the Discovery Channel, and NOVA. They are also the founders and sponsors of the Elder Care Concert Series in Reno, Nevada, administered by the Sierra Arts Foundation.

Dallas Smith is a lifelong musician, writer, and business owner. He is a professional jazz flutist, saxophonist, and clarinetist. He is a decades-long student of North Indian classical music, having performed on numerous music tours in India and Scandinavia. Mr. Smith is the co-author, with his wife Susan E. Mazer, of *Sound Choices* (published by Hay House) as well as a regular travel blogger at www.mazerandsmith.com. Mr. Smith is the co-founder (with Susan Mazer) of Healing Healthcare Systems, which produces *The C.A.R.E. Channel*, a 24-hour relaxation channel broadcast for patients in hospitals in all fifty states. He lives in Reno, Nevada, with Susan E. Mazer.

CHAPTER 10

THE IMPACT OF PROGRESSIVE DOCTORAL EDUCATION TRAJECTORIES OF ALUMNI CAREERS
As Reflected In Data From LinkedIn

Judith Stevens-Long, PhD
Fielding Graduate University

This article will document the third phase of an extensive evaluation project that began over ten years ago at Fielding Graduate University. The aim of the research is to investigate the impact of mid-career doctoral education on graduates of a program oriented toward scholar-practitioners. We presented phase one at the American Association of Higher Education Assessment Conference (McClintock and Stevens-Long, 2002). The second phase was published in Adult Education Quarterly (Stevens-Long, Schapiro and McClintock, 2012) and the third phase, presented here, was completed in early 2017. Data from the first phase outline the cognitive, emotional and behavioral changes that alumni attribute to their doctoral study at Fielding.

The second phase offered data on the events and people at Fielding that alumni suggested were responsible for developments they described in phase 1. The current data highlights changes in career path and work arrangements that might illuminate behavioral development. Phase three of this extensive, and we believe innovative, evaluation project is reported here. The data for this report is taken from current postings of our alumni on the website LinkedIn. We are also executing a longitudinal study (phase 4) that will track the cognitive development of systems thinking from entry through graduation using an instrument designed to measure level of cognitive function.

For this phase three study, names of alumni were selected from a roster of graduates provided by the University. Participants were selected from a list of those who graduated from Fielding's doctoral programs in Human and Organizational Development after the year 2000. Participants were selected partly based on the assumption that these programs strongly reflects Fielding's values and enrolls students from a broad range of professions in the corporate, private, non-profit and government sectors, potentiating career changes when compared to our PhD in clinical psychology (many of whom are already in private practice) and our EdD (which enrolls individuals who are strongly committed to education).

The researcher selected every 10th name from the roster of individuals who completed a doctoral degree in Human and Organizational Development programs between 2000 and 2016 until the number of participants equaled 70. This is the approximate size of the previous samples in our project and seemed likely to produce redundancy in the data. Once the names were selected, the researcher signed into LinkedIn and used the search function to discern whether a particular graduate had created an individual page. The results suggest that LinkedIn is an invaluable tool in following the careers of graduates.

We discovered that over 80% of our sample had created LinkedIn pages. A LinkedIn page is quite similar to a resume. It lists the individual's current occupation, previous occupation(s), educational achievements, publications and awards. It also offers a list the member may use to reflect their current skill set. The skills Fielding graduates highlighted most often include leadership and leadership development, organizational change and development, management and change management, coaching and teaching. In our previous survey work, return rates were about average for survey research, hovering around 15%. Clearly, LinkedIn data can provide more rounded results on career than most survey work.

In developing the results here, we were focused on two basic issues: Can LinkedIn yield interesting and productive data about the lives of our students after graduation and what kinds of postgraduate career change might be reflected in these data? We were looking for evidence that our graduates become the kind of scholar-practitioners the HOD programs were designed to encourage. Scholar-practitioners do work that is informed by research and theory, and produce research and theory that reflects and informs work in the world. We looked at the kinds of communication they created for both academic and professional audiences as well as the changes they reported in their career trajectories.

Results

Over half (36) of these 70 graduates indicated that they had published since graduation, and nearly half of them (34) reported accepting a university or college position either while enrolled at Fielding or after completing their doctoral program. Most of the academic positions were described as part-time or adjunct. A number of participants, however, reported tenure track positions, full-time positions and administrative positions in academic settings. More specific information about these individuals is reported in Table 1.

As reflected in Table 1, about half of the participants (36) entered their doctoral program while holding full time positions in corporate America. Their occupations ranged from Human Resource specialist to the director level of management, engineering and finance. Another 27% (19 participants) reported running their own business when they entered and 5 of these people held adjunct position in colleges and universities positions when they matriculated. Nine percent (6 participants) came from the government sector. Six people did not list a previous occupation on their LinkedIn page but did list current occupations. There were two participants, both of whom owned their own business, who posted no discernible signs of change before and after graduation.

Table 1 also presents post-graduate occupational status as reflected by self-report on LinkedIn. By the time people graduate, many of those who came from corporations have left those organizations. Only 23% of the entire sample remained in corporate life. Nearly half of them (42%) reported publishing after graduation. Four of those who remained in

Table 1: Participants by Sector at Entry and Current Position

SECTOR AT ENTRY	CURRENT POSITION		NUMBER OF PARTICIPANTS	NUMBER OF PUBLICATIONS
Corporate			36	15
	Corporate	8		2
	Corporate and Own Business	3		1
	Corporate and Full or Part-time Academic position	4		3
	Corporate and Own Business and Adjunct position	1		1
	Own Business	5		1
	Own Business and Full or Part-time Academic Position	12		4
	Government	2		2
	Full time Academic	1		1
Own Business			21	
	Own Business	9		6
	Own Business plus Adjunct position	6		3
	Own Business plus Full-time Academic Position	4		2
	Full-time Academic Position	2		2
Government			7	
	Government	2		1
	Government plus Adjunct positons	1		1
	Government plus own business	2		
	Own Business	1		1
	2 Part-time academic positions	1		
Unknown			6	
	Own Business	3		2
	Own Business plus Full-time Academic position	1		1
	Corporate	1		
	Religious	1		

corporations added an academic position and one more added an academic position plus a personal consulting business as well. Of those who leave corporations, most open their own businesses (53%). Twelve of those 19 people (63%) added an academic position to their repertoire. Two of those from the corporate sector moved into government and one moved into a full time academic position.

Turning our attention to those who entered the program as proprietors of their own consulting business, all but two continued to run their own businesses (often changing the titles to reflect their new skill set. Some added a second business that seemed to reflect their course of study). The two who no longer listed a personal business had accepted full-time academic positions and were published. Nine of those who continued their own businesses added a part-time or adjunct academic job and five of them published. Overall, 75% of those who entered while running their own businesses were published after graduation. Details about these publications are discussed later in this report. Two people entered the program with their own businesses and an academic position. These people did not change sectors and remained in both their businesses and academic rolls.

Finally, of those who entered the program from the public sector (6), most (4) stayed in government jobs. Of those four, one added a personal business and one added an adjunct academic position. Two graduates left the government, one for a full-time academic position and that one also taught as an adjunct at another institution. The other one that left the government opened a personal business. Three of these six participants listed publications.

Two individuals in the sample of 70 indicated no discernible changes in career. Of those, six did not list of previous occupations, one listed the current occupation as a pastor; the other entered a corporate job. The other four listed personal businesses; two of them also held adjunct positions, and one held a full-time academic position. It seems likely that those who did not list a previous occupation were now in positions that had little to do with the jobs they held previously.

Table 2 presents a complete list of publications by category from full length books to white papers published on LinkedIn or by various organizations.

TABLE 2: LIST OF ALUMNI PUBLICATIONS

(2009) *The Coaching Connection.* Amazon Publishing

(2011) *How to Work for an Idiot.* 2nd Edition (NY Times best seller list)

(2006) *How to Sell to an Idiot.* John Wiley and Sons

(2004) *How to Live with an Idiot.* Career Press

(2007) *Leadership when the Heat's on.* 3rd Ed. McGraw Hill

(2009) *Collins Best Practices: Difficult People.* Harper Collins

(2009) *Collins Best Practices: Time Management.* Harper Collins

(2013) *Bullwinkle on business.* St. Martin's Press

(2008) *The Art of constructive conflict.* John Wiley and Sons

(2008) *Unleashing Leadership Career Press*

(2012) *Seize the Day: How to be an extraordinary person.* Career Press

(2001) *The Gift and Calling of God.* Lulu press

(2015) *Tomorrow's change makers: Reclaiming the power of citizenship.* Eagle Harbor Publishing

(2007) *Taming the abrasive manager.* Jossey Bass

(2017) *Authentic leadership and followership.* Palgrave McMillan

(2013) *The Generative Team.* International association of management

(2004) *From scientist to leader: Opportunities and challenges.* Genomic/ proteomic technology.

(2014) *New rules for women: Revolutionizing the way women work.* Ann Litwin and associates.

(2010) *From workplace to playspace.* Jossey Bass.

(2015) *The agility shift: creating agile and effective leaders, teams and organizations.* Bibliomotion

(2006) *A career for the 21st century.* ICMI press.

(2012) *Leading business change for dummies.* Dummies press

(2006) *The voice of your company.* ICMI Press.

(2007) *Frontline leadership in the call center.* ICMI press

Book Chapters

(2012) Sista abuse: The prevalence of Black on Black female buying in the workplace. In C.B. Fitzgerald and L.M. Geraci (eds). *Bullying: An assault on human dignity.* Oxford Press.

(2016) On crossing sacred and profane boundaries in time and place. In *Leading effective change in the workplace.* ISPCAN press.

(2008) Untitled chapter in *Transformational Phenomenology.* Lexington Press.

(2010) Untitled chapter in *Creating spiritual and psychological resilience.* Routledge.

(2012) Lost wisdom, lost ROI: Causes and consequences of failed global mobility. *Encyclopedia of HR management.* Pfeiffer.

(2009) Management development for wellbeing and survival. In *Work and Health Psychology.* 3rd Ed.

(2004) Diana's dilemma: The promotion stumbling block in organizational behavior. In *Emerging realities for the work*place. 4th Ed.

(2004) Untitled chapter in *Health and Wellness Coaching*, 2nd. Ed. Springer. (18)

(2014) An integral map of sexuality. *In Integral Voices on sex, gender and sexuality. SUNY press.*

(2002) Design and facilitate roles and responsibilities clarification in cross-functional teams. *In Team and Organization Development Sourcebook.* McGraw Hill.

Journal Articles

(2009) Boundary dynamics: Implications for building parent-school partnerships. The *School Community Journal.*

(2009) Workplace bullying? Mobbing? Harassment? *Consulting Psychology Journal.*

(2019) Personal inner values. *Journal of Executive Education.*

(2000) Introducing organizational development in a human services organization. *Administration in Social Work.*

(2009) holistic human development. *Journal of Adult Development.*

(2010) Epistemology and metamethodology in religious fundamentalism research. *Integral review.*

(2009) Developing and delivering an effective eCompliance curriculum. *Journal of Interactive instruction development.*

(2016) Getting to the root of the problem in experiential learning. *Journal of Management Education.*

(2013) An empirical examination of mega-event volunteer satisfaction. *International Journal of Sport and Society.*

(2012) retention and reengagement: Talent engagement strategies during mergers and acquisitions. *People and Strategy.*

(2006) Principles and practice of servant leadership. *John Ben Sheppard Journal of Practical Leadership.*

(2004) The roles of values and leadership in organizational transformation. *Journal of Human Values.*

(2012) What business student really need to learn. *Journal of Higher Education Theory and Practice.*

(2004) The roles of values and leadership in organizational transformation. *Journal of Human Values.*

(2013) Building consensus on defining success of diversity work in organizations. *Consulting Psychology Journal of Practice and Research.*

(2013) Diversity work in organizations. *Journal of psychological issues in organizational culture.*

(2012) Managers' interpersonal skills and their role in achieving organizational diversity and inclusiveness. *Journal of psychological issues in organizational culture.*

(2010) Addressing today's diverse learners. *Journal of psychological issues in organizational culture.*

Miscellaneous papers, online publications and trade magazine articles (14)

Creating successful change at the department of child and family services with appreciative inquiry. Independent white paper available at LinkedIn

(2005) *Ethical considerations in qualitative coaching research.* Proceeding of the 3rd annual coaching research symposium

(2012) *Living out loud.* Creative Thought Magazine

(2015) *Experiences of positive growth and energy at work.* LinkedIn com/pulse

(2006) *Revising the learning organization.* Social services consortium.

(2009) *Lost wisdom: Capturing expatriate knowledge.* HR Times

(2004) *Lessons from a problem-plagued learning initiative.* Training Technology and HR.

(2003) *Caution: Mixed generations at work.* Canadian HR Reporter

(2012) *Evidence from the field: OD tools and methods that positively impact mergers and acquisitions.* OD Practitioner

(2002) *Defining a diversity initiative.* Inside Supply Management

(2002) *Understanding workforce diversity.* Sharing Diversity.

(2013) White paper: The patient experience and C.A.R.E. *Healing health systems*

(2011) *The role and perception of privacy and its influence on patient experience.* The Beryl Institute.

(2003) Leadership development: A sound investment for biotech companies. *Biotechnological Focus.*

Finally, in Table 3, we present the academic positions our graduates indicated were part of their current career mix.

TABLE 3
LIST OF ACADEMIC POSITIONS AND INSTITUTIONS

Position	Institution
Adjunct faculty	Fielding Graduate University
Undergraduate Mentor	University of Puget Sound
Faculty	International training intensive
Dean of Academic Affairs	California International University
Adjunct faculty	Argosy
Doctoral adjunct faculty	Capella University
Director of Master of Science in Negotiation and Conflict Resolution	Columbia University School of Continuing Education
	Columbia University
Co-Chair Advanced Consortium on Cooperation, Conflict and Complexity	
Adjunct faculty	Cleveland State
Adjunct faculty	New York University
Faculty, School of Business	Capella
Mentor, doctoral faculty, Business Administration	Capella
Professor	Chicago School of Professional Psychology
Adjunct faculty	Fox Valley Technical College
Adjunct MBA faculty	Concordia University
Adjunct faculty, psychology	William Jessup University
Faculty	Intercultural Communication Institute/University of the Pacific
Part-time lecturer	Waseda Graduate School of Asian Pacific Studies
Professor	Rikkyo Graduate School of Intercultural Communication
Adjunct professor	Coles College of Business
Adjunct professor and sessional instructor	University of Victoria
Assistant Academic Program Manger	Post University
Faculty Project Supervisor	Royal Roads University
Director, career and self-awareness program	Post University
Associate Professor of Business	NYAK College
Faculty	Harvard, T.H. Chan School of Public Health
Associate Professor of Management	University of Dallas
Associate Professor	New Hampshire Bureau of Education and Training
Lecturer	Springfield College, School of Continuing Studies
Adjunct faculty	Springfield College School of Human Services
Associate professor	State of New Hampshire

Department Chair, MS Leadership	Trident University
Adjunct professor	Capella
Director, Center to Advance Education for Adults	DePaul University
Visiting faculty	DePaul University
Provost/ Chief Academic Officer	University of the Rockies
Vice Provost	University of the Rockies
Director of Diversity	University of the Rockies
Director of Academic Affairs	Phoenix Institute of Herbal Medicine and Acupuncture
Assistant Professor of Management	Westminster college
Adjunct	University of San Francisco
Instructor of Business Rhetoric	Santa Clara University
Associate faculty MA in Leadership Program	Royal Roads University

Illustrative Examples

Selected various examples of individuals entering in each of the sectors illustrate both the kinds of changes the participants made and the way we scored entries taken from Fielding selected alumni's public self-reported LinkedIn accounts; however, we have used pseudonyms here to comply with FERPA guidelines.

Trajectories of those entering from the private sector

Louise began her course of study while she was employed as VP of Global Risk Management at GlaxoSmithKline pharmaceuticals. By the time she graduated, she had become a board member of the Association of Audit Committee Members, Inc. as well as the FHL Bank's Office of Finance. She had accepted a position at Drexel University in the LeBow College of Business and opened her own business. She now describes herself as a consultant in enterprise and social risk management, social media and organizational systems. She has recently been appointed to the advisory board for the Drexel University Center for Corporate Governance.

Carl began his work at Fielding while the CEO of the American Red Cross for the Great Lakes region. He graduated in 2006. In 2005, he took a post as associate professor of behavior sciences at Queens University of Charlotte and in 2016, he become the Director of Graduate Programs for Queens University. In 2010, he added an adjunct professor position at American University. He continues to run his own consulting business (a company he had opened before entering Fielding). Recently, he published a book called about coaching for Routledge. Carl describes himself as a specialist in change management, organizational development, executive coaching and leadership development. His profile demonstrates a decision we made to categorize non-profit employment as "corporate." It seemed most efficient since there were relatively few participants working for non-profits and since non-profits experience the same kinds of external market forces as most corporations, and offer similar upward mobility.

In a typical trajectory for those who stay in the corporate world, Elana entered Fielding while working as a training specialist for Kobe Steel. She graduated in 2008. In 2005, after she began her work in the program, she accepted a position as Director of Talent Management and OD, Global Biologics Supply Chain for Johnson and Johnson Family of Companies. Two years later, she became the Director of Organizational Development for Qualcomm, a position she currently inhabits. In her Qualcomm job, she is currently leading learning and development, strategic and operational leadership for all sites in India.

In a shift from corporate life to government, JoAnne entered Fielding while working as the Director of Global Talent for McCain Foods Limited, a Canadian company. During her enrollment at Fielding, she was promoted to Director of Global Careers Center of Expertise, the Director of Global Workforce Planning for McCain. In 2015, she entered Ontario Public Service as a Senior Talent Management Consultant and in 2016, became an Executive Coach for that organization. She graduated a year later, in 2017. She describes herself as a human resource leader with deep expertise in integrated talent management, organizational development, career and succession management and performance management as well as coaching. She has posted an article "Experiences of Positive Growth and Energy" on LinkedIn.

Barbara presents an interesting profile. When she entered Fielding, in

2011, she worked as a consultant to the 50:50 programs for the Vancouver Canucks. She also owned two consulting businesses that focused on providing experiential learning programs for corporations and a third that focused on strategic philanthropy for major league sport teams, including the Calgary Flames and the Chicago Bulls. In 2008, she closed these businesses and opened a company that created solutions for problems of organizational alignment. She entered Fielding three years later and now describes her business as "designing and facilitating multi-stakeholder collaborative processes to development sustainable solutions to complex systems issues." After graduation, she continued to run her own business and accepted an adjunct professorship at the University of Victoria. Her work at entry was coded as "corporate" since she had been worked for the Vancouver Canucks from 1994 to 2013 and had closed her private businesses in 2008.

Trajectories of those entering as proprietors of their own business
Jane entered Fielding while running her own consulting firm, a psycho-educational service practice. She graduated in 2003, reframing her business while enrolled at Fielding from evaluations and counseling of adolescents with trichotillomania and victims of bullying, including body-focused repetitive disorders and NSSI (nonsuicidal self-injury). In 2009, she published a book for Aardvark Publishing called *Do It Yourself Trichotillomania Toolkit*. Trichotillomania is a form of Obsessive Compulsive Disorder. During her enrollment at Fielding, she also accepted a position as Adjunct professor of psychology at Farquhar College at Nova Southeastern University where she now teaches interpersonal communication and human development.

Sally sold a business in East Asian medicine and opened her own consulting practice in leadership six years before she entered Fielding. After graduating from Fielding, she opened a second business that specializes in leadership development for underserved communities and produced several tools, methods and practices she now features along with stories and videos based on projects in 26 different countries. Last year, she accepted a full time faculty position in the M.A. program in Organizational Development at Sonoma State University. She has also been working as a facilitator in the PhD, MBA and MsX students in the Women in Management program at Stanford University. She received a doctoral scholarship from the Organization Change Division of the Academy of Management for her dissertation work.

By the time he started his program am at Fielding, Steve had left IT at Philip Morris to open his own consulting business focused on management. After graduation, he changed the nature of the business and the name. The new mission was offered innovative and measureable web-based and mobile solutions for healthcare professionals who manage personal wellness. He also took a position as a faculty member in the school of business at Capella. Two years ago, he broadened his business again to include "strategy and operations" advice designed to increase global market share through innovative management. He now specializes in culturally sensitive strategic planning in physical and virtual environments. Two years after graduation, he published a chapter in a handbook by Routledge on care during disaster relief after hurricane Katrina.

When Sandra entered Fielding in 2007, she described herself as a management consultant/coauthor and co-founder of the Seattle based "National ParentNet Association." After graduation, she became a contributing writer to Psychology Today on youth development and opened a business as a researcher, author and speaker in Seattle. She has trademarked a framework called "The Compass Advantage"™ for educators who are want to understand how children and adolescents can become more engaged citizens and ethical leaders. She now also writes a blog for Edutopia, a website for educators sponsored by the George Lucas Education Foundation and has published a book called *Tomorrow's Change Makers: Reclaiming the Power of Citizenship for a New Generation"* by Eagle Harbor Publishing. In 2009, she wrote an article on boundary dynamics in the creation of parent-school partnerships for *The School*

Community Journal.

Trajectories of those entering from the public sector

Diane entered Fielding as a Social Worker II employed by L.A. Country Department of Children and Family Services where she served as assistant director. Since graduation, she has opened her own business and describes her work as analysis of workflow and business processes, behavioral healthcare administration and the development of soft-skills. She has advanced to Social Worker III and now works with the Los Angeles Police Department, Newton Division, as a co-located liaison. She has published a chapter on bullying in the workplace that was published in an Oxford handbook and has posted a number of articles on Linked-in, including one on sacred and profane boundaries. Other writings discuss the CPS worker as the other, and the bullying of social workers and criminalization of the social workers in child protection services.

Elizabeth graduated in 2009, having entered Fielding as a public information officer with the New Hampshire retirement system and an adjunct faculty member at Springfield College. During her enrollment at Fielding, she became an Associate Professor for the State of New Hampshire Bureau of Education and Training and accepted a position as a lecturer at Springfield in the School of Professional and Continuing Studies. After graduation, she also served as the Bureau Chief for the New Hampshire Bureau of Education and Training.

In 2006, David graduated from Fielding while he served as Director of the-Share-in-Savings Program Office for the General Services Administration of the federal government. That year, he became the Director of Strategic Human Capital Management for Health and Human Services; two years later, he became Director of Acquisition Policies and Programs for the Department of Veterans Affairs. In 2010, he was appointed the Executive Director for Management Integration of the US Department of Homeland Security. In 2006, he published a book with Google called *Adoption of Paradigm Shifting Change in the Public Sector* that outlined his dissertation research on stretching investment dollars while he was at the SiS program (Share in Savings).

Finally, Carol, who graduated in 2009, entered Fielding as Organizational Readiness Director for the Treasury Board Secretariat of the Government of Canada. Just prior to graduation, she opened her own business dedicated or organizational change management and public intervention. In 2018, she was appointed Honorary Consul to the Republic of Slovenia where she serves as the primary interface between Slovenia and British Columbia, helping to develop business, cultural and educational opportunities for Slovenia and solving problems for Slovenians residing in B.C.

Each of these illustrations was chosen from the names selected for the study by pulling the profile of the 5th name on the list of graduates in a given sector. Some consideration was given to finding diversity in the illustrations as well.

Discussion and Conclusion

In our 2012 paper, we reported that, when asked about changes in their thinking, personal development and behavior, graduates talked about development toward more critical thinking, ability to suspend judgments, and think systemically. They also described themselves as more tolerant of self and others, better able to see the perspective of others, and became more empowered and autonomous. They described themselves as more comfortable with complexity and ambiguity, better able to appreciate diversity, and more aware of the ways in which the world is socially constructed. The data reported here extends these findings and demonstrates how these changes appear to be reflected in career development. In our 2012 paper, we noted the need for doctoral education to meet the broader societal needs, as well as the personal and professional goals of graduate students (Carnegie Foundation for the Advancement of Teaching, 2003) to balance the current hyper-specialization of most graduate curricula. We defined transformational learning as a whole person process that is accompanied by changes in cognition, emotional life and behavior. As noted, the graduates of 2012 reported change in all three areas. They saw themselves as more reflective and critical. They felt more confident of their own ideas, more empowered and autonomous. In terms of behavior development, they talked about new skills, roles and products, continuous learning and experimentation, the ability to cope with change and attune their behavior to others.

This study demonstrates behavior changes that seem to accompany the cognitive and emotional change noted in our previous work. Only two of the 70 alumni did not report clear changes in their career trajectories, suggesting that increased ability to cope with change might result in everything from finding the time and courage to publish to changing their jobs. The patterns documented here suggest a kind of pastiche career life reflected in such popular terms as the "gig economy." In more academic circles, such a pattern is often referred to as a "protean career." The consistent listing of such skills as leadership development and executive or management coaching suggest an empowered or autonomous sense of self, attunement to others and the ability to see multiple perspectives, to diagnose situations and think systemically, as reported in the 2012 study.

As we wrote in 2012 "the behavioral aspect of graduate study is difficult to assess by self-report alone, yet it is arguable the most important outcome in relation to the societal value of education" (Stevens-Long, Shapiro and McClintock). At Fielding, we claim to help our students develop the skills and behaviors of a "scholar-practitioner." That is, to be reflective in action Schön (1987) to inform their work in the world through research and theory in the field and to contribute to research and theory through their work. The data from the current study demonstrate that, at least in self-reports, our alumni make career choices that reflect this definition. They engage in consultation across a wide variety of corporate and non-profit activities; they take up academic life; they publish and they move into positions that offer more complex challenges and a wider span of authority.

Although few people enter a doctoral program at midlife, our students seem to have exploited the opportunities that followed their attainment of an advanced degree. Perusing these results, one might suggest three basic dimensions to the trajectories of our graduates, regardless of the sector from which they entered Fielding:

- *Autonomy:* They move up in organizations, enter teaching and their own businesses

- *Variety:* They engage in a wider range of activities in their professional lives after graduation.

- *Impact:* They reach a wider audience or move toward a wider span of authority.

In 2012, graduates often reported that they felt more confident about what they knew and also clearer about what they did not know. So, descriptions of the consulting practices our alumni own often became more specific, for example moving from vague descriptions like "corporate alignment" to "analysis of workflow and business processes." At the same time, they began to describe their clients as "multinational or multicultural" and to emphasize the importance of coping with "diversity."

In the corporate world, they moved from local or regional leadership positions that entailed national or global responsibilities. This kind of change was often reflected in those who entered in the government sector as well. These changes suggest that self-reports of more systemic thinking are behaviorally consonant with increasing span of authority, a more systemic view and an opportunity for greater impact.

Adding adjunct or part-time positions in colleges and universities to their careers as consultants and in corporate and government management, or taking on academic administration suggests both the desire for variety as well as the need to function independently and expand the audience for one's work. The surprising range and variety of publication also suggests the desire to reach a broader audience, particularly to bring research and theory to the world of practitioners in leadership, coaching and management. A teaching position offers a wider audience and the opportunity for greater impact.

Over all, our 2012 findings about our graduates increased confidence in their own abilities and knowledge certainly seems reflected in the numerous and often large career changes our graduates embraced. One would suppose that embarking upon the doctoral education at the age of 40 or 50 reflects a desire to grow and develop as a scholar practitioner. At Fielding, our mission refers to the creation of a community of scholar practitioners who are interested in personal, organizational, societal, and global concerns in the service of creating a more just and sustainable future. The postgraduate careers of our alumni appear to reflect the success of this mission and to underscore the potential of a scholar practitioner model of midlife doctoral education.

References

Carnegie Foundation for the Advancement of Teaching. (2003). *Carnegie Initiative on the Doctorate*. Retrieved from http://www.ams.org/notices/200305/comm-carnegie.pdf.

McClintock, C. and Stevens-Long, J. (2002). *Assessing Ineffable Learning Outcomes in Graduate Education*. American Association of Higher Education Assessment Conference, Boston, Mass.

Schön, Donald A. (1987). *Educating the Reflective Practitioner*. SanFrancisco:Jossey-Bass.Stevens-Long, J., Schapiro, S., & McClintock, C. (2012). Passionate scholars: Transformative learning in doctoral education. *Adult Education Quarterly*, 62, 180-198.

About the Author

Judy Stevens-Long is an internationally known researcher in adult development, the author of four editions of *Adult life, developmental processes,* and a new guidebook to the last stages of adulthood, *Living Well, Dying Well* as well as numerous journal articles and handbook chapters. She has taught developmental psychology for all of her career, and has consulted to professional groups and universities in team building and communication. She has helped design graduate level programs in human and organizational development, including a Master's Degree in Organizational Design and Effectiveness, a certificate in Evidence-Based Coaching, and a variety of continuing education programs. She was a founding faculty member of the University of Washington, Tacoma. She has served on the editorial boards of several journals, including the *Journal of Adult Development,* and served as co-chair of the *Society for Research in Adult Development.*

PART II

FIELDING'S ACADEMIC VISION: AN INDEPENDENT GRADUATE SCHOOL TAKES SHAPE

CHAPTER 11

LEARNER-CENTERED GRADUATE EDUCATION

Monique L. Snowden, PhD
Fielding Graduate University

In the Learning Core

It is common for college and universities to unequivocally pronounce their student-centeredness, while paradoxically adopting ideologies and enacting models that situate faculty at the center of students' learning. Conversely, from the onset of Fielding's founding, learner-centeredness has been a fundamental characteristic of the relationship between its faculty and students. Metaphorically speaking, Fielding faculty invite our students in from the periphery of their education into the co-inhabited learning core amongst their faculty. Students' initial response to this empowering learning proposition, and their subsequent participation in their own learning process, illuminates different learner types.

Tough (1971, 1979) and Knowles (1975, 1980) emphasized that adult learners become increasingly self-directed as they mature. It is a misnomer, however, that the archetypal "adult student" is necessarily self-directed in their learning (Schrader-Naef, 2000). An inaccurate assumption in this regard can impose strain on the student-faculty relationship. On one side, there may be misaligned student expectations, in terms of faculty "teaching" role, style and strategies. On the other side, faculty may view "facilitating" learning as their role, in terms working with adult students. Achieving optimal balance between the two sides necessitates both parties attaining a nuanced understanding of the adjustments needed to meet student and faculty expectations. As a related aside, the grand narrative of a monolithic Fielding learning model makes for interesting folklore.

However, it fails to convey the situational balancing that occurs in the aforementioned learning core.

Hershey and Blanchard's (1988) situational leadership model stimulated theories about situational learning, with respect to educators personalizing their styles to meet the developmental needs of learners. For example, Grow (1991, 1994) promotes a Staged Self-Directed Learning (SSDL) model with four distinct learner stages: 1) dependent, 2) interested, 3) involved, and 4) self-directed (see Figure 1). The model offers both an organizing learner typology and generative process for integrating learning experiences in a situational nature. Altogether, curricular and instructional design of particular *learning models* may be more or less suited for different learner types. Furthermore, it is important to take into considerations the complex and entangled bricolage of *learning theories* (e.g., informational learning, transformation learning, and experiential learning), *learning assessment methods* (e.g., diagnostic, formative, and summative) and *learning assessment mechanisms* (rubrics, portfolios, and observations).

Figure 1: Learner Stages/Typology

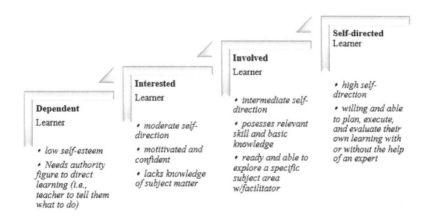

The co-construction of a learning milieu—as a consultative and collaborative process between faculty and students—is not easily realized. In fact, cooperative structuring of active learning environments sets Fielding apart from other institutions offering online, hybrid and blended learning delivery (i.e., distributed programs). For many Fielding students, their learning experiences transcend the transactional delivery and consumption of curricular and program components. Conversely, our students interact with faculty by way of a personalized learning nexus that is intensely felt and passionately described by those who engage in and witness the mutual relationship. Deep and affecting connections between Fielding faculty, their extant students, and former students incites transformative experiences in the learning core. Furthermore, an array of complementary support services are situated at learning perimeters to augment students' educational goals and objectives attainment.

A Learning Centric Mission and Ethos

The Malcolm Knowles Endowed Chair in Adult Learning was initiated in 2005 to honor the work of Knowles, who was a founding faculty member of the former School of Human & Organizational Development (HOD), and a renowned scholar in the area of adult learning and social change. The application of "andragogy" (Knowles, 2012) continues to make a substantial contribution to adult learner-centeredness in Fielding's innovative academic programs. Thus, it is not happenstance that learning is prominent in Fielding's current mission statement: "We provide exemplary interdisciplinary programs within a distributed and relational learning model grounded in student-driven inquiry and leading to enhanced knowledge. This community of scholar-practitioners addresses personal, organizational, societal, ecological, and global concerns in pursuit of a more just and sustainable world."

The last sentence of the mission statement warrants close attention, in terms of how Fielding's learning ethos facilitates institutional vision fulfilment: "Educating leaders, scholars, and practitioners for a more just and sustainable world." That is, if an essential purpose of Fielding's existence is to provide and cultivate environments and opportunities for learners to recognize, evaluate, understand and contribute to global justice and sustainability, then reflective practice, reflexivity, and critical reflection are integral components of a Fielding learning experience. Furthermore, connecting the university's mission and vision to the following institutional values crystallizes the distinctive nature of learning in adulthood at Fielding, with the intent of promoting and aiding personal and social change:

- **Learner-centered Education**: We create an interactive experience that responds to the interrelated personal and professional lives of our students.

- **Transformational Learning**: We inspire a re-examination of one's world view and underlying assumptions to enable a deeper understanding of self and society.

The previously referenced SSDL model (Grow, 1991, 1994) opens space to view self-directed learning as both developmental and situational. In this regard, Hammond and Collins' (1991) self-directed learning model reflects complementary process components developed by Tough, Knowles and others (*see* Garrison, 1997; Stockdale & Brockett, 2011). Their expanded model is critically oriented, in that its "ultimate goal is to empower learners to use their learning to improve the conditions under which they and those around them live and work" (1991, p. 14). Their seven-component framework is comprised of three learner initiatives (italicized emphasis added) that focus on social and personal learning goals and contexts (see Figure 2).

Figure 2: Self-Directed Learner Actions

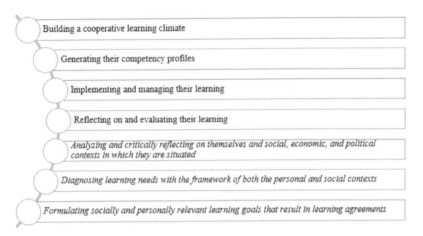

Building a cooperative learning climate

Generating their competency profiles

Implementing and managing their learning

Reflecting on and evaluating their learning

Analyzing and critically reflecting on themselves and social, economic, and political contexts in which they are situated

Diagnosing learning needs with the framework of both the personal and social contexts

Formulating socially and personally relevant learning goals that result in learning agreements

Learning is the transcendent mission of education. Therefore, placing primacy on learners and learning is an explicit reminder that individuals engage in education with particular learning outcomes in mind. John Dewey proclaimed, "Education is not preparation for life; education is life itself." One of the laudable goals of postsecondary education is to nurture individuals' life-long relationship to learning. Fielding decisively and intently occupies a special place amongst institutions who offer distributed graduate and professional education. Moreover, as one of few nonprofit independent graduate universities designated by the Carnegie Foundation for the Advancement of Teaching with the Community Engagement Classification, Fielding has evidenced a catalytic learning ethos that yields personal and social change (see Figure 3).

Figure 3: Fielding Learning Ethos

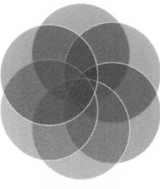

1. Responds to the educational needs of individual learners; stewards and promotes diverse learning ideologies, environments and delivery

2. Accentuates the benefits of graduation education and learning in adulthood, with respect to critical examinations and enactments of knowledge construction, socialization, integration, internalization and externalization

6. Recognizes that learning dimensions, assessments and reflections on individual learner's and learner collectives' experiences yield meaningful and impact learning outcomes

5. Clarifies goals, objectives, and associated understandings of learners' common and distinct skills, knowledge, insights, wisdom and experiences; informs learner-related actions with such understandings

3. Develops content-and context-specific learning outcomes, taking into consideration the educational needs of society— individuals, groups, organizations, communities and professions

4. Values and engages humanist modes of inquiry; places foci on learning to inform impactful actions that yield personal and social change

There is an unequivocal "passion for adult learning" at Fielding (Melville, 2016). At this momentous juncture in the university's history, the vision set forth for the institution is deliberately grounded in Fielding's innovative past and promising future—in learning domains. It is therefore incumbent on academic leaders and faculty to develop educational offerings and devise associated enrollment strategies to reach new and diverse learner populations—sans subjugating Fielding's strength with regard to learning in adulthood. Toward that end, a plausible next step is to develop and operationalize learner-centered academic planning, which is arguably a more interactive and organic approach than the normative production of a static academic master plan. This particular institutional action is an implicit declaration that distributed learning advanced by Fielding in 1974—and adopted by many institutions since its founding— is merely a method by which our most prominent innovative characteristic remains distinct. Learning!

References

Hammond, M., & Collins, R. (1991). Self-directed learning: Critical practice. New York: Nichols.

Hershey, P., & K. Blanchard (1988). *Management of organizational behavior: Utilizing human resources* (5th ed.). Englewood Cliffs, NJ: Prentice Hall.

Garrison, D. R. (1997). Self-directed learning: Toward a comprehensive model. Adult education quarterly, 48(1), 18-33.

Grow, G. (1991). Teaching learners to be self-directed: A stage approach. *Adult Education Quarterly*, 41(3), 125-149.

Grow, G. (1994). In defense of the staged self-directed learning model. *Adult Education Quarterly*, 44(2), 109-114.

Knowles, M. S. (1975) *Self-directed learning*. New York. Association Press.

Knowles, M. S. (1980) *The modern practice of adult education: From pedagogy to andragogy* (2nd ed). New York: Cambridge Books.

Knowles, M. S., E. F. Holton & R. A. Swanson (2012). *The adult learner: The definitive classic in adult education and human resources development* (8th ed). London: Elsevier.

Melville, K. (2016). *A passion for adult learning*. Santa Barbara, CA: Fielding University Press.

Schrader-Naef, R. (2000). Foundations of self-directed lifelong learning. In G. A. Straka, *Conceptions of self-directed learning* (pp. 143-169). New York: Waxmann

Stockdale, S. L., & Brockett, R. G. (2011). Development of the PRO-SDLS: A measure of self-direction in learning based on the personal responsibility orientation model. *Adult Education Quarterly*, 61(2), 161-180.

Tough (1971). *The adult's learning projects: A fresh approach to theory and practice in adult learning*. Toronto: Ontario Institute for

Studies in Education.

Tough (1979). *The adult's learning projects: A fresh approach to theory and practice in adult learning* (2nd ed). Toronto: Ontario Institute for Studies in Education.

About the Author

Monique L. Snowden, PhD, is Provost & Senior Vice President at Fielding Graduate University and faculty in its School of Leadership Studies. She is also teaching faculty for the University of Southern California Race and Equity Center Equity Institutes. Dr. Snowden is a Commissioner on the WASC Senior College and University Commission (WSCUC) and an American Council on Education (ACE) Fellow. She served as Vice President for Access and Equity on the American Association of Collegiate Registrars and Admissions Officers' Board of Directors from 2014 – 2017. Her scholarship focuses on enrollment logics that guide higher education practices, with respect to linkages between accreditation, institutional stainability, enrollment efficacy, learning assessment and student learning outcomes. She is an expert on strategic enrollment management, with particular focus on developing and leveraging enrollment and learning analytics to enhance institutional and educational effectiveness.

CHAPTER 12

STRENGTHENING A CULTURE OF SCHOLARSHIP, PARTNERSHIP, AND SOCIAL JUSTICE AT FIELDING GRADUATE UNIVERSITY

Charles McClintock, PhD
Director of the Institute for Social Innovation, Dean Emeritus

Orlando L. Taylor, PhD
Vice President for Strategic Initiatives and Research

As co-authors of this chapter, both of us came to Fielding Graduate University for similar reasons and to accomplish common goals. Founded in 1974, Fielding is an institution with rich roots and promising prospects for continued evolution as a distinctively high-quality, free-standing graduate school. In this chapter, we outline the ways in which our entrepreneurial efforts to increase external funding and partnerships enriches Fielding's scholar-practitioner environment and commitment to social justice.

Fielding Graduate University has evolved from an institution that eschewed external entanglements to one that has had to adapt to the environment of accreditation, financial aid, and other forms of regulatory reach. Fielding could not afford to stay "under the radar," as it had in its early years. The University prospered by earning a widely acknowledged reputation for a pioneering approach to graduate education (Melville, 2016), especially PhD-level learning, that deepened intellectual, personal, and professional development (Stevens-Long, et al., 2012).

Both before and after the creation of the Internet, Fielding's model was a blend of in-person and distance learning that, because of its comparatively low residency requirements, broadened access to graduate education for mid-career professionals. While curricula have become more formalized, graduate students are still able to customize their education by working in tutorial relationships with faculty mentors that build on and deepen their previously acquired knowledge and expertise, and they can pursue their education while maintaining residence and employment in their home communities.

In an effort to strengthen these distinctive educational features, we see our work as furthering two fundamental Fielding values: the scholar-practitioner model of graduate education (McClintock, 2004), and social justice, diversity, and inclusion (http://www.fielding.edu/who-we-are/vision-mission-values/). Our entrepreneurial efforts to increase external resources and partnerships are grounded in these values and are aimed at strengthening opportunities for faculty, students, and alumni to deepen their scholarly pursuits. Extramural support also enhances Fielding's intramural funding for faculty and student scholarship. The sum of these factors lends credibility to Fielding's primary effort: graduate education that is strongly rooted in research and that distinguishes the University from many similar schools.

The Institute for Social Innovation (ISI)

Prior to 2001, when Dr. McClintock came to Fielding as dean of what was the School of Human and Organizational Development, and in 2015 evolve into now the School of Leadership Studies—offering multidisciplinary programs in education, human and organizational development, and coaching. Fielding had received little formal grant or contract funding for research or professional development. Upon receipt of several grants from the Irvine Foundation to do cross-training of professionals from the fields of program evaluation and organization development (Campbell & McClintock 2002), Fielding created the Institute for Social Innovation (ISI) to promote and house grant and contract work.

Over the ensuing years, ISI sponsored over 60 projects for research, professional development, and organizational consulting (http://www.

fielding.edu/our-programs/institute-for-social-innovation/). These projects have been undertaken in Santa Barbara to strengthen Fielding's ties to its home community, as well as nationally and internationally, drawing upon the globally distributed nature of faculty, students, and alumni. Funding for these projects came from more than 30 foundations, corporations, and community agencies, as well as individual donor contributions.

ISI projects formed an important foundation for a major achievement in 2010 when Fielding became the first free-standing graduate school to earn the Carnegie Classification of Institutions of Higher Education as a Community-Engaged institution (Rogers & McClintock, 2010). This honor was renewed in 2015 through 2025 based on Fielding's alignment of its university mission, culture, leadership, resources, and practices that support exemplary and innovative practices of community engagement.

ISI continues these efforts through its Fellows program for Fielding alumni who want to remain engaged in research and continuing education projects. ISI fellows receive Institutional Review Board (IRB) and consulting support for external funding research proposals as well as assistance in offering continuing education units through their consulting businesses. Most recently, ISI created the Dianne Kipnes Endowment Fund for Social Innovation through a generous gift from a Fielding alumna. This annual award provides funding for alumni projects that demonstrate innovation and collaboration to improve the lives of individuals, organizations, and communities.

Office of Strategic Initiatives and Research

ISI's efforts have emphasized community-based projects with modest funding. In 2014, Fielding created the Office of Strategic Initiatives and Research to strengthen its profile through national-level extramural funding and partnerships for research and professional development. There was renewed attention to the fact that the first word in scholar-practitioner, especially at a PhD-granting institution, is "scholar," and that scholarship is a costly enterprise. The costs of sound scholarship are borne by recruiting a largely full-time faculty who are active scholars with funded research. However, the direct and indirect costs of research should not be primarily supported by student tuition. For these reasons, Fielding took the opportunity to create an Office of Sponsored Programs that would manage larger extramural funds, especially from Federal government agencies. This office coordinated the establishment of a grants management infrastructure for submitting, receiving, and monitoring Federal grants, while simultaneously providing professional development to faculty, students, and alumni on grant-seeking and grant-writing.

Dr. Orlando Taylor, a highly respected leader in higher education with longstanding grants experience, was recruited in 2014 to serve as Fielding's first vice president of Strategic Initiatives and Research. Fielding subsequently created the University's first negotiated indirect cost rate. Consistent with federal government requirements, these indirect cost recovery funds from grants are designated to defray costs for conducting grants, including those for the management and accounting of awards, and to recover costs associated for purchasing, space, depreciation, and utilities associated with the execution of grants.

At the same time, Fielding approved a distribution plan that uses a portion of its indirect cost recovery for an internal faculty and student grants program and to provide incentives and technical assistance for those seeking external grants. These efforts have resulted in a marked increase in the number of faculty members, students, and alumni who have submitted grant applications to both federal and private funding agencies and organizations.

Most notably, Fielding has recently been awarded several grants, principally from the National Science Foundation (NSF), totaling several million dollars. The largest of these is a five-year award to establish the national Center for the Advancement of STEM Leadership (CASL), a partnership project to study and promote leadership practices that underlie student success in science, technology, engineering, and math (STEM) programs at Historically Black Colleges and Universities (HBCUs).

Its ultimate goal is to use the research findings and current literature in leadership studies to produce a new generation of leaders to broaden participation in STEM at HBCUs and ultimately throughout American higher education (Mack et al., 2014). Other NSF grants have supported leadership development programs for African American, Latinx, Asian American, and Native American STEM women faculty and emerging leaders (Engerman & Luster-Teasley, 2017).

Under Dr. Taylor's leadership, the Office of Strategic Initiatives and Research has achieved several additional goals, including the creation in 2015 of the Marie Fielder Center for Democracy, Leadership, and Education. This Center honors Dr. Marie Fielder, a distinguished African-American civil rights pioneer in California and one of Fielding's founding trustees, as a university-wide entity to advance research, education, and advocacy on issues related to social justice, diversity and inclusion. The Fielder Graduate Scholars Program supports current doctoral student research under faculty supervision on topics related to educational innovation, race and culture, public policy, and social justice. It also provides basic training for Scholars in grantsmanship and modest funding to present papers at national or regional professional conferences. In addition, partnerships have been established to further research and education programs, including with the American Association of Colleges and Universities, Los Angeles Harbor College, North Carolina State Agricultural and Technical University, the University of the District of Columbia, and the University of the Virgin Islands.

Some Concluding Reflections

In addition to Fielding's faculty and students, alumni have contributed much to the University's social justice impact through their scholar-practitioner work as ISI Fellows. An illustrative list of topics would include positive aging; public engagement; dialogue and deliberation; healthcare transformation; coaching; sustainability; nonprofit leadership; organization development and evaluation; integral studies; and the World

Café, an inclusive group dialog and brainstorming process developed by Fielding students, alumni, and faculty. As noted earlier, these projects have contributed to Fielding's stature and Carnegie designation as a community-engaged university.

At age 45, Fielding is still a young organization within the higher education sector. Recognizing that it takes time to advance quality, the University has increased its investment in and begun to reap rewards from activities of the Institute for Social Innovation and the Office of Strategic Initiatives and Research. Building upon the long-standing strength of its regional and professional accreditations, these investments have strategically helped the University deepen its research base, create national institutional partnerships, and mark significant progress toward social justice, all of which will further distinguish Fielding Graduate University as the premier scholar-practitioner university of its kind.

References

Campbell, M., & McClintock, C. (2002). Shall we dance? Program evaluation meets OD in the nonprofit sector. *OD Practitioner, 34*(4), 3-7.

Engerman, K., & Luster-Teasley, S. (2017). *Women called to lead.* Santa Barbara, CA: Fielding Graduate University Press.

Mack, K., Taylor O., Cantor, N., & McDermott, P. (2014). If not now, when? The promise of STEM intersectionality in the twenty-first century. *Peer Review, 16,* 2.

McClintock, C. (2004). The scholar-practitioner model. In A. DiStefano, K. E. Rudestam, & R. J. Silverman (Eds.), *Encyclopedia of Distributed Learning* (pp. 393-396). Thousand Oaks, CA: SAGE Publications.

Melville, K. (2016). *A passion for adult learning.* Santa Barbara, CA: Fielding University Press.

Rogers, K., & McClintock, C. (2010). Higher education and community engagement: Strengthening democracy through a university institute. *Higher Education Exchange* (pp. 58-68). Dayton, OH: Kettering Foundation.

Stevens-Long, J., Schapiro, S., & McClintock, C. (2012). Passionate scholars: Transformative   learning in doctoral education. *Adult Education Quarterly, 62*, 180-198.

About the Authors

Charles McClintock, PhD, is Senior Advisor, Professor, and Dean Emeritus at Fielding Graduate University. He served as Dean from 2001-2012 and founded Fielding's Institute for Social Innovation in 2002, which he currently directs. His scholarship focuses on educational leadership, graduate education, and organizational change. Dr. McClintock was professor and Associate Dean at Cornell University from 1974-2001. He serves on the Substantive Change Committee of the Western Association of Schools and Colleges (WSCUC). He was President of the Occidental College Alumni Association and a Trustee from 2016-18, and is an Advisory Board member for public broadcasting station KCLU.

Orlando L. Taylor, PhD, is Vice President for Strategic Initiatives & Research at Fielding Graduate University and Executive Director of the National Science Foundation-funded Center for the Advancement of STEM Leadership. He is a national leader for diversity and inclusion in higher education, including preparing the next generation of faculty and leaders for the nation's colleges and universities, particularly in STEM disciplines. He has authored many publications and been awarded millions of dollars in grants to support this work. Dr. Taylor earned a PhD from the University of Michigan, served as professor and Graduate Dean at Howard University, and has received seven honorary doctoral degrees.

CHAPTER 13

THE ALONSO CENTER FOR PSYCHODYNAMIC STUDIES: FIELDING'S LEGACY IN PSYCHODYNAMICS

Margaret A. Cramer, PhD, ABPP
Fielding Faculty, Director

Samuel Osherson, PhD
Fielding Faculty Emeritus, Former Director

"So that, someday, there will be someone to talk to." With these words, Anne Alonso, PhD, (1934-2007), Fielding Graduate University graduate and faculty emerita, established the endowment that funded the Alonso Center for Psychodynamic Studies.

Anne was the quintessential Fielding graduate: an adult learner; an accomplished psychologist; a leader in the field of group psychotherapy (a former President of the American Group Psychotherapy Association); the author of several books (including a classic on psychotherapy supervision to be reprinted by the Fielding University Press in early 2019); a professor of Psychiatry at Harvard Medical School; a feminist; and a sought-after psychotherapist, teacher, and supervisor.

She had the brilliance of a scholar, the fearlessness of an entrepreneur, and the stamina of a distance runner. Anne's boundless energy, generosity to junior faculty, and compassionate wit made her not only an effective teacher and advocate, but also an honored one.

She believed, as we do, and as the research pertaining to common factors for positive outcomes in psychotherapy has now confirmed, that it is not one's theory, or manuals, or programs that help human beings to heal their psychological injuries, but elements of the therapeutic relationship that actually "do the trick." That "special something" that heals is related to what researchers have termed "nonspecific variables"—characteristics of the therapist that appear to be most responsible for positive treatment outcomes in psychotherapy.

Contemporary psychodynamic theory and practice puts the focus on the internal capacities of the therapist by emphasizing the ability of the therapist to listen in an active, empathic, and nonjudgmental way, to be aware of the telltale signs of the past masquerading as the present in the patient's actions, conflicts, and narratives, and to be able to bear painful feelings in the patient and in themselves in the course of treatment. A central notion of contemporary practice is that nothing is as powerful in creating the environment for change as the experience of being profoundly understood by another human being. Indeed, the basic elements of psychodynamic treatment principles assume that the dynamic unconscious is always at work for both members of the treatment dyad, that the treatment relationship is both the arena in which the patient's core conflict comes to life as well as the vehicle for cure, and that deep emotions are central to the success of treatment.

The central focus of the Alonso Center is to support our understanding of the important role of strong therapeutic relationships in mental health. Upon Anne's retirement from Fielding, the University approved the creation of a new Center to support these goals and to name the Center after Anne Alonso, whose endowment made the many activities of the Center possible.

Sam Osherson became the first director of the Alonso Center. Under his direction, the Center initiated the practice of hosting events at every Winter National Session that promote the understanding of psychodynamic ideas in the arts and in academic scholarship, within the Fielding community and for the public at large. Previous symposia have focused on such topics as the creative lives of psychotherapists, Three Approaches to Psychotherapy (comparing psychoanalytic, CBT, and humanistic therapies) and presentations by renowned contemporary psychoanalytic contributors, such as Justin Frank, Nancy McWilliams, Irving Yalom, and Vamik Volkan. Psychodynamic theory's long association with and appreciation of the use of the unconscious in the creative process has led to sponsoring events that have showcased the work of creative artists, including, among many others, a showing of the movie *Tangerine*—a moving exploration of the lives of transgendered sex workers—accompanied by a discussion with its writer-director, Sean Baker. The event that explored the creative lives of psychotherapists showcased the artistic work of Fielding faculty in literature, poetry, and the visual arts. The event planned for winter session 2019 will feature a presentation by psychoanalyst Donna Orange, PhD entitled, "Climate justice and psychotherapy."

Center events have also included two retreats held for Fielding students who wanted to deepen their understanding and experience of psychodynamic theory and therapy. These events allowed students and alums already familiar with dynamic ideas and practice to explore the latest theories and to share clinical experiences.

To support the scholarly efforts and development of current students, the center offers the Frieda Fromm-Reichmann award to the student whose paper demonstrates excellence in the understanding and extension of psychodynamic ideas and practices. It is named after the psychoanalyst who successfully applied psychodynamic principles and modified dynamic clinical interventions in the treatment of severely ill patients at Chestnut Lodge Hospital. This honor is awarded annually and includes a cash prize in addition to formal recognition at the National Session.

To further highlight the scholarly work of psychodynamic students and faculty at Fielding, Dr. Sherry Hatcher, another Fielding faculty member and Center faculty member, along with Sam, co-edited the Center's newsletter, *Talking Cures*. The newsletter offered a forum for faculty commentary and writing, highlighted the scholarship of Fielding students within the psychodynamic track, and updated the community about psychodynamic ideas regarding films and current events. Through their efforts, the work of the Center and the value of psychodynamic treatment were brought to a wider audience.

In 2004, the Osherson family also endowed a Fellowship within the Center that has brought two established professionals from the fields of education, social work, and journalism to attend a National Session to study psychodynamic theory along with the rest of the Fielding community. Each Winter National Session, two Osherson Fellows participate in seminars, mingle with faculty and students, and learn about the theory and practice of psychodynamic psychotherapy.

Upon Sam's retirement in 2016, Margaret became the director of the Center and continues to help fulfill its mission of promoting psychodynamic psychotherapy, the oldest and most enduring form of talk therapy. The Center now sees its future directions as continuing our traditions, while emphasizing the expansion of membership both within the Fielding community and in the public at large, as well as providing ongoing support for psychodynamic research and therapy through research opportunities with Center faculty and awards. With the support of President Katrina Rogers, the Center has invited Fielding alums, staff, students, and faculty to join in the mission and philosophy of the Center. Together, we look forward to the ongoing conversation about this way of listening so that, to paraphrase Anne Alonso, there will always be someone to talk to.

About the Authors

Margaret A. Cramer, PhD, ABPP, is a member of the Fielding faculty in the clinical psychology program, a psychoanalyst, and a teacher and supervisor at Massachusetts General Hospital in Boston. She is also on the faculty of the Boston Psychoanalytic Society & Institute.

Sam Osherson, PhD, is an emeritus faculty member at Fielding and is on the faculty of the Stanley King Counseling Institute. He is the author of a number of books, most recently, *The Stethoscope Cure*, a novel about war and psychotherapy.

CHAPTER 14

FIELDINGS FOUNDING VISION: THE POWER OF DISRUPTIVE INNOVATION

Keith Melville, PhD
Fielding Graduate University

"There is nothing more difficult to take in hand, more perilous to conduct, or more uncertain in its success than to take the lead in the introduction of a new order of things." – Machiavelli, *The Prince, 1532*

Forty-five years after the founding of what was originally called the Fielding Institute, it is easy to forget how radical and innovative it was. Almost a half century after it was started in 1974—and at a time when many aspects of Fielding's model have become familiar parts of mainstream institutions—it is worth recalling how bold its founders were, how clear-sighted they were about trends that would transform American higher education, and how audacious they were to think they could succeed with their upstart venture.

It was from the beginning an against-the-odds venture, unlikely to succeed. In retrospect, it seems remarkable that Fielding's founders managed to persuade a talented group of scholar-practitioners to join a fledgling institution that had no campus, very little start-up capital, and just a few dozen adventurous students.

Fielding's story is particularly pertinent today, a time when there is growing recognition of flaws in the mainstream model of higher education and the need to address them. Over the past few years, higher education has come under growing criticism. Dozens of recent books with titles such as *College Unbound, Academically Adrift, What Is College For?* and *Designing the New American University* illustrate a rising tide of institutional scrutiny. At a time when the cost of higher education continues to spiral upward, many are asking what students gain from their educational experience and what social benefits justify this nation's significant investment in higher education. The traditional learning model is criticized on the grounds that it has not adapted to keep up with the changing needs of students, in particular older students who need programs that are more convenient and flexible. Employers increasingly criticize higher education institutions for not producing graduates with the skills needed in today's workforce. In colleges and graduate schools, educators are under growing pressure to demonstrate what students learn in the course of their studies, pressures for accountability that many educators have resisted.

As Goldie Blumenstyk, a columnist for the *Chronicle of Higher Education* writes, at a time that can be characterized as "higher education's era of the re-set, 'disruption' may well be the key buzzword" (*American Higher Education in Crisis*, Oxford, 2014). The term "disruptive innovation," which was coined by Harvard Business School professor Clayton Christensen, refers to a process in which innovations introduced at the margins of an established industry work their way into the mainstream and eventually displace well-established competitors.

At a time when many traditional institutions are scrambling to innovate, creative disruption is clearly apparent in higher education. Innovations that were introduced in programs formerly regarded as outliers are now taken seriously, and have been incorporated into the learning delivery model of hundreds of mainstream institutions. In particular, increasing attention is paid to innovative programs whose learning models feature no-frills, low-residency programs that offer convenient, high-quality education at lower cost.

The experience of the Fielding Institute, which started as a one-of-a-kind program, is particularly instructive in this regard. It was a pioneer in important respects, and not just in the sense that it was one of the first graduate programs to recognize the potential of the Internet and employ it as an integral part of its learning model. The founders anticipated and appreciated the importance of a handful of significant developments:

1) They anticipated that higher education (part of it, at least), which has traditionally been geared to young adults in their 20s, needs to be redesigned to respond to the influx of adult, mid-career learners, who have different needs and bring a different set of experiences to their graduate education.

2) Recognizing that many mid-career adults who pursue a doctorate degree are not able to interrupt their lives to attend residential campus-based programs, they anticipated the need for distributed learning, a delivery model now called "low-residency" programs.

3) At a time when the cost of higher education was starting to increase rapidly, they recognized how important it is to pare down the amenities and accoutrements offered in campus-based programs to keep costs down and make doctoral education accessible to a broad group of students. What happened over the next few decades showed how prescient the Fielding founders were. Over the next 30 years the cost of tuition at public and private universities and colleges more than doubled in inflation-adjusted dollars, which partly led to the current crisis of affordability and staggeringly high levels of student loan debt.

4) Fielding's founders saw that a higher education system based on course credit or "seat time" is a misleading and inaccurate way to assess what students know and what they have learned. From the beginning, Fielding's model was assessment-based, which anticipated by several decades the national movement toward outcome-based learning.

5) They anticipated that doctoral programs, which have traditionally been devoted to the task of preparing graduates for academic careers, do not respond to the needs of a growing number of students who seek a graduate education that they intend to apply in other ways, as practitioners in a wide variety of fields. Fielding's doctoral programs in clinical psychology, media psychology, organization development, infant and early childhood education, human development, and education stand as hallmarks of the University's scholar-practitioner orientation.

6) They recognized that most graduate programs, which are intended to prepare students for academic careers in specific academic disciplines and focus their curricula on discipline-specific knowledge, are not always well suited to the needs of many people entering graduate programs. Fielding has combined both approaches to meet the needs of a diverse population of adult learners through its discipline-based School of Psychology and its inter-disciplinary School of Leadership Studies.

7) They recognized that learning—especially at the doctoral level—is not likely to be effective if it is faculty-centered, featuring professors as sage-on-the-stage experts. Learning is more effective when it is based on agreements that are mutually developed by faculty and students. The shift from faculty-centered learning to student-centered learning signals a fundamental departure from the way higher education has been organized over the past century.

8) Finally, the founders recognized that one of the chief weaknesses of mainstream doctoral programs is that they focus almost entirely on scholarly knowledge and concepts. What has been neglected is what a well-educated person should be able to *do*. These include fundamental scholarly competencies such as research skills, and the ability to make critical assessments of knowledge claims.

As Fielding's co-founder and first president Frederic Hudson noted on various occasions, the evaluation matrix for doctoral learning should also include the ability to demonstrate high levels of professional competence in applied settings, as well as what he called "developmental knowledge of oneself and others," by which he meant the ability to demonstrate "emotional skills, decisional skills, and communication skills," among others (Hudson, "Assessment of knowledge skills in an external degree graduate school," address to CAEL, November 29, 1984).

The term "visionary" is often used, sometimes quite loosely. In the case of Fielding's founders, it is accurate and well-deserved. They identified major trends and imagined the future of higher education several decades before these trends were widely recognized, and they asked fundamental questions: What is higher education's purpose? How do people learn best? What kind of learning environment is best suited to adults as they re-tool for the third and fourth quarters of their lives? Does it make sense to organize higher education according to academic disciplines? Far from being captive to traditional ideas about how doctoral students should be educated, Fielding's founders put forward a bold new approach to graduate studies.

They set out to reinvent doctoral studies for a new generation of graduate students, many of whom enter graduate programs not as a pathway to scholarly careers but as a way to become more effective and insightful practitioners. To use a phrase that has become a key element in Fielding's approach and its brand, they aspire to become scholar-practitioners. As the founders recognized, it is no easy matter to achieve that goal. Indeed, it requires a substantially different approach to doctoral studies. Fielding was part of the most recent wave of the progressive education movement, which crested in the late 1960s and early 1970s. Most of the institutions that featured progressive ideas were undergraduate programs. Fielding's notable distinction was that it was one of the first fully accredited graduate programs to embody progressive ideas.

Fielding opened its doors in March 1974, the same week the Watergate indictments were handed down by Special Prosecutor Leon Jaworski, which led to President Nixon's impeachment. It was a time of rapidly eroding trust in the presidency and public institutions generally; a time of growing interest in educational reform; a time when feminism, the Pill, the sexual revolution; and the human potential movement all signaled rapid cultural change. During the 1970s, fundamental assumptions and institutional arrangements were called into question, and countercultural themes of protest and nonconformity reverberated throughout American culture.

In many ways, Fielding was a response to those developments. The institution's founders were deeply influenced by the counterculture and the humanistic aspirations of that era. In some respects, they set out to form a utopian learning community, which bore a certain resemblance to Thomas Moore's original Utopia, a community devoted to lifelong learning. As Hallock Hoffman later acknowledged, there was a moment when he, Frederic Hudson, and Renate Tesch considered forming a learning community for adults that would offer no degrees. This idea and several of the founders' other ideas about how their new doctoral program should operate were quickly abandoned.

An upstart in the tradition-bound world of higher education, Fielding met sustained resistance in its quest for acceptance as a legitimate educational institution. After it cleared the hurdle of regional accreditation, Fielding not only survived, it grew and thrived. Whatever else might be said about visions that were not fully realized or principles that were compromised, this is an against-the-odds success story, and a narrative about a group of visionaries who left a remarkable legacy by forming an institution whose impact has created a legacy of scholar-practitioners that influence their respective professions.

This article was excerpted from *A Passion for Adult Learning: How the Fielding Model revolutionized doctoral education* (Fielding University Press, 2016). Reprinted with permission.

About the Author

A PhD sociologist who graduated from Columbia University, **Keith Melville** has been a faculty member at the Fielding Graduate University since 1983. In that capacity, he has been chair or faculty member on more than 100 doctoral dissertations. Throughout his career, his main interests have been in the areas of public policy, higher education, and applied social science.

He has worked in the White House, where he was a writer and staff member for the President's Commission for a National Agenda for the 1980s. Subsequently, he was a senior vice president at Public Agenda in New York, founded by former Secretary of State Cyrus Vance and pollster Daniel Yankelovich. He has worked for more than 30 years with the Kettering Foundation, where he is a senior associate. His first trade book, *Communes in the Counter Culture*, was a featured selection of the Book of the Month Club. He is the author of a college-level textbook, *Marriage and Family Today*, which over the course of four editions was a leading text in that field. Dr. Melville is currently an advisor to the National Issues Forums Institute and a member of the editorial group that produces the issue guides used in this nationwide network. Currently he is writing about public views on immigration, and a book about the major challenges facing democracy.

CHAPTER 15

AN INTERVIEW WITH DEAN EMERITUS, DR. RON GIANNETTI: APA, LUCY THE CAT, AND HANGING CHADS

Sherry Lynn Hatcher, PhD, ABPP
Fielding Graduate University

In 1999 I was seeking a new academic position, having taught at the University of Michigan for many years. At a holiday party in Ann Arbor, the host mentioned a psychology faculty opening at Fielding, noting that their clinical program was APA-accredited. I had not heard of Fielding, let alone that it offered an APA-accredited psychology doctoral program. I knew nothing of Fielding's geographically distributed faculty and not a thing about its blended, combined residency and online education model. Nonetheless, I decided to apply, partly in order to learn more about this intriguing-sounding institute called Fielding. Subsequently, I was invited to interview at a couple of different venues, including with the then School of Psychology Dean, Dr. Ronald Giannetti. He and I had a wide-ranging, lively conversation about teaching, technology, multi-site research, and more—all of which I found quite interesting. Not long thereafter, Dr. Giannetti called me to say I was hired if I wanted the position—and I accepted.

Fast forward 19 years to another especially meaningful conversation I had with Dr. Giannetti, this time over Zoom, a video conferencing platform that Fielding uses for some webinars and virtual meetings. For Fielding's 45th anniversary monograph, I wanted to be able to share Ron Giannetti's many contributions to Fielding that endure to this day, which include: our first APA accreditation (that has continued since 1991), his role in the origination of Fielding's Media Psychology Program, his support in developing our Clinical Psychology Respecialization Program (RCP), his creating a Director of Internship Advising position, and sponsoring the original iteration of Fielding's Writing Center. The last two of these initiatives are ones on which I was invited to collaborate.

APA Accreditation

Dr. Giannetti, a Fellow in APA Divisions 1, 12, and 46, was hired in 1988 in the position of "Chair of the Psychology Program" with a specific mandate to help the Clinical Psychology Program gain accreditation from the American Psychological Association (APA). In undertaking this mission, Dr. Giannetti succeeded in ways that have benefitted generations of Fielding Psychology students. As he noted, "When I took the job there had been one attempt at accreditation and it was close. We got our first accreditation on appeal. Fortunately, we had a totally unbiased appeal panel; they really listened to both sides carefully. Accreditation was way simpler then." When I then asked Dr. Giannetti if it was accurate to say that our first APA accreditation was around 27 years ago, he responded with a chuckle—and without missing a beat: "It was July 17, 1991."

Ron Giannetti also helped initiate the very successful and thriving Media Psychology Program. He said that at first: "I had no idea what Media Psychology was. At that time my idea of media psychology was Joyce Brothers." He was, however, "inspired and informed by a published study of potential career paths in that field." Giannetti said he heard about the study at a conference where the keynote speaker was Dr. Bernie Luskin, who had worked administratively at community colleges and with master's students; still, there had been no media psychology programs above the master's level. So, Dr. Giannetti, in collaboration with Dr. Luskin, developed the proposal for a Media Psychology doctoral program and presented it to Fielding's Board of Trustees, complete with a budget, a recommended curriculum, selection criteria, and research requirements, "the whole package." The Board of Trustees approved their proposal and "we got more students on the first pass than expected. Traditional nonclinical PhD programs don't have that many students a year," noted Giannetti. While he credits others with bringing this idea to his attention, Giannetti describes himself as "the organizational ringleader."

In addition to Media Psychology and as part of an overall initiative to create new Programs at Fielding, Giannetti helped initiate a Respecialization Program in Psychology (RCP), whereby quality PhDs, already awarded a doctorate in another field of psychology, could work toward earning a certificate in clinical psychology. Interestingly, in the late 1970s, Dr. Giannetti had completed the equivalent of a Respecialization Program while working on a post-doctoral grant at the Salt Lake VA and the University of Utah College of Medicine; it was a program arranged by his supervisor specifically for him. Fielding's RCP Program, originally developed by Giannetti in concert with Fielding faculty members Dr. Richard Stuart and Dr. Anne Alonso, was created using the clinical courses that were a subset of the PhD Program plus practicum and internship, thus not requiring additional funds. Over time, Fielding's RCP has ended up attracting a good number of students and is now administered by current Psychology Program Director, Dr. Marilyn Freimuth.

Lucy the Cat

At one point in our interview, Ron introduced me to his cat, Lucy, who had climbed up on his desk; "Meet my cat," he said. He credits Lucy with periodically "changing my computer settings." In the process of meeting and greeting Lucy, I was reminded of what a wonderful sense of humor Ron Giannetti has. It was something that made his tenure as Dean memorable and enjoyable for faculty. Periodically he would send the Psychology faculty timely pictorial messages, such as one I recall that was a cartoon of "hanging chads" (which gained notoriety around the time of the 2000 presidential election in Florida). He sent this to us when the faculty couldn't agree on some pressing issue that required a majority vote. Altogether, Ron's dry humor was facilitative of the many warm relationships among faculty and it was a quality we anticipated and appreciated, whether generated via an email cartoon or an in-person witticism.

Recalling the "hanging chads" and other levities, I wondered aloud to Ron about his rumored youthful enterprise in a troupe that performed comedy on stage. He told me that during his college years at UC Berkeley, he'd spent some summers in Chicago where he and three friends formed a "Second City" type group that presented humorous skits in coffee houses between folk music sets.

Fielding "Unprecedented"

I asked Ron what made him move to Fielding from his prior position as Chair of the Virginia Consortium for Professional Psychology at the Eastern Virginia Medical School in Norfolk, Virginia (before that, he was Director of the Psychology Internship Training Program at the Eastern Virginia Graduate School of Medicine). To that he replied:

> If you take a look at my personal history, I tended to be involved in things that were unprecedented and Fielding was sort of the extreme example of that. But when I interviewed for the job, I had no idea what I was going to experience because I could not imagine how it worked, which is part of the problem. People on the outside can't figure it out; and sometimes, for people on the inside, it takes a couple of years for them to figure it out.

But, he went on to say,

> It was exciting, it served a population that had no other opportunities at the time. The students were very interesting compared to what I experienced in the past. Students at the previous place I ran tended to be a bit older, but Fielding was a jump. The average student age was 40 at the time and I was 42.

He said he'd wondered: "What would it be like starting a doctoral program at this point in my life?"

Giannetti said he was further intrigued by the electronically mediated aspects of Fielding's program because, together with another researcher, he had earlier developed an online computer system for comprehensive evaluations of applicants for mental health services. As a self-described "part-geek," he also authored a very useful social history program, *Quikview Social History* (QVW), still featured as one of the Pearson Clinical Assessment products. (I used this program in one of my seminars to very positive student reviews.)

Given his history with computer-assisted assessment and a prolific range of publications in that area to his credit, Giannetti affirmed that "the whole technological aspect [of Fielding] interested me. So, it was a good combination for me; that's what I found exciting about it." He went on to say that he

> . . . enjoyed the job, [though] dealing with external issues was extraordinarily difficult. Internally I really loved the faculty. It was a cast of characters you rarely see anywhere—from all over the country, all kinds of backgrounds, varied strengths. And the students—that was really fun. It was great while it lasted.

Keeping Up With Ron

Whenever I travel to Santa Barbara for Winter Session or for a New Student Orientation there, I arrange to have a lunch with Ron Giannetti. We have remained friendly, both online and in person. I admire Ron greatly, not only because of all he has done for Fielding, but also for his intellect, kindness, modesty, and that wonderfully wry sense of humor.

Recently Ron has shared with me some exquisite photographs he'd taken of Santa Barbara flowers that he gave me permission to enlarge and frame. Several of these are hung on the wall of my study. During our interview for this article, I turned the computer camera in the direction of his photographic artwork, so Ron could see how lovely his photography looks in the room where I do my Fielding work most days.

Photography is one of Ron's retirement projects—that and new travel adventures with Carolyn, his wife of 43 years. They didn't have much time to travel while Ron was Dean at Fielding but, in the last few years, they have taken trips to Alaska, Italy, Portugal, and Spain; they have a fall trip planned to Vienna and Prague—and Spring, 2019 travels are scheduled to Israel and Jordan. Carolyn's and Ron's 42-year-old son, Tony, is a talented biochemist with a doctorate who worked as a Senior Scientist at Google in Mountain View, California and now owns an independent scientific consulting firm called Fringe Discovery Sciences. From that title, it sounds like exploring "the unprecedented" may be something Tony shares in common with his father.

Why I Wrote This Article

I wanted to write this article for Fielding's 45th anniversary celebration monograph because I believe our University owes a great debt to Dean Emeritus, Dr. Ronald Giannetti. It is more than likely true that most of our current students (and perhaps some of our newer faculty as well) are unaware of his groundbreaking and lasting contributions to Psychology at Fielding. Without the accumulated decades of successful APA accreditation, for which he first achieved success—and even with all the continuing bumps in that road—Fielding would not have attracted many of the quality students it has now graduated, and we might not have had a thriving Media Psychology Program or a respected Respecialization Program. Those of us whom Ron hired (many of whom are still on the Psychology faculty) would likely not have found an academic home at a university that privileges values of social justice and spawns uncommonly warm collegial relationships, along with encouraging creative mentorship for training our doctoral students to produce impactful research and competently help their psychotherapy clients achieve improved quality of life.

About the Author

Sherry Lynn Hatcher, PhD, ABPP is a member of the doctoral faculty and formerly Faculty Chair in the Clinical Psychology Program at Fielding Graduate University. She was previously on the faculty at the University of Michigan, where she received three Excellence in Education Awards. Dr. Hatcher was the recipient of a Woodrow Wilson Fellowship for College Teaching. This year she was honored with a scholarship created in her name that was generously endowed by Fielding alumna Dr. Elizabeth Hardy and Mr. Rick Omlor, for the benefit of Psychology students' research. For many years, Dr. Hatcher served on the Michigan Psychological Association Ethics Committee. She has published on topics including psychotherapy research, the psychology of women, and adolescent development, in journals such as *Psychotherapy*, *Teaching of Psychology*, *The Journal of Youth and Adolescence*, *The Qualitative Report*, and *Psychiatry*. Dr. Hatcher previously served on the Editorial Board for the APA journal *PsycCRITIQUES*.

CHAPTER 16

SYSTEMS INTENSIVES, COLLABORATIVE FACILITATION, AND THE SYNERGY OF EXPERIENTIAL LEARNING: THE POWER OF TRANSFORMATIVE ADULT EDUCATION AT FIELDING GRADUATE UNIVERSITY

Rich Appelbaum, PhD, Frederick Steier, PhD, David Blake Willis, PhD
Fielding Graduate University

In the beginning, there was La Casa de Maria. . .

La Casa de Maria

When Fielding Graduate University was founded in the mid-1970s, its summer and winter sessions were held at La Casa de Maria, an interfaith spiritual retreat and conference center spread among 26 wooded acres in the Montecito, California foothills of the Santa Ynez Mountains. The area that housed La Casa, as we fondly called it as if it were our home, was once an oak woodland from which the Chumash Indians harvested their staple food, acorns, which were ground into flour for soup and bread. We at Fielding did not harvest acorns but, like the Chumash, we did experience the peace that pervaded La Casa—leafy walkways, chapels and wooded glens for prayer and meditation, the sound of waters gently flowing in San Ysidro Creek.

La Casa and Fielding shared much in common: a deeply-committed belief in experiential learning; the importance of being sensitive to a fragile ecology; a commitment to social and ecological justice (La Casa was the home of the former Sisters of the Immaculate Heart, who had been defrocked for their radical ideas); and an emphasis on the bonding power of a shared and open community. As faculty, our experiences at La Casa were personally transformative. It provided a setting where learning from the heart as well as the head had a deep, primal resonance. When Will McWhinney, one of our founding faculty members (a systems maven and La Casa enthusiast) passed away, an oak on the property was dedicated to his memory. In addition, when our founder Frederic Hudson passed, a memorial service was conducted on the property.

Faculty members David Willis and Fred Steier

During the early morning hours of January 9, 2018, La Casa de Maria ceased to exist as we had known it. A few weeks earlier the Thomas Fire—at the time the largest in California history—had denuded the mountains above Montecito. A powerful rainstorm that night triggered massive debris flows that raged down once-dry creek beds, carrying with them house-sized boulders, trees, and cars. Large swaths of Montecito, from the mountains to the ocean, were laid waste. Twenty-three people perished; hundreds were injured. Four hundred houses were destroyed, including half of the buildings at La Casa de Maria. Pristine San Ysidro Creek, now a deadly torrent, covered half of La Casa with boulders, trees, and deep mud. La Casa closed its doors, confronted with the costly and seemingly impossible task of rebuilding.

Context and Culture: Creating a Systems Intensive

On this same January 9th of 2018, Fielding Graduate University was holding its annual Winter Session just a few miles away from this unfolding tragedy, experiencing nothing more than a brief, heavy rain. Before we knew the extent of the destruction, our focus had been on planning for a March System Intensive the three of us had scheduled at La Casa. We had already hosted a highly successful Systems Intensive at La Casa the previous March, and we were looking forward to somehow replicating that experience. That earlier Intensive, which included a dozen students, was structured around small group experiences in the Santa Barbara area, with students divided into several groups for a range of detailed assignments. Two different kinds of field trips were organized over two different days, in addition to the students working in small groups, to bring systemic insights into case situations that they had shared with each other prior to the Intensive.

The first field trip was largely unstructured; students were urged to observe and reflect on anything they chose, with the stipulation that they were observing systems in action in public spaces that included the interplay of people and place, whether it be mountain trails or downtown businesses. The second field trip, with new groupings being formed, was more structured and prearranged.

One group focused on issues of housing and homelessness, attending a Santa Barbara City Council public hearing on homelessness, meeting with Santa Barbara's Mayor and the director of the Housing Authority, and talking with activists from various nonprofit organizations. A second group focused on local environmental issues stemming from the seven-year drought, meeting with the leaders of Santa Barbara's leading environmental organization and the manager of the city's water system. A third group focused on education, meeting with the president of Santa Barbara City College (himself a Fielding graduate) and City College's Chief Development Officer. Students were instructed to view all of these experiences in systems terms, both through small group discussions and in written reflections.

The field trips also provided opportunities for reflecting on practice—what interventions might be appropriate, from a systems perspective, to address the challenges under discussion. In one of the small group experiences, the students were able to draw on their own OD skills to effectively solve a serious problem that had just arisen in the organization they were visiting. The conversations the students had in their posted reflections continued with a high level of energy during the Intensive itself. Student observations and recognition of the importance of process in a group provided everyone with a model of systems learning. Their ability to sustain deep and multivalent conversations about systems ideas and their shared observations about their cases also spoke well to the importance of mutuality in systems. The students actively supported each other and had strong dialogues both during the session and also in their post-Intensive conversations.

Whatever planning we had done for the second Intensive clearly had to be rethought in light of the night of January 9, 2018. We could no longer meet at La Casa, whose spirit had been central to the previous years' experience (and indeed to the Fielding Institute's early history). Much of Montecito was cordoned off, as the community took stock of the destruction and began to dig itself out. Most importantly, the weight of loss hung heavily in our minds. How could we approach this Systems Intensive in a sensitive way, less than three months after the disaster? Finding another place to stay was not difficult; there was a small hotel, a few blocks from the waterfront, with many amenities but none of the spirit (or, we are tempted to say, magic) of La Casa. We again organized small structured group field trips, this time around what we termed "creative spaces" (such as the new Santa Barbara Impact Hub), environmental issues, and education. We then came together again as a group to explore patterns that connected these different forms of systems and learning, including our own evolving relationships as a learning system. Our participation as students and facilitators in all of these diverse systems conversations was an important aspect of the success of the Intensive.

Sobering Lessons: Humans, Systems, and Trauma

But the core of the experience was a sobering field trip into Montecito, hosted by a key first responder who drove us in a county bus into the closed-off areas. We saw entire neighborhoods that had disappeared: the remains of small bungalows and large mansions that had been pummeled by boulders and swept downstream; a once narrow, verdant creek that was now a barren scar plunging out of the mountains, a hundred yards wide and a dozen feet deep. We then attended a follow-up panel discussion that included first responders, people from both the county and private organizations who were working with traumatized victims, and a representative of the "Bucket Brigade"—a group of local citizens that spontaneously emerged shortly after the disaster who, initially armed with only buckets and shovels, went into Montecito to help dig people out. The Bucket Brigade quickly grew into a thousand volunteers, received funding from a local relief organization, acquired backhoes and other equipment, and played a now-legendary role in the recovery, a case study in the effectiveness of self-organizing systems.

We next met with Ed Keller, a UCSB geologist who was running a long-term research project on debris flows in California. He explained not only the geology of the event, but also its historical predictability. This was yet another reminder of the different time scales of our physical and human ecologies, that we are very recent visitors in an ever-changing environment. That same message was conveyed after dinner, although in more spiritual terms, when we were joined by Marcus Lopez, a Chumash elder and leader whose ancestral home and associated structures, along with those of his relatives, were lost or damaged in the debris flow.

He reminded us in a compelling narrative of his experience of the debris flow and its effect on the local Chumash community as a system of the importance of living in harmony with nature, whose power must never be taken for granted. On reflection, we learned about different ways of knowing, and of storytelling. We realized that what might have been "heard" as a highly non-linear telling of the history of the Chumash engagement with their home, and the tragic events of the debris flow, replete with redundancies and folding back on itself, was a gift to us—a transformative gift inviting us into alternative and meaningful ways of telling and listening.

All of these experiences brought systems perspectives to us in varied, complex ways, as we learned about observing systems in times of natural disasters.

Systems Practices and Systems Learnings: Identity, Stability, and Change

One of the key themes of systems practice is how a system, whether it is a family, a community, an organization, an institution, or even a nation, balances its identity with either transformation or stability with change. While this issue is a theme of our learning in the Intensives, it also is one that applies to organizing the Intensive itself. In our description of the two above Santa Barbara-based Systems Intensives, we honored the earlier Bethel Systems Intensive in bringing conceptual work together with doing systems, with the latter including creating opportunities to understand ourselves as a learning system, as well as making a contribution—even if a small one—to the community in which we met. The identity may thus be one that balances inward looking and outward looking, action and reflection, as well as knowing in many senses.

To that end, the "placeness" of La Casa could not be replicated. This includes its history and our history with it; its campus, with its soundscape inviting a contemplative and yet dialogic milieu; and its staff, eager to share its mission and values with us. In a strong sense, we could say the same about how we sought to build on the Bethel Systems Intensives with the Eco-Village Intensives, the Anacostia DC Intensive, the LA Intensive in Boyle Heights, and others. But perhaps the identity of the System Intensive lies not in specific places or people but in the very process of trying to create a way of being together for learning and doing systems—a way that recognizes the affordances of place, as well as building learning relationships among ourselves and all of our fellow participants. In the face of the disaster at La Casa, the question of how to engage all participants in bringing about such a learning space was paramount. This meant also recognizing the affordances of the local space.

One of the other features of our Systems Intensives has been a focus on movement and embodied learning. At an earlier Systems Intensive in Bethel, Maine, we had a local movement therapist whose work resonated with systems principles meet with us, choreographing exercises on the house floor as an opener each day. At La Casa, body work with Dr. Roger Jahnke, a doctor of Oriental Medicine, hiking in the rugged hills above La Casa, and morning contemplative walks on the campus set the stage for the day.

Experiential Education: Making a Non-Place a Place

In the Systems Intensive in March 2018 we were near the ocean, so bringing the Pacific and the dramatic Santa Barbara Channel into our learning made sense. But then how to do this in a way that also would fit with our overall learning was a question we asked ourselves, as the affordances of place were important to our Intensive.

This question often surfaces as *how to make a non-place* (those spaces we move through every day in our rush to get from home to work, for example, without engaging with them) *into a place* that has meaning for us. The space itself near the ocean and the beach became an important part of our systems learning as we had the opportunity to blend the conversational with the contemplative. During the Systems Intensive, we explored key systems principles and continued our small group conversations centered on the presentation of new systems learning from our case situations.

We were fortunate to be near a significant landmark on the beach, the Burton Mound. Although the landmark is one that many people pass by every day, perhaps glancing at it as they cycle or skateboard by, mostly they do so without noticing or engaging with it. On the walking path by the beach is a beautiful mosaic representing this mound and the long-vanished vibrant community that was there. Built into the ground in a circular form, the Syuxtun Story Circle is a mosaic that depicts in rich visual form the myths, legends, and history of the local Chumash—the very group whose ancestral homeland was severely impacted by the Montecito Debris flow. Its visual display invites us to appreciate the ecological wisdom of the Chumash. We chose this location that had deep meaning for some to also become meaning-*full* to us, as a place to meet in the early morning to do activities that might bring movement to our Systems Intensive. We took this as a gift to us from the Chumash.

As we formed a circle around the Syuxtun Story Circle in the early morning, we tried out different exercises. On several occasions, Rik Spann, a visiting jazz musician/improvisational artist from The Netherlands who joined us for the entire Intensive, led us in some serious play as passersby smiled (and perhaps wondered about joining us). Led by another of our colleagues, we played a novel form of a collaborative hands-on children's game that enabled us to reflect on boundaries of the self. We also engaged in exercises, also from improvisational work, brought in by student participants that involved stability and change in movement. We hoped that we honored the Syuxtun Story Circle with our activity that also brought to life the importance of ritual and performance in learning systems, as well as bringing to life the readings we had done.

A key focus of systems is how to balance identity and transformation, stability and change, and the flow of different narratives for the same events or phenomena in the face of often turbulent environments. This is the "identity of our Systems Intensive" and can go in several different directions as we describe the stories from our learning together. Collaborative facilitation of this learning is a key element helping students (and ourselves) focus on different levels of systems in the Intensive: from interpersonal/organic to cultural/world, and with these played out in the rhythm of the Intensive. This also leads into our looking inward (our group) and outward (bringing value to the community in which we hold the Intensive), and playing with the relationship between the two but doing this with stories of what we did, rather than just abstractions.

Transformative educational experiences such as this are called Intensives for a reason: they provide an opportunity for a small group of students and faculty to get together for several days and share experiences that can be intense in myriad ways that open our minds, hearts, and lives. Extended face-to-face contact, with time for reflection, processing, and writing, creates a learning environment where ideas can be shared in real time. They are organized around a highly experiential format that requires learning not only about the content of advanced systems principles and practices, including ecological systems, but also about systems process issues, including our own group learning process. On our final day of the Systems Intensives, for example, after initially returning to our groups to reflect on the group learning within those groups, we came back together as a group as a whole to explore patterns that connected the variety of systems in which we had engaged, and focused on our own evolving relationships as a learning system. This included reflections on our learning spaces and the importance of space in systems learning.

Transformation occurs, moreover, not only in the student experience, but in the faculty experience as well. Collaborative teaching is not merely the sum of two or three teachers but has a multiplier effect on students, teachers/facilitators, and other participants alike in the synergy it produces. As faculty we learned both from our students, as they made deep sense of their experiences, and from the shared experiences themselves. Having three of us facilitate the Intensives brought additional depth as well; apart from making it possible for us to more effectively engage with students in small groups, each of us brought our own academic knowledge and practical experience to the nightly discussions, which no single one of us could have provided alone. With variety being so important to systems, including for sustainability, our own variety—of arenas for systems practice, of interactional styles, for example—was seen by the students as affording the kind of dialogue that, for them, was key to being in a learning system.

Another key principle of systems thinking and its concrete and deliberate manifestations is an appreciation of recursion and circularity, a central concern of cybernetics. In particular, we have come to realize that although the physical space of La Casa has been lost for quite some time, the spirit of La Casa and the story with which we began this brief reflective essay continues to guide our learning and planning for future collaborative learning journeys. The cross-pollinating groups, observing and acting in *systems*, and understanding ourselves as collaborative *observing* systems, while rooted in dialogue that values difference *and* shared experience, has provided a rich transformative experience that we hope to continue through future Fielding Graduate University's Systems Intensives in Santa Barbara and beyond.

About the Authors

Richard P. Appelbaum, PhD, is a professor at Fielding Graduate University, where he heads the doctoral concentration in Sustainability Leadership. He has published extensively in the sociology of work and labor; science, technology, and society (with a focus on China's turn to technology-based economic development); the globalization of business; urban sociology; and social theory. He is author or co-author of more than a dozen scholarly books and nearly two hundred articles and book chapters. His most recent books include *Innovation in China: Challenging the Global Science and Technology System* (Polity Press, 2018) and *Achieving Workers' Rights in the Global Economy* (Cornell University Press, 2016). He is also co-author of a widely used introductory textbook, *Sociology* (W.W. Norton, 2018). Dr. Appelbaum received his B.A. from Columbia University (1964), his MPA from Princeton University's Woodrow Wilson School of Public and International Affairs (1966), and his PhD from the University of Chicago (1971). He is also Distinguished Research

Professor Emeritus and former MacArthur Foundation Chair in Global and International Studies and Sociology at the University of California at Santa Barbara.

David Blake Willis, PhD, is Professor of Anthropology and Education at Fielding Graduate University and Professor Emeritus of Anthropology, Soai Buddhist University, Osaka, Japan. He taught and did research at the University of Oxford and was Visiting Professor at the University of Washington and Grinnell College. His interests in anthropology, sustainability, social justice, and immigration come from 38 years living in traditional cultural systems in Japan and South India. His scholarly work is on transformational leadership and education, human development in transnational contexts, the creolization of cultures, transcultural communities, and Dalit/Gandhian liberation movements in South India. His publications include *World Cultures: The Language Villages (Leading, Learning, and Teaching on the Global Frontier)* with Walter Enloe (2017); *Sustainability Leadership: Integrating Values, Meaning, and Action* with Fred Steier and Paul Stillman (2015); *Reimagining Japanese Education: Borders, Transfers, Circulations, and the Comparative* with Jeremy Rappleye (2011); *Transcultural Japan: At the Borders of Race, Gender, and Identity* with Stephen Murphy-Shigematsu (2007); and *Japanese Education in Transition 2001: Radical Perspectives on Cultural and Political Transformation* with Satoshi Yamamura (2002).

Frederick Steier, PhD, is a professor in the School of Leadership Studies at Fielding Graduate University. His work focuses on systemic approaches to social/ecological systems, with attention to learning, communication, and design. He has directed participatory action research programs in a wide variety of settings, ranging from government institutions, including NASA, to science centers, such as the Museum of Science and Industry (MOSI), in Tampa, Florida, where he was also a scientist-in-residence. He is the editor of the volumes *Gregory Bateson: Essays for an ecology of ideas* (2005) and *Research and Reflexivity* (1991), and is a past president of the American Society for Cybernetics. He has been on the faculty of the University of South Florida (where he was also Director of Interdisciplinary Studies Programs), Old Dominion University (where he was also Director of the Center for Cybernetic Studies in Complex Systems), the University of Oslo (Norway), and the University of Pennsylvania. He has also had the honor of being a King Olav V Fellow with the American-Scandinavian Foundation. Dr. Steier received his doctorate in social systems sciences from the Wharton School of the University of Pennsylvania in 1983.

CHAPTER 17

CROSSING BORDERS: PATHWAYS TO SCHOLARSHIP, SOCIAL JUSTICE, AND OPEN HEARTS THROUGH ADULT TRANSFORMATIVE EDUCATION

David Blake Willis, PhD, Jerry Snow, PhD, Stephen Murphy-Shigematsu, PhD, Connie Corley, PhD, Lenneal Henderson, PhD, and Harry (Rick) Moody, PhD
Fielding Graduate University

Crossing Borders—A Concept, Seminar, and Discussion

Crossing Borders is an increasingly important theme for all human societies in the 21st century. Mobilities, migrations, and movements are all challenging our notion of the journey of being human. Along with the crossing of national, regional, or local political borders are those cultural, social, psychological, and spiritual borderlands we experience as we travel to contexts dramatically different from those we may be familiar with and where we meet the Other. For many of us these borderlands are encountered, negotiated, and lived on a daily basis throughout our life course.

The purpose of our Crossing Borders Seminar, held at Fielding's Winter Session in Santa Barbara since 2010, has been to construct an overview of the landscapes of the life course and human development. We have utilized the lenses of social change, social psychology, spirituality, aesthetics, and anthropology as we have examined human development, life course, mobility, and identity. Our main texts have been works by those of us who have organized the workshop, along with a range of scholars, including Gene Cohen, George Vaillant, Barbara Rogoff, Benedict Anderson, Anna Lowenhaupt Tsing, Gloria Anzaldua, and others. We have explored and integrated ideas from positive and integral psychology, together with aging research, to frame our multicultural lived experience. The ideas of creolized, mixed lives, and life courses have emerged again and again during our seminar, adding a rich texture of complexity and intersectionality to the study of human development.

The seminar has been interactive, with an expectation that students, alums, and faculty would bring their experiences and perspectives to our time together as well as engage deeply with our texts. We have been interested in what the crossing of borders means in terms of lifespan and in the contexts of aging and human development, especially the lived intersubjective and "we-experience" over time in multicultural, transnational contexts. After framing this topic initially through several theoretical perspectives in each workshop, we began a process of dialogue and reflection that enabled us to determine possible research questions to pursue.

Transcultural mobilities, transnational lives, identity development, and encounters with the "Other" have been some of the primary topics we have examined. Identities and, in particular, the ways identities are enacted through creolization and in creolized contexts have been of special interest. After framing this topic initially through several theoretical perspectives in each seminar from 2010 to the present, we began a process of dialogue and reflection that would enable us to determine possible research questions to pursue that will enable us to grow and develop.

Our study together of human development and consciousness of course always begins with our own epistemologies, where we have come from and what we are looking for that might inform our journey of knowledge construction in new ways. Mindful contemplation of the here and now, of how we got to this point, what it means for us, and where we might go together next are important themes. Human development and consciousness are ongoing natural processes that manifest themselves at certain points in our lives in powerful, focused moments that some cultures have called epiphanies. These are, first of all, individualized experiences, but they also take place in the context of our societies and cultures at key points in our development. Our cultures are central to our meaning-making as we develop as humans. Moreover, the process of human development and consciousness continues throughout our adult lives, as reflected in the work/adult transformative education of many of us in the Fielding Graduate University community.

What follows are thoughts from our experience with Crossing Borders as facilitators of these Winter Session events, whether through the Crossing Borders Seminar itself or from larger issues of journeys across borders. We also include a number of photographs from our times together and those images that emphasize the mobile nature of who we are, where we have come from, and where we are going.

Reflections on Crossing Borders (Jerry Snow)

From the beginning, students in the Human and Organizational Development program are introduced to the notion of "becoming a PhD, rather than getting a PhD." This distinction highlights the transformational nature of the program and the curriculum; it's a journey as well as a destination. Because much of the curriculum is elective, the student is largely in charge of their own transformation . . . it is personal and cohort-based. Crossing borders provides a way of thinking about the discrete components that make up the curriculum and one's engagement with it. For me, it was an enjoyable deep consideration of a literal and figurative aspect of my existence. You see, I'm an American living in Baja California, Mexico and in Encinitas, California, a Mexican immigrant, legal alien, expatriate, and American citizen. Traveling across the busiest border in the world every few weeks, literally allows the mind to contemplate, figuratively about this "lived experience."

The mind is inhabited by awareness, concept, and imagination. These manifest in thought and language through metaphor, a form of thought that recognizes similarity in the dissimilar. Crossing borders is a metaphor, a primal form of communication, native to all languages and made up of visual and conceptual elements. In the Crossing Borders seminar, we asked what borders were of interest. There were many. Every field of interest has borders, obstacles, or concerns that act to frame it. The "other side" may be seen as a fearful unknown, an adversary, or a place filled with foreign novelty and attraction, suggesting adventure. The grass may be greener on the other side.

In the seminar, we initially only used concepts and research from the fields of anthropology, social psychology, and developmental psychology to frame the topic. After the initial launching in 2010, however, it was clear that the conversation and interest of the participants was broader and included many unique borders of both geographical and social interest. Some considered career changes, life-partners, life stages, and even fabric design as borders of interest. In turn, the experiences of divergent participants provided points of view from one border that helped to understand another. We saw the dialectical, metaphorical process in action.

The area surrounding a border, often called the borderlands, were an interesting component in the Crossing Borders seminar. These can be likened to liminal spaces, the in-between of hybrids, mixtures, cocktails, and stews. Borderlands have elements of both sides of the border, and many of us identify easily with being a mixture, a mongrel. Maybe that's a clue as to why these borderlands are of special interest: we can easily identify with being in the middle of things. Just as the "now" is surrounded by the past and the future, we have layered identities of experience and imagination. Beings-in-the-world the existentialists called us, and of course a "being-in-transition" is a common identity of students, with earning a PhD as an especially complex journey. Borderlands are places ripe for creating innovative solutions, new forms of art, and original scholarly works.

Borders vary in their degree of porosity or permeability. How easily can one move back and forth through them? Borders with greater porosity seem to have larger borderlands and greater liminality. Borderlands, the liminal spaces that surround a border, are places where creativity thrives.

They are the in-betweens on either side of the border. Borders can act as filters that catch and hold some while letting others through. Human borders, such as the Mexican-American one, have processing criteria that allow some to pass through more easily than others. If one has gone through the background checking and been cleared for "SENTRI" or "Pre-Approved," then passing through is significantly easier—even privileged with designated lines or ports. Border crossings can be facilitated in one direction and restricted in another (in fact, they usually are). One of the radical alternatives to a border is a bridge, wherein one passes over the border, or a tunnel where one goes under the border.

Clearly, politics play a significant role in how borders and border crossing is perceived, and the extent to which borders are perceived as a protective measure, a goal line to be crossed, or a cage to imprison. We started the seminar in 2010, during the Obama administration, and in the academy we were mostly encouraged to be innovative, open-hearted, and global. Hard-headedness was more commonly seen in concerns with the lack of evidence-based claims and rigor in softer, more idealistic possibilities. Context matters.

The current administration has made immigration and the porous borders an enemy, emphasizing scarcity of resources and fear of the other. Now we are in a period of great concern about being too open, and with hardening our borders. Caution or fear of the other have again become a rallying cry for the "base." We have been shown that power can trump truth, that alternative facts can have sway over science and majority opinion. What new implications can we develop from the notion of crossing borders in this ever-changing political landscape?

Mastery and Mystery (Stephen Murphy-Shigematsu)

When I was a child, people would ask me what I wanted to be when I grew up. The answer was always the same: "A doctor!" I could imagine nothing better than a life serving others in need. But when I began to volunteer in hospitals I was shocked to find that doctors weren't the compassionate heroes I imagined them to be. I was further disillusioned when I discovered that mainstream medicine was unable to help me with my own health problems, and my dream faded away.

Some years later I saw a film, *Redbeard* that opened my eyes to a new way of understanding illness and healing. The story shows the historical convergence and integration of East Asian medicine and European medicine in 17th century Japan, each system with their strengths and weaknesses. I was a college student when I saw *Redbeard*, and it was a time of expanding consciousness through the spread of yoga, meditation, and Zen. Acupuncturists had begun practicing in the U.S. and I was able to personally experience the benefits of these healing arts and see the possibilities of integrative medicine. My dream of being a doctor returned and I set out in search of knowledge.

The search for knowledge about health and illness led me into academia and the confrontation with its way of distinguishing what is real knowledge from what is fake. Certain knowledge is acceptable and that which falls outside of the boundaries is considered not to be real knowledge. Scientific standards, empirical research, and evidence-based data are employed in determining what can be taught at universities.

As a graduate student, while I respected academia, I also sensed its limitations. My study of East Asian healing arts had taught me to recognize that there were forms of knowledge that the academic system would respect and include only grudgingly and slowly. As I studied clinical psychology I realized that certain theories and therapeutic practices were considered knowledge while others were not. I learned the major approaches while also respecting so-called alternative and complementary ways of viewing human development, illness, and healing. These ways were often indigenous, somatic, intuitive, and compassionate, contrasting sharply with the ways I was being socialized in the university to be professional by valuing knowledge based in cognitive, rational, technical, logical, analytical methods of inquiry.

Since then, I have existed in a liminal space in academia, balancing mastery and mystery. Mastery is our striving for control, certainty, predictability and trust in what we know. Mystery is our letting go, not knowing, intuition, and wonder. We cross borders by respecting diverse forms of knowledge. Today, as our government attacks science, we are reminded of the importance of respecting its immense importance in helping us to determine best practices for human survival and flourishing. We are also reminded of the dangers of blind faith in technology and the need to trust in the mystery and revel in the wonder of humanity. We can engage in the pursuit of knowledge unburdened by dualism, not separating what belongs together, embracing visible and invisible, marginal and mainstream, human and divine.

Crossing Borders—One Path Via Crossing Bridges (Connie Corley)

In the fall of 2015, a gathering of faculty, students, and alumni of Fielding Graduate University focused on exploring the borderlands of the Boyle Heights neighborhood of Los Angeles. This led to the next phase of creating a multi-day Intensive, which was a segue to the Winter Session 2016 "Crossing Borders" workshop. Building on the concept of *communitas* and emerging as a new phase of the Fielding-funded ISI Grant for "Cruzando Puentes: Crossing Bridges" Social Transformation Project, we gathered for a day in Santa Barbara to discuss the borders we have crossed individually. Then we collectively explored a retirement community in Boyle Heights that was the first to be licensed as such in California (Hollenbeck Palms), Mariachi Plaza and environs, and then went on to Homeboy Industries headquarters.

Our team of 11 included participants whose home countries were as varied as Ukraine, India, Canada, the U.S., Japan, and Taiwan, and we immersed ourselves in historic Boyle Heights, which has been called "the Ellis Island of the West." Many cultural and ethnic groups established homes there until the disruptions of World War II (displacement of Japanese families to internment camps) and postwar "progress" (the building of multiple freeways slicing up neighborhoods; redlining preventing people of color from owning homes) led to rapid social change and gentrification. Our multi-day Intensive led us to dine together in Chinatown and Little Tokyo and connect with elders at the Hollenbeck Palms retirement community.

"Crossing Borders Ethnography" became a course and some of the participants took it for credit as part of the Intensive; it was also a course that is part of the completion of the Creative Longevity and Wisdom Doctoral Concentration. Emerging from the presentations that the students prepared following the Intensive, a symposium at the Society for Applied Anthropology was presented in Philadelphia in April, 2018 (*Cruzando Puentes*: Crossing Cultural Bridges to Sustainable Futures). Several of the students who presented also co-authored with Corley and Willis for a chapter in an edited volume on resilience titled *Cruzando Puentes/ Crossing Bridges: Building Resilience through Communitas* (Corley, Willis, Dobberteen, & von Baeyer, in press).

The Crossing Borders impact starting from one-day gatherings and emerging into a multi-day Intensive has impacted me personally through the annual gathering of community into short but meaningful periods of engagement (*communitas*) to the fuller engagement of academic colleagues at conferences including S4A and the Gerontological Society of America and the Academy of Gerontology in Higher Education. In Los Angeles my intersections with California State University, Los Angeles as an Emeriti Faculty member brought in students and faculty from a university intersecting with Boyle Heights, hence crossing another border of the virtual with the "brick and mortar" to create a Community of Practice.

Crossing Borders: Pathways to Scholarship, Social Justice, and Open Hearts Through Adult Transformative Education (Lenneal Henderson)

In 1991, I made my first journey to Casa de Maria in Santa Barbara to participate in the Fielding Institute's Admissions Contract Workshop (ACW, now called New Student Orientation or NSO). Much like our new doctoral students, I experienced the sensation and elation of being admitted to something novel and promising. I had joined the faculty of the "program" in human and organizational development.

I had been a college professor for more 22 years at venues such as St. Mary's College of California, the University of San Francisco, Howard University, and the University of Baltimore. But little of this experience prepared me for the new vistas, dynamics, and mission I experienced at this session. I journeyed across at least five new boundaries in this first live encounter with Fielding.

First, students truly were the core and heart of all that occurred at Fielding. "Student-centered" was almost a reflex utterance at other colleges and universities, but at Fielding, programs, interpersonal activity, and even fun derived from and returned to what students needed. Second, faculty were on a fervent mission to serve students. Faculty such as Don Bushnell, Barbara Mink, Anna DiStefano, Jody Veroff, Elizabeth Douvan, Argentine Craig, Will McWhinney, Leo Johnson, Judy Stevens-Long, Valerie Bentz, Keith Melville, Frank Friedlander, and others brought full and diverse scholarly, practitioner, and civic experience to their roles. Since 1991, I can think of very few faculty members who did not meet this exceptional standards set by those core faculty members in Fielding's youth. Interaction with them was a major boundary crossing for me, because I had little of the experience of these stalwarts.

Third, my research and training at the University of California, Berkeley, was substantially influenced by the behavioral science movement. This movement featured an emphasis on quantitative analysis of human experience and behavior. If it could not be quantified, it not only could not be measured but it did not exist! The Fielding Institute warmly welcomed me to the world of qualitative research. Phenomenology, ethnography, appreciative inquiry, auto-ethnography, action and participatory action research, narrative analysis, and focus groups were new research orientations and tools I learned from both faculty and student colleagues over my years at Fielding. I have come to know advances and new approaches in these orientations and tools as well as those in the more quantitative sciences through work with students on courses and dissertations.

Fourth, from the beginning Fielding has been about social and ecological justice. When I arrived in 1991, although there were only four African American and two Latino faculty members, the leadership and faculty were sufficiently introspective and honest to place diversity high on the agenda. One of the Fielding founders, Dr. Marie Fielder, mother of faculty member Nicola Smith and a giant I met at Lowell High School in San Francisco, helped Fielding to move forward in its diversity aspirations. In 1993, I persuaded Dr. Willy DeMarcell Smith, a faculty colleague of mine at Howard University, to apply for the position of Associate Dean of what now is the School of Human and Organizational Development. Three years later, he became the Founding Dean of the new School of Educational Leadership and Change. Cohort agreements between this new school and incoming students of Latinos from New Mexico, Navajos from Arizona, and African Americans from Cambridge College in Massachusetts and Lincoln University of Pennsylvania brought color and new social and ecological justice perspectives to Fielding. Much of the faculty and administrative leadership of the new School came from stellar graduates of the School of Human and Organizational Development.

Dynamic souls and minds such as Judy Witt, Jennifer Edwards, Mark Scanlon-Greene, Rena Palloff, and other HOD alumni joined with intellectual and social change scholars such as Szabi Ishtai Zee, Anthony Holliday, Don Jacobs (Four Arrows), Yolanda Gayol, Nicola Smith, Shawn Ginwright, Joyce Germaine Watts, and Sheila Gregory to elevate the profile of Fielding throughout the nation and to significantly diversify its curricular, teaching, scholarship and civic contributions. Four Arrows raised our consciousness not only about scholarship and teaching but about indigenous and ecological wisdom. Crossing, archiving, and learning *about* and *from* boundaries became more and more inherent in the Fielding ways of doing, knowing, and learning.

Fifth, for me, Fielding enabled me to cross international boundaries on many occasions. My first Fielding doctoral committee was chaired by the Thai scholar Chalintorn Burian, who commuted between the United Nations and Bangkok while completing her PhD in a record 18 months. A faculty development grant in 1993 allowed me to journey to Maastricht, The Netherlands for the formal signing of the new European Community agreement. For three consecutive years, I joined Don Bushnell in coordinating travel to the Czech Republic with 12 to 15 students each May to chronicle how a former Soviet Warsaw Pact member was in the process of becoming a progressive democracy. Thanks to HOD alums Rena Palloff and Keith Pratt, I was able to teach research methods and international political economy in Singapore, Malaysia, and Hong Kong. And, as an ELC faculty member, I joined Kitty Kelly Epstein twice in Ethiopia to teach action research at Unity University.

Sixth and finally, Fielding is now a community—a community with the challenges, conflicts, and occasional disruptions likely to befall the best of communities but a community in constant reflection, striving, and struggle. Fielding was and is a transformative dynamic in my life. The community has encouraged me to see borders not as difference or subtraction but as addition and multiplication. In my gratitude, I am committed to remain involved in any way I can.

Crossing the Border Into Age (Harry "Rick" Moody)

How old would you be if you did not know how old you are?

– Satchel Paige

When do we "cross the border" into age? It's a question I've pondered for 47 years, since I first began teaching elders (or whatever we call them— or ourselves). Now that I'm 73 years old myself the question has become more personal, but I still don't know the answer. Maybe this essay should stop right here with that admission. But I will continue, with a personal story that illuminates the question about crossing the border into age.

I remember well when I turned 65 and went to a movie theater, delighted at last to qualify for the senior discount. As I reached for my wallet, the ticket taker quickly said to me, "Oh you don't need to do that. You clearly qualify." I was startled, and not altogether pleased with her response.

As a gerontologist, I know well that there is a (modest) literature on what is called "age identification": namely, when do people feel that they are old? The answer is actually obvious: we cross the border into age when other people regard us as such or when we have experiences—such as personal illness or bereavement of age-peers—that remind us that we have now become a "person of a certain age."

But what is that border into old age and does it matter? Is crossing the border into age merely a question of attitude—"You're only as old as you think"? Or is that very sentiment a form of denial? I had the great privilege of working for Dr. Robert Butler, who invented the term "ageism." In the half-century since Butler coined that term, the reality of age discrimination has remained undeniable. Ageism has remained, even though one traditional "border" of old age—65 years for retirement—has become less relevant. But other borders— for example, age 18 for voting—as well as other age-based borders have, seemingly, been eroded, at least for more fortunate members of society. Indeed, we hear that "60 is the new 40." Cosmetic surgery and anti-aging medicine have become ever more popular. It seems at times as if age itself has come to fall more and more under the sphere of action and control. Companies in Silicon Valley, as well as mainstream researchers in bio gerontology, increasingly see age not as fate or limit but as a problem susceptible to human and technological intervention. Some go so far as to see aging itself as a disease. From this perspective, the very question of "crossing the border into old age" seems out-of-date.

"Out-of-date"—a provocative phrase, like the "Sell By" expiration date for food or drugs. It's a warning to us. We don't want to believe it (denial?). If age as a border is ambiguous or malleable, it opens up other questions. Look more deeply at the concept of "border" itself. We know what it means as a demarcation between countries—for example, the U.S. and Canada. But if were walking near the border in say, Montana or some other remote area, there would be a large region where there is no physical demarcation between two sovereign areas. In that sense, a border can be arbitrary, a human construction, often invisible. Increasingly, it seems that is what age has become today. For the "healthy-wealthy-and-wise" (exemplars of "successful aging"), individuals can feel themselves to be ageless, even at 90 or beyond. By contrast, for those in Hollywood or Silicon Valley, turning 30 can be a catastrophic transition. Even if borders are invisible, they become all too real by virtue of the action, or social construction, among others in society. As in these examples, it is possible for some people to feel "ageless" while others are victims of age discrimination (ageism) at ever younger ages. Crossing the border into age invites us to look critically at all borders and limits.

This description of our social and cultural environment, and its contradictory signs of ageism, is important because, in gerontology and demography, we customarily make reference to the Age-Period-Cohort connection. In brief, this framework reminds us that when we look at individuals, age-based characteristics are linked to more than chronological age. There is another temporal dimension, a historical trajectory, embedded in age-based characteristics. Our chronological age reflects the time in which we grew up and the epoch in which we were socialized and went through distinctive life events—in short, cohort characteristics, which of course vary with other elements (gender, social class, ethnicity, etc.). Our chronological age also reflects the time in which we are living in later life: for example, medical treatment of geriatric conditions, pensions and the economic foundations of retirement, and so on. When we look at any kind of variable or behavior, we have to take account of the interaction among age, period, and cohort. In analytic terms, it becomes difficult to disentangle these three factors in specific cases. Thus, it becomes difficult indeed to establish where the "border" of age is to be found.

To speak about borders reminds us that we need to pay attention to where we are looking. To speak of the Age-Period-Cohort conundrum is to look outside, at social, cultural, and historical elements. But can we also look inside? Each of us has our own sense of time in our lives—for example, "feeling young" or "feeling old." This individual trajectory can be something discovered with surprise, as in my case when the theater ticket-taker told me I "clearly qualified" for the senior discount. How do we make sense of our inner sense of crossing the border into age?

Jungian psychology, more than many other psychological frameworks, has understood that "crossing the border" into age means turning our attention to the inner trajectory of our lives. Jung distinguished between two central archetypal elements: the *Puer* (eternal youth, Peter Pan, etc.) and the *Senex* (the Saturnian element of age). What is important about Jung's contribution is less its truth-value than the fact that it points us toward a dimension of "border-crossing" usually overlooked: namely, the possibility of conscious aging.

Modern and post-modern cultures celebrate "successful aging" and "productive aging," ideals that implicitly uphold values linked to youth or mid-life: namely, success and productivity. If later life brings infirmities or deficits that work against those values, then crossing the border into age must seem to be a disaster. But a third element to be remembered is what we can call "conscious aging," and it is not vain to hope that crossing the border into age can open up possibilities not disclosed earlier in life. As Jung put it well:

> A human being would certainly not grow to be seventy or eighty years old if this longevity had no meaning for the species. The afternoon of human life must also have a significance of its own and cannot be merely a pitiful appendage to life's morning.

Crossing Borders—Some Closing Thoughts

As we can see from these essays, our life course is both an individual quest and a social journey, stories that contain the wisdom of our ancestors as well as the seeds of our future. Major themes that we have discovered as important for human development and consciousness in the context of crossing borders include *cultural transmission* (from one generation to another); *individual and social transformation; growth* (and the many ways in which it is measured); *wisdom*; and *change*, especially the *social change* that we support and encourage in our environments and the movements for social justice.

Framing is critical for those of us crossing borders, with boundaries/ borders and their creation having a signal effect on our evolving selves (which also include the observation the borders themselves are evolving). The intentionality of creating boundaries and borders thus reveals an awareness of unconscious, preconscious, and conscious lives. *Self as a verb* is something we become aware of, too, noting the dynamism of being human—that we are not only "civilized" citizens-in-place in cities, but that we range widely.

As we are doing this and *experiencing border processes, mobility* and its *relationships and interactions* become a focus point for understanding, too. And in these the *character traits, states*, and *stages*, whether they are *vertical, horizontal*, or *chronological*, highlight once again the importance of *boundaries/borders* and their crossings. These are, in the end, our *co-presence* of *living in the borderlands*, a powerful and inspirational state and position to be in as we enter the exciting—even as it is fraught and challenging—world of our future together.

We look forward to continuing our Crossing Borders Seminar together at Fielding Graduate University!

References

Anderson, B. (1994). *Imagined communities: Reflections on the origin and spread of nationalism*. London: Verso.

Appadurai, A. (1991). Global ethnoscapes: Notes and queries for a transnational anthropology. In R. G. Fox (Ed.), *Recapturing anthropology: Working in the present* (pp. 191-210). Santa Fe:

School of American Research.

Anzaldua, G. (1987). *Borderlands: The new mestiza = la frontera.* San Francisco: Aunt Lute Books.

Appiah, K. A. (2006) *Cosmopolitanism: Ethics in a world of strangers.* New York: Norton.

Bateson, M. C. (2010). *Composing a further life: The age of active wisdom.* New York: Vintage.

Bhabha, H. (Ed.). (1997). "Front Lines/Border Posts." *Critical Inquiry, Spring, 23*(3).

Butler, R. (1975, 2005). W*hy survive? Being old in America.* Baltimore: Johns Hopkins University Press.

Cohen, R., & Toninato, P. (2009). *The creolization reader: Studies in mixed identities and cultures.* London: Routledge.

De Gray, A. (2008). *Ending aging: The rejuvenation breakthroughs that could reverse human aging.* New York: St. Martin's.

Hannerz, U. (1992). *Cultural complexity.* New York: Columbia University Press.

Hannerz, U. (1996). *Transnational connections.* London: Routledge.

Hanson, R. (2009). *Buddha's brain: The practical neuroscience of happiness, love & wisdom.* Oakland: New Harbinger Publications, Inc.

Harvey, D. (2009). *Cosmopolitanism and the geographies of freedom.* New York: Columbia University Press.

Hillman, J. (2000). *The force of character: And the lasting life.* New York: Ballantine.

Hillman, J. (2006). *Senex and puer, Uniform Edition,* Vol. 3. Putnam, CT: Spring Publications.

Martinez, O. J. (1994). *Border people: Life and society in the U.S.-Mexico Borderlands.* Tucson: University of Arizona Press.

Matsuda, T. (Ed.). (2001). *The age of creolization in the Pacific: In search of emerging cultures and shared values in the Japan-America borderlands.* Hiroshima: Keisuisha.

Mignolo, W. D. (2000). *Local histories/global designs: Coloniality, subaltern knowledges, and border thinking.* Princeton: Princeton University Press.

Moody, H. R. (2002). Conscious Aging: A strategy for positive development in later life, in J. Ronch & J. Goldfield (Eds.), *Mental wellness in aging: Strength-based approaches.* Baltimore: Health Professions Services Press.

Moody, H. R. (1997). *The five stages of the soul: Charting the spiritual passages that shape our lives.* New York: Anchor Books Doubleday.

Mooney, C. G. (2000). *Theories of childhood: An introduction to Dewey, Montessori, Erikson, Piaget & Vygotsky.* St. Paul, Minnesota: Redleaf Press.

Morrow-Howell, N., Hinterlong, J., & Sherraden, M. (Eds.). (2001). *Productive aging: Concepts and challenges.* Baltimore: Johns Hopkins University Press.

Murphy-Shigematsu, S. (2002). *Multicultural encounters: Case narratives from a counseling practice.* New York: Teachers College Press.

Nederveen Pieterse, J. (2004). *Globalization & culture: Global mélange.* Lanham, MD: Rowman & Littlefield.

Nederveen Pieterse, J., & Parekh, B. (Eds.). (1995). *The decolonization of imagination: Culture, knowledge and power.* London: Zed Books.

Papastergiadis, N. (1997). *Tracing hybridity in theory.* In P. Werbner & T. Modood (Eds.), *Debating cultural hybridity.* London: Zed.

Papastergiadis, N. (2000). *The turbulence of migration: Globalization, deterritorialization and hybridity.* London: Polity.

Phinney, J., & Rotheram, M. J. (Eds.). (1987). *Children's ethnic socialization: Pluralism and development.* Newbury Park, CA: SAGE.

Rogoff, B. (2003). *The cultural nature of human development.* Oxford: Oxford University Press.

Root, M.P.P. (Ed.) (1996). *The multiracial experience: Racial borders as the new frontier.* Thousand Oaks: SAGE.

Rowe, J., & Kahn, R. (1999). *Successful aging.* New York: Dell.

Stonequist, E. V. (1937). *The marginal man: A study in personality and culture conflict.* New York: Russell and Russell.

Urry, J. (2003) *Global complexity.* Cambridge: Polity.

Urry, J. (2005). *Complexity.* Special issue of *Theory, Culture and Society, 22,* 1-274.

Urry, J. (2008). *Mobilities.* Cambridge: Polity Press.

Vaillant, G. E. (2000). "Adaptive mental mechanisms: Their role in Positive Psychology." *American Psychologist, 55*(1), 88-98.

Vaillant, G. E. (2002). *Aging well: Surprising guideposts to a happier life from the landmark Harvard Study of Adult Development.* New York: Little, Brown and Company.

Vaillant, G. E. (2008). *Spiritual evolution: A scientific defense of faith.* New York: Broadway Books.

Vertovec, S., & Cohen, R. (Eds.). (2003). *Conceiving cosmopolitanism: Theory, context, and practice*. Oxford: Oxford University Press.

Wenjiang, F. (2018). A *practical guide to Age-Period-Cohort Analysis*. London: Chapman and Hall.

Werbner, P. (1997) "Introduction: the dialectics of cultural hybridity," in P. Werbner and T. Modood (Eds.), *Debating cultural hybridity>* London: Zed Books.

Werbner, P., & Modood, T. (1997). *Debating cultural hybridity*. London: Zed Books.

Willis, D. B. (In press). "Creating culture: How we form our social and cultural identities," Chapter 2 of *Crossing borders: Learning and teaching in a transcultural world*.

Willis, D. B., & Murphy-Shigematsu, S. (Eds.) (2009) *Transcultural Japan: At the borderlands of race, gender, and identity*. London: Routledge.

Willis, D. B. (In press). "Unusual learning in unusual places," Chapter 1 of *Crossing borders: Learning and teaching in a transcultural world*.

Willis, D. B., Enloe, W., & Minoura, Y. (1994). Transculturals, transnationals: The new diaspora. *International Schools Journal, XIV* (1), 29-42.

Zachary, G. P. (2000). *The global me: New cosmopolitans and the competitive edge—Picking globalism's winners and losers*. Washington, DC: Public Affairs.

Zack, N. (1995). *American mixed race: The culture of microdiversity*. Lanham, MD: Rowman & Littlefield.

About the Authors

David Blake Willis, PhD, is Professor of Anthropology and Education at Fielding Graduate University and Professor Emeritus of Anthropology, Soai Buddhist University, Osaka, Japan. He taught and did research at the University of Oxford and was Visiting Professor at the University of Washington and Grinnell College. His interests in anthropology, sustainability, social justice, and immigration come from 38 years of living in traditional cultural systems in Japan and South India. His scholarly work is on transformational leadership and education, human development in transnational contexts, the creolization of cultures, transcultural communities, and Dalit/Gandhian liberation movements in South India. His publications include *World Cultures: The Language Villages (Leading, Learning, and Teaching on the Global Frontier)* with Walter Enloe (2017); *Sustainability Leadership: Integrating Values, Meaning, and Action* with Fred Steier and Paul Stillman (2015); *Reimagining Japanese Education: Borders, Transfers, Circulations, and the Comparative* with Jeremy Rappleye (2011); *Transcultural Japan: At the Borders of Race, Gender, and Identity* with Stephen Murphy-Shigematsu (2007); and *Japanese Education in Transition 2001: Radical Perspectives on Cultural and Political Transformation* with Satoshi Yamamura (2002).

Connie Corley, MSW, MA, PhD, has a long history in the fields of gerontology/geriatrics as a graduate of the University of Michigan, Ann Arbor. Dr. Corley leads the doctoral concentration in Creative Longevity and Wisdom in the School of Leadership Studies. She is Professor Emeritus at California State University, Los Angeles. A Fellow of both the Gerontological Society of America and the Academy of Gerontology in Higher Education, Dr. Corley has engaged in multiple programs as a mentor and leader in curriculum development. Work involving creativity in later life (emerging out of a national study of Holocaust survivors, led by Roberta Greene, PI) led to the "Experience, Engagement, Expression" model of creativity based on life course experiences. *Cruzando Puentes* ("Crossing Bridges") was launched in 2015 as an intergenerational and intercultural mutual mentoring program in diverse communities of Los Angeles. Dr. Corley co-hosts and produces a radio show (www. ExperienceTalks.org), interviewing people seasoned in life.

Lenneal J. Henderson, PhD, was born in New Orleans and raised in the housing projects of San Francisco, California. He received his AB, MA, and PhD degrees from the University of California, Berkeley and has conducted additional postdoctoral study at the Paul Nitze School of Advanced International Studies at Johns Hopkins University and as a post-doctoral scholar in science, technology, and public policy at George Washington University. He is the author of numerous books and articles, including *Black Political Life in the United States*, *Administrative Advocacy: Black Administrators in Urban Bureaucracies*, *The New Black Politics: The Search for Political Power*, *Public Administration and Public Policy: A Minority Perspective*, and, most recently, *Dimensions of Learning: Education for Life*. To commemorate the 50th anniversary of the Topeka, Kansas Supreme Court decision, Brown vs. The Board of Education, he researched and wrote *Thurgood Is Coming*, a one-man play, and performed the role of Thurgood Marshall. These performances have taken place in Maryland, Texas, North Carolina, and California and have been used as a fundraisers for charitable organizations.

Harry R. Moody, PhD, retired as Vice President for Academic Affairs with AARP and is currently a Visiting Faculty member at Fielding Graduate University and Tohoku University in Japan. He previously served as Executive Director of the Brookdale Center on Aging at Hunter College and Chairman of the Board of Elderhostel (now Road Scholar). He is author of many scholarly articles and books including as the co-author of *Aging: Concepts and Controversies*, a gerontology textbook now in its 9th edition. His boo, *The Five Stages of the Soul* was published by Doubleday and has been translated into seven languages worldwide. He is the editor of *Human Values in Aging*, published by Fielding Graduate University. In 2011 he received the Lifetime Achievement Award from the American Society on Aging and, in 2008, he was named by the *Utne Reader* as one of "50 Visionaries Who Are Changing Your World."

Stephen Murphy-Shigematsu, PhD, received a doctorate in counseling and consulting psychology from Harvard University and has taught there, at Temple University, the University of Tokyo, Fielding Graduate University, and Stanford University for 30 years. At the University of Tokyo, he was professor at the International Center and Graduate School of Education. The founder of the Stanford Heartfulness Lab, a transformative education program in Health and Human Performance, School of Medicine, he is also faculty in Comparative Studies in Race and Ethnicity. He is the author and editor of books in English and Japanese, including *From Mindfulness to Heartfulness: Transforming Self and Society with Compassion* (2018) and, in Japanese, *The Stanford Way of Ultimate Leadership* (2019).

Jerry J. Snow, PhD, retired as Associate Dean of Student Development for Fielding Graduate University in 2014. He travels monthly between Baja California, Mexico and Encinitas, California. For the last few years he has been practicing contemplative photography (*Miksang*), and mindfulness to understand and express the art of aging and individuation. He continues to enjoy gardening, spirited conversation, and the companionship of others.

Chapter 18

The Development of a New Discipline: Media Psychology

Karen Dill-Shackleford, PhD, and Jean-Pierre Isbouts, DLitt
Fielding Graduate University

When Fielding Graduate University launched the world's first doctoral program in media psychology in 2003, one key challenge confronting its faculty was to determine the academic boundaries of this new discipline. Where should this brave new realm of inquiry begin, and where should it end? How to define the parameters of this ever-changing landscape?

Today, more than 10 years on, with nearly a hundred of our PhD graduates active in academia as well as public and private enterprise, we find that the answer to this question is still elusive. Perhaps we should conclude that the boundaries of media psychology will continue to move as long as the intersection of media and human behavior continues to shift as well, powered by astounding technological innovation, always disrupting established practice, while actively stimulating new areas of human endeavor.

A Media Psychology cohort in 2012

Just by way of an example, in recent years we have seen the rapid growth of phenomena that few of us could have anticipated in 2003, including things such as social media, mobile computing, and streaming video-on-demand (VOD). All of these new platforms have radically changed the way we behave as human beings, in our relationships at home, at work, and within society at large.

To illustrate the range of topics that the media psychology discipline can encompass, we would like to cite the dissertation research of several media psychology alumni from Fielding Graduate University.

For example, Gordon Goodman's study examined one medium of entertainment long ignored by psychologists, namely the stage. An accomplished actor and director in his own right, Dr. Goodman asked whether stage fright, popularly associated with young and inexperienced actors, continues to vex accomplished, veteran actors. Given his broad network of contacts in the Broadway industry, Dr. Goodman was able to sample 136 elite actors, many with credits in motion pictures and television as well as theater. Contrary to popular perception and some of the literature, his data showed no significant association between stage fright and age, years of experience, or even personality in actors.

Jennifer Johnston developed a groundbreaking study on childhood exposure to pornography, a dominant genre in virtually all media, and the effects of such exposure on sexual satisfaction in adulthood. Remarkably, Dr. Johnson's findings, which were based on a national sample of adult Americans, showed that early exposure to pornography *can* increase sexual satisfaction when mediated by sexual experience—i.e., the number of lifetime sexual partners—but that this correlation is stronger for men than for women.

Jonny White's phenomenological inquiry addressed the realm of storytelling. Narrative psychology holds that the way we tell our self-story influences our life. It follows that a professional author's incarnation of his self-story is perhaps an important root of that author's creativity. Based on five in-depth interviews with accomplished authors of fiction, augmented by additional case study material, Dr. White concluded that authors benefit from stepping outside of their societal narrative conventions in order to develop new perspectives for storytelling.

Cynthia Vinney studied the role of identity in television experiences among 790 fans of *Buffy the Vampire Slayer*. Fans watched a montage of important moments from the show, and answered questions about the strength of their identity as fans and their thoughts and feelings in reaction to the show. Results showed that those with stronger identities as fans experienced more reflective thoughts and more mixed and meaningful feelings in response to the show. Mixed and meaningful feelings have been shown to indicate that a person is making meaning from a media experience such as this one. All told, what Vinney's dissertation demonstrated is that fans of a show take away ideas and feelings that are meaningful to them, and that the greater their identity as fans, the deeper the experience can be.

Media Psychology students used this film lab to master the art of digital editing.

Kristin Hopper-Losenicky also studied popular culture narrative, but she focused on how women who worked in STEM fields drew inspiration from the people in their lives, as well as from people they met on screen. Hopper-Losenicky interviewed twelve women using a narrative inquiry qualitative research approach. Interviewees listed many media characters from which they drew inspiration in their work. These ranged from classic characters like Mary Poppins and Nancy Drew, to current media favorites like Daenerys Targaryen from *Game of Thrones* and Olivia Pope from *Scandal*. When asked what type of characteristics these women found inspirational, they listed traits and skills such as "leader, optimistic and problem solver" (Mary Poppins) and "bold, strong values and defends others" (Targaryen). These character paradigms were particularly helpful in women imagining themselves in jobs in traditionally male-dominated fields.

Lastly, Ivone Umar examined the role of the Internet in an area largely overlooked by American scholars: the ability of students born in Latin America to integrate within an American college community in the United States. This question of acculturation is particularly significant in view of the growing numbers of foreign students who matriculate into American campuses for undergraduate and graduate studies, and often feel an acute sense of isolation. Using a sample of 104 Latin American students, Dr. Umar's data show that the use of the Internet in the host language— English—was a positive factor in the acculturation process, whereas the use of the Internet in the student's native language was correlated with a slower acculturation on an American English-speaking campus.

Our hope is that the media psychology program will continue to support a growing recognition of the role of modern media in changing human psychology; not only in American and international academia, but also as an extension of our pursuit of human wellbeing and the key role that public and private sectors play therein.

Note: this introduction was originally published as part of the monograph *New Directions in Media Psychology* by Fielding University Press. Republished with permission.

About the Authors

Karen Dill-Shackleford, PhD, is a social psychologist who studies the role of media in everyday life, particularly focusing on how we are moved by and make meaning from what we encounter in the media. Some of her special areas of interest include narrative engagement and persuasion, entertainment-education, violence and violence prevention, portrayals of race and gender, and fandom. She has testified twice before the U.S. Congress about the psychology of media use. Dr. Dill-Shackleford is the author of *How Fantasy Becomes Reality* (2009, in press) and the editor of the *Oxford Handbook of Media Psychology* (2013). She teaches media psychology, especially research methods and the social psychology of media, at Fielding Graduate University in Santa Barbara, California.

Jean-Pierre Isbouts, DLitt, was a founding member of Fielding's Media Psychology program in 2003. A humanities scholar, Dr. Isbouts served as Editor-in-Chief of the *Bertelsmann Multimedia Lexikon*, published in German, and the *Standaard Multimedia Encyclopedie*, published in Dutch. He has written on a number of subjects, including American cinema (*Charlton Heston's Hollywood*, 1998); Renaissance art (*Young Leonardo*, 2017 and *The Da Vinci Legacy,* 2019); comparative religion (*From Moses to Muhammad: The Shared Origins of Judaism, Christianity and Islam*, 2010); and biblical archaeology, including two National Geographic bestsellers: *The Biblical World,* 2007, and *In the Footsteps of Jesus,* 2012. He has also directed a number of films and TV specials for ABC, History Channel, A&E and the PBS network.

CHAPTER 19

THE SILVER AGE OF PHENOMENOLOGY AT FIELDING GRADUATE UNIVERSITY

Valerie Malhotra Bentz, PhD, David Rehorick, PhD, James Marlatt, PhD, Ayumi Nishii, PhD, Barton Buechner, PhD, and Carol Estrada, Doctoral Student
Fielding Graduate University

A Short History of Phenomenological Research and Practice at Fielding

The history of phenomenological research and practice at Fielding can be depicted in two stages that are situated within the broader educational history of Fielding as described by Keith Melville (2016). The "formative stage" of phenomenology at Fielding culminated in the description of the foundations of *mindful inquiry* in social research by Valerie Bentz and Jeremy Shapiro (1998) and the emergence of a Fielding phenomenological research program created by David Rehorick and Valerie Bentz. The latter development stemmed part, from Bentz and Rehorick's long-term collaborative association with the Society of Phenomenology and Human Studies (SPHS). The "transformative stage" of phenomenology demarks the "Silver Age" of applied phenomenology at Fielding that started in 1996. The "Golden Age" of phenomenology arose at the New School for Social Research in New York City from 1954 to 1973 (Embree & Barber, 2017). During the "Golden Age," European phenomenology was introduced to the North American doctoral program, in which researchers engaged in phenomenological investigations on social matters, as opposed to the trend in Europe or elsewhere in North America, where phenomenology itself was the center of the study. During the "Silver Age,"

David Rehorick, Valerie Bentz and their students developed an innovative phenomenological turn through the co-creation of *Transformative Phenomenology* that was more than just following the pathways generated by "Golden Age" scholars. The "Silver Age" is characterized by extensive applied phenomenological research by doctoral students at Fielding and the emergence of *Transformative Phenomenology* as a form of applied socio-cultural research and practice that supports positive change in the lifeworld (Rehorick & Bentz, 2008a).

The Formative Stage (1974-1995)

Phenomenology has been part of Fielding from its founding in 1974. One of the Fielding founders, Renata Tesch, wrote about and taught phenomenology, and recognized it as being "transformative" (Tesch, 1980). The late Donald Polkinghorne was a faculty member during part of this stage. Will Kouw carried phenomenology on in psychology for more than two decades and left a scholarship for phenomenology in his name. Faculty member Jeremy Shapiro and others developed study guides informed by phenomenology and hermeneutics. Valerie Bentz was an associate dean for research and wrote *Mindful Inquiry for Social Research* with Jeremy Shapiro (Bentz & Shapiro, 1998). *Mindful Inquiry* invokes phenomenology, hermeneutics, critical theory, and Buddhist principles as key elements for social research.

The story of the emergence of phenomenological inquiry at Fielding involves the intersection of two "scholarly lives" holding a deep interest in introducing phenomenological research and practice to mid-career professionals who chose to pursue doctoral research. Valerie Bentz and David Rehorick describe the evolution of their scholarship founded in inspiration from Helmet Wagner, George Psathas, Kurt Wolff, Richard Owsley, and Richard Jung (Rehorick & Bentz, 2017a). Bentz and Rehorick also attribute their long-term involvement with SPHS as an important part of their scholarly evolution and bringing their students to phenomenological inquiry through introductions to the SPHS community

(Bentz, 2002; Rehorick, 2002). David Rehorick acted as an editor for the SPHS *Human Studies* journal for several years during this period while teaching at the University of New Brunswick. Bentz edited the *SPHS Book Review Journal* that was published by Fielding Graduate University between 1993 and 1996. Bentz and Rehorick's long-time professional association led to the introduction of a seminar on phenomenology for doctoral students at Fielding in 1996.

The "Silver Age" Transformative Stage (1996-Present)

David Rehorick joined Fielding as Research Faculty in 1995. Valerie and David taught the Advanced Research Module in Phenomenology and supervised doctoral students from 1996 through 2012, when David Rehorick retired from full-time work. Thereafter, David and Valerie continued to co-teach the seminar until 2016. We call this period, and beyond, the "Silver Age" of phenomenology. During this period, Professors Bentz and Rehorick continued their association with SPHS, contributing articles and reviews, and presenting and organizing doctoral student panels at annual meetings. They also led seminars in phenomenology and somatics at Fielding research and practice sessions.

From 1996 to 2016, Bentz and Rehorick supervised over seventy-six doctoral dissertations at Fielding that were informed by phenomenology and/or hermeneutics. External doctoral committee members associated with the SPHS community were also engaged, including Kurt Wolff, George Psathas, Gary Backhaus, Carlos Belvedere, Phil Lewin, and Michael Barber. Rehorick and Bentz characterize these dissertations as phenomenologically-inspired, phenomenologically-informed, and phenomenologically–based research patterns (Rehorick & Bentz, 2017a). The extensive body of phenomenological research by Fielding scholar-practitioners provides a permanent record of how phenomenology can transform ourselves, our lifeworlds, and professional practice (see Appendix B in Rehorick and Bentz, 2017b for a listing of the phenomenological or hermeneutic dissertations at Fielding from 1996 to 2016).

The publication of the edited volume *Transformative Phenomenology: Changing Ourselves, Lifeworlds and Professional Practice* by Rehorick and Bentz in 2008 (Rehorick & Bentz, 2008b), with a forward by George Psathas, offered an introduction to the nature of an applied phenomenology that can instill personal and professional transformation (Rehorick & Bentz, 2008b). The editors and alumni contributors describe the essence of transformation that can be achieved through the application of the methodology and methods of a transformative somatic-hermeneutic-phenomenology in the lifeworld.

| 1998 | 2008 | 2016 | 2017 |

20 years of Transformative Phenomenology

Fielding University Press published *Expressions of Phenomenological Research: Consciousness and Lifeworld Studies* in 2017 (Rehorick & Bentz, 2017b). This volume, edited by David and Valerie, with a forward by Michael Barber, situates 20 years of applied phenomenological research at Fielding from 1996 to 2016 within the context of the broader phenomenological movement. Rehorick and Bentz provide an assessment of this body of doctoral research, describe their "lereogic" adult learning model, identify 10 qualities of transformative phenomenologists, and provide evidence of a mature curriculum for "teaching" transformative phenomenology.

Former students contributed chapters to both of the edited volumes that outline the transformative impact of phenomenology on their research, practice, and lives. These authors provide rich stories of the diverse practices that embody *truthful* communication to address practical concerns in the lifeworld from the diverse vantage of the executive coach, human development professionals, leadership specialists, company executives, directors of medical organizations, professional musicians, community social innovators, and more.

With the publication of the edited volume *Contemplative Social Research: Caring for Self, Being and Lifeworlds* by Fielding University Press in 2016, Valerie Bentz situates transformative somatic phenomenology within the emerging multi-disciplinary and cross-cultural contemplative-based-inquiry movement that recognizes the "deep oneness of humanity" (Bentz, 2016; Bentz & Giorgino, 2016). Through "Transformative Phenomenology as an Antidote to Technological Deathworlds," Bentz and collaborative authors illustrate the value of *Transformative Phenomenology* for consciousness-raising and social change in complex times (Bentz, Rehorick, Marlatt, Nishii, & Estrada, 2018, in press).

Valerie Bentz currently teaches somatics and phenomenology at Fielding through the Somatics Phenomenology and Communicative Leadership (SPCL) curriculum concentration with the support of Fielding alumnus Barton Buechner, and students and other alumni. The emerging SPCL community-of-practice is active and continues to evolve through monthly teleconferences and face-to-face interactions. Opportunities to "teach" *Transformative Phenomenology* have recently been extended to collaborations with the University of the Virgin Islands and the University of Lodz, Poland.

David and Valerie continue to support phenomenological research and practice by "Silver Age" alumni and students through collaborative writing, attendance at Fielding workshops and events, and engagements with the SPHS, the European Sociological Association, the Schütz Circle, and other communities. The creation of opportunities for projects, presentations at conferences, and interactions with Fielding students is a sustaining activity for the SPCL community. In the next section, we offer a short description of some of the unique aspects of *Transformative Phenomenology*, including excerpts from Bentz et al. (2018, in press).

Community-of-Practice in action

Part 2: Characteristics of Transformative Phenomenology

What Is Transformative Phenomenology?

We describe *Transformative Phenomenology* as a somatic-hermeneutic-phenomenology that is put into action in the lifeworld. It is an application of phenomenology—the study of consciousness and phenomena— that can lead to personal, professional, organizational, and social transformations. *Transformative Phenomenology* is founded on the eidetic phenomenology of Edmund Husserl, the social phenomenology of Alfred Schütz, the embodied phenomenology of Maurice Merleau-Ponty, the ontologic-existential phenomenology of Martin Heidegger, and the reflective hermeneutic methods of Hans-Georg Gadamer (Bentz & Rehorick, 2008a).

Somatics has been a part of the lineage of phenomenology since its birth. *Transformative Phenomenology* places emphasis on somatics, not only from the philosophical tradition, but also through healing practices such as yoga, meditation, and mindfulness that considers the interconnected nature of the body, mind, and spirit. Transformative phenomenologists understand the body as wisdom and develop their conscious awareness of the body from within (Bentz, 2003; Hanna, 1988). For example, Valerie Bentz offers retreats through the Fielding Somatics in Human and Organizational Development course for students, alumni, and other like-minded people to experience a range of modalities such as creative visualizations and meditations, Kundalini yoga, dance, Tibetan bowl sessions, and drum circles, for enhancing somatic awareness.

Heidegger inspired Gadamer to develop a form of philosophical hermeneutics that involves the search for meaning through the interpretation of texts and life that include conversations, relationships, and social interaction. The interpreter is reminded to reflect on her cultural and historically sculpted prejudgments and prejudices, and to move beyond them when they are encountered during inquiry (Bentz & Shapiro, 1998). Rehorick and Bentz developed the metaphor of the wild horse, to illustrate Gadamer's three levels of hermeneutic understanding (Rehorick & Bentz, 2008a). In the first level, texts are interpreted within the context of the lifeworlds upon which it exists. This is like seeing and describing the wild horse from a distance. At the second level the interpreter responds to the multiple voices connecting and challenging each other within the text, and even poses questions of the texts. The interpreter gets closer to the wild horse and observes it running, walking, and engaging with other horses. At Gadamer's third level the interpreter might experience personal transformation as a result of engaging with the texts. The interpreter jumps on the wild horse and tries to ride. This can be a risky endeavor that might take the rider away from their intended destination. The rider might even be thrown and injured. "But this is the nature of entering into phenomenological inquiry where one must embrace ambiguity and uncertainty as part of the process of coming to see, as though for the first time" (Rehorick & Bentz, 2017, p. 22).

Sometimes transformative phenomenologists dare to ride on wild horses and run to a new and open horizon to its extreme in their research and practice. *Transformative Phenomenology* can expand the boundary of social science research and practice to the boundary of the humanities and arts, and even the natural sciences—creating a new horizon without losing the integrity of the scholarship and practice. For example, Valerie Bentz wrote a philosophical and historical romance novel fusing intellectual and literary realms through the illumination of her fascination with pragmatic philosopher George Herbert Mead and existentialist Martin Heidegger (Bentz, 2014). David Rehorick called upon students in the immediate experience of an earthquake to record and discuss their lived experiences, leading to an awareness of how social phenomenology can inform public safety, in addition to traditional approaches that are reliant on the science of seismology (Rehorick, 1986).

George Psathas states that, "phenomenology is many things to many people" and that "phenomenology can restore, affect, influence, and change persons" (2008, p. xi). "Phenomenology becomes an artful, assimilative experience for those who take it seriously and incorporate its premises, methods, orientations, and perspectives—boldly, affectively, cognitively, and assumptively" (p. xi). For the learner, the process of *Transformative Phenomenology* brings phenomenology to consciousness and offers the opportunity for the learner to incorporate it into their lifeworld. We believe that phenomenology transforms anyone who cares to engage with it in a deep way.

> Transformative phenomenology may be the way to show how we can experience renewal—through our readings, our study, our interviews, our organized protocols, our hermeneutic exploration, our understandings; in short, through all of the mysteries entailed in the transformative process. (Psathas, 2008, pp. xii-xiii)

Husserl reminds us that the phenomenologist engages in a perpetual effort to understand things like a beginner, finding an entry point into the philosophy again and again (Natanson, 1973). For the beginner at Fielding, the focus is not on an exploration of a more exclusive, theoretical, kind. Any number of philosophers, methodologies, and methods can serve as entry points into the phenomenological realm—Husserl, Schütz, Merleau-Ponty, Heidegger, Gadamer, Wolff, van Manen, Wagner, and Psathas. Barber (2017) observes that Fielding scholar-practitioners do not restrict themselves to one version of phenomenology but use phenomenology to explore their interests, through a multidisciplinary lens, to a greater or lesser degree as they see fit:

> As if phenomenology itself precludes any absolutizing of itself . . . these authors are unwilling to abide within the comfortable bounds of phenomenological philosophy itself. Instead, they seek to bring its resources to bear on a variety of practical concerns in such a way that it is impossible to think of them in any other way than as the "Scholar-Practitioners" that they call themselves. (Barber, 2017, pp. 7-8)

It is this openness to finding new entry points to phenomenology that is characteristic of the Fielding scholar-practitioner. Where the past "awaits new interpretations to help reconceive it . . . blocking attempts to predict with any certainty the future the past will yield" (Barber, 2017, p. 7).

Writing, and the interpretation of texts, is central to the process of *Transformative Phenomenology*. Learners become immersed in their research project from a first-person perspective. They often experience a thoughtful, disorienting incoherence in coming to phenomenology for the first time through the development of their protocol statements, conducting their interviews, engaging with hermeneutic explorations, and reflecting on lived experience (Rehorick & Taylor, 1995). The allure of phenomenology and hermeneutics grows over time. The veiled nature of the taken-for-granted is acknowledged and the "unclouded phenomenological eye" emerges.

> A person's view of the lifeworld, understandings, and situations of others are clouded by his preconceptions, scientific and popular constructs, and media images and distortions. Over time, these may blind us to what is apparent to the unclouded phenomenological eye, much as cataracts impair one's vision. (Rehorick & Bentz, 2008a, p. 21)

The ineffable process of personal learning and transformation is realized with the endless opportunity to return to the philosophy, again and again.

A Fielding Education and the Emergence of the "Leregogue"

> Leregogy is a term coined to try and bridge the indomitable severing of roles between teacher and learner. It implies a transactional and shifting set of "roles" wherein both people, are at various times and sometimes synchronously, both teachers and learners. (Rehorick and Taylor, 1995)

Barber (2017) suggests that the openness that Fielding phenomenologists exhibit toward their research might be attributed to the leregogic method (attitude) of teaching that Rehorick and Bentz have adopted. They offer leregogy as an alternative collaborative learning model to that of the teacher-directed focus of pedagogy, and the self-directed focus of andragogy.

The neologism "leregogy" as conceived by David Rehorick (Rehorick & Taylor, 1995) describes the guiding and supportive stance between a teacher and a learner that is founded on trust, devoid of power, accepting of faultiness, and conscious of the impact of reward and criticism. A leregogic educator walks beside the learner as an equal; thus the dichotomous differentiation between student/teacher and mentor/mentee falls away. It is a relationship where social distance and dialogue mitigates dependence and spawns creativity. The teacher and learner acknowledge that there are many possible avenues to the learner's destination. In a leregogic relationship, the teacher learns from, and with, the learner as they engage in a unique self-directed journey of scholarship and self-discovery (Rehorick & Bentz, 2017a; Rehorick & Rehorick, 2016).

Whether or not a leregogic attitude is innate to the learner, we contend that such an attitude is a natural outcome of the adoption of qualities (competencies) that arise, implicitly, through an education in *Transformative Phenomenology* as modeled by Rehorick and Bentz. Students who experience a phenomenological education through leregogic mentorship can emerge as transformative phenomenologists-in-action, expressing leregogic qualities. A leregogic education can lead to the emergence of a phenomenological way-of-being that shows deep respect for the experience of others and is focused on recognizing "inner value."

Qualities of Transformative Phenomenologists

Transformative phenomenologists seek positive changes in self, lifeworlds, and professional practice for the benefit of society. They are educated in the principles of *Mindful Inquiry*—developing a capacity for mindful thought, interpreting situations in the context of history and culture, attempting to alleviate suffering by critiquing the sources origins of oppression, and pulling back epistemological blinders by going back to the things themselves (Bentz & Shapiro, 1998).

Rehorick and Bentz (2017a) identified 10 qualities (competencies) of phenomenological scholar-practitioners based on their analysis of phenomenological research completed at Fielding from 1996 to 2016. These qualities are illustrated in Figure 1. Writing rich descriptions and collaboratively interpreting meaning is a foundational activity. Additional qualities include adopting phenomenology as a way of being and embracing embodied consciousness, wonderment, and authenticity.

Phenomenological scholar-practitioners are focused on looking beyond the taken for granted, with awareness that lifeworlds are constructed through patterns of communication. Transformative phenomenologists seek to transcend the reality of everyday lived-experience in service of generating common understanding among others. In the next section we explore the impact that *Transformative Phenomenology* has had on some of the current and former students of Valerie Bentz and David Rehorick.

Figure 1. The qualities of transformative phenomenologists

The Impact of Transformative Phenomenology—Our Collective Story

It's typical to hear Fielding students and alumni describe their studies as transformational. I expected no less from my Fielding experience. Yet looking back today, 10 years later, I am struck by how utterly life-changing my studies and dissertation process were and continue to be. Each time I have faced another new challenge. . . I have been able to draw upon the insights, perspective, and strengths gleaned from my study and practice of phenomenology. (Lori)

In writing this section of this chapter, we contacted Fielding phenomenologists (students and alumni) and asked them to reflect on the impact they experienced through the practice of *Transformative Phenomenology*. Lori's comment above exemplifies the voices from the 19 phenomenologists who responded with their reflections. For them, in Ann's words, "it stretched my thinking in new and unique ways, opening new pathways for my intellectual development. Transformative Phenomenology has expanded my way of being in the world." The question posed by Max van Manen became real: "The question isn't what will we do with phenomenology. The question is what will phenomenology do with us?" (David H.). We explored the question of what phenomenology did with "us," the Fielding students and alumni. It transformed our ways of thinking and being in the world. But what does it mean? This section narrates a collective story of our experience of transformation.

For some of the students and graduates, *Transformative Phenomenology* opened the door to legitimizing, confirming, and expanding what they had already known as the embodied knowledge, or the knowing within. For many "this journey has unlocked the power of multiple ways of knowing through the mind, body and spirit" (Valerie N.), and "open[ed] windows of insight for making sense of otherwise ineffable experience" (Bart). Theresa could go to "a deeper reflection on my research question" with "new meaning" after attending a joint event where Fielding phenomenologists and administrators, as well as residents of a social innovation facility for citizens recovering from drug addiction and facing homelessness intermingled, and "where communication relied not on words but on interpersonal connections of spirit" (Theresa).

One of the catalysts for transformation through phenomenology is the shift from asking "why" questions to asking "what" questions. Frank vividly narrated the transformation of his way of thinking by the acknowledgement that "This culture of inquiry was new to me. Historically, my preferred culture of inquiries is oriented to answering 'why' questions. In my life as a scholar and practitioner, I have been most concerned with cause and effect." Frank was to give a presentation about his life at the aforementioned Fielding event, and he was approaching this with a "cause and effect" and "explaining" mindset, and avoiding *understanding* when he was preparing for his talk. He wrote, "I was approaching this conference mechanically. That was my defense mechanism. It was my efforts to avoid reconciling whom I am versus where I am. I was avoiding understanding, or truly doing a phenomenological exploration." But looking at his life through a phenomenological lens and presenting it were a liberating experience for him: "I cannot speak for anyone else there, but I changed after I was done [the presentation]. I have a better understanding of who I am. I am comfortable with me. Most importantly, I learned I mattered" (Frank).

Frank is not the only one who experienced "I learned I mattered." The sense of *I matter* is an implicit part of the phenomenological practice, especially with Gadamarian hermeneutics, as *self* is an integral part of the interpretation. Interpreting the text or the lifeworlds does not exist in a vacuum; the phenomenologists bring their preunderstandings to the forefront (or in Husserlian epoché, phenomenologists consciously make them aware of their preunderstandings so that they can bracket them). As Lee put it, "Transformative phenomenology reminds us of the traditions and prejudices that we bring to our research and the multiple realities influencing our life worlds."

The phenomenological students and alumni have learned to work with multiple ways of knowing, and it led them to "a mindful awareness of the value of looking beyond the taken-for-granted" (James) and "second and third loop learning" (David H.). "I became aware of a phenomenon I had taken for granted," said Evelyn. "Entering the world of transformative phenomenology led me to research I would never have otherwise undertaken and has deepened my practice of Sacred Circle Dance. I am forever grateful for this awakening" (Evelyn). Through *Transformative Phenomenology*, the students and alumni could *let things reveal themselves*, see what their texts (study participants' voices) are telling. Lee also reported, "This approach made it possible for me to uncover aspects of [Nelson] Mandela's lifeworld that may not have shown themselves under other qualitative research conditions."

It is not only their ways of thinking that have transformed. The practice of *Transformative Phenomenology* deepened the level of awareness of self, others, and contexts, and expanded the way of being as a personal transformation, in addition to the changes in their scholarly and professional work. The students and graduates dwell in the phenomenological being wherever they go. Carol L. expressed:

> There isn't a day that goes by that I don't think about how things are affecting both my and people's consciousness around me, in terms of interpretation of meaning. . . . In my professional and family life, from the boardroom, to day to day operations, coaching, mentoring and strategizing with staff, reviewing student's writing assignments and watching my adult children grow through their journey in the world, I carry my transformative phenomenological lens.

The phenomenological qualities and attitudes have become a part of the students' and alumni's being. For example, Ayumi noticed:

> As the phenomenological qualities and attitudes becoming a part of my habit, I reflect my *fore-structure* (biases, preknowledge, or ladder of inference) more often and deeper, and this act makes me appreciate others as precious human-fellows who have their own fore-

structures. It is not that I did not do this before, but the experience of *doing* phenomenology definitely put me on a higher level of consciousness.

For Tetyana, "enjoyment of wonderment" became a new habit: I began listening to my intuition. I gave myself permission not to know in advance, not to rush and enjoy simply being present. Marveling at the ordinary, gradually I ran into unspeakable, into transcendent. Wandering in wonderment became my door to different realities.

As the students and graduates have learned "to be patient and to let the insights reveal themselves as they may, with the passage of time" (Lori), they have grown certain virtues in their characteristics. Using Carol L.'s expression, "I believe *Transformative Phenomenology* has taught me how to be humble and have patience in everyday life, resulting in what I interpret as a sense of inner calmness."

Learning about self and reaching to a higher level of awareness brought a revelation to Evelyn as a leader and teacher of self-development through dance:

To my great surprise, I also became aware of less positive thoughts and feelings (some judgments of myself and others) I was having while dancing, which made me realize that my authentic experience was far more complex than I had first intuited and that for an experience to be transformative it need not be entirely positive. I already understood that this dance was a vehicle for coming to consciousness in relation to self and other, but now I found myself becoming more aware in ways that made me a more sensitive leader who could help others awaken.

As with Evelyn, the students and graduates find their ways to bring positive transformations to their fields of practice (including scholarly ones). Luann emphasizes the importance of scholar-practitioners taking an advocate role "for the topics and paths less traveled." As she described it, "*Transformative Phenomenology* encouraged me to actively integrate practice-based techniques and helped me to legitimize my clinical knowledge base. In the process, I embraced the identity of scholar-practitioner-advocate and became transformed myself."

Many of the scholar-practitioners apply their learning from *Transformative Phenomenology* to assist with others' self-development or leadership development, through the modalities rooted in multiple ways of knowing. As Adair put it, "My research was personally transformational and enabled me to engage my students in embarking on similar paths of self-development." The impacts on the students and graduates are carried on to more people through the phenomenologists.

After the Fielding doctoral program, Bart, who is an advocate for healing posttraumatic stress disorder (PTSD) for veterans, teaches phenomenology as a research methodology in a military psychology program. Bart sees profound impact in his students:

> As one Vietnam veteran I worked with in a writing workshop put it at the end of a poem that he wrote afterwards, "phenomenology is good for veterans." When asked what this meant, he tearfully stated (in essence) that if what he had just experienced (in a space of shared and open phenomenological co-inquiry in community of other veterans) had been available when he returned from Vietnam, the last forty years of his life would not have been as painful as they had been for him. This is a transformative conversation worth continuing and expanding.

Through the experience of *Transformative Phenomenology*, Valerie N. started to incorporate art, storytelling, and other creative techniques in her leadership development programs, and she sees that "something has fundamentally shifted in how they [her clients] see the world and who they are." Valerie continued:

> I have discovered that creating the space for curiosity, courage and deep connection invites the creative soul, the collective heart and moral leadership. I believe that phenomenology provides a critical gateway to understand restore and transform humanity in the evolving complexity we are living into.

The work of phenomenology is indeed a doorway to humanity, which is much bigger than self, scholarly conversations, or customers and clients in the professional arena. The reflections of the students and alumni collectively point to the deep quality of humanity in a world where all humans and other living and non-living beings belong together. This includes "the lifeworld(s) of other human beings and even animals to a lesser extent" (Dan). It is a paradox—the more we, the phenomenologists, go deeply inside of self, the closer we get to humanity and the whole world.

The students and alumni have developed a community of practice, and "opportunities to collaborate on writing projects, seminars, and conference presentations continue to build awareness about how our community of transformative phenomenologists can lead social change in complex times" (James) and it motivates them to move forward. Phenomenology may be felt as enigmatic when one starts the journey. Dan confessed "When I first heard the word—phenomenology—it sounded complex, forbidding even." But its philosophy, concepts, and practices are not far away from us engaging with daily activities as a human. It is "practical" (Dan) and "an expressed act of caring, an intentionality to know that which is most essential to our being in the world" (Lee).

Sergej thinks that he was not a phenomenologist per se when he was a doctoral student, but notices now that "in retrospect, I experience a double helix where I have co-evolved with this idea and this community." The circle of *Transformative Phenomenology* has a permeable boundary and it is not an exclusive club: it is open to anyone who wishes to test the water by wetting one foot, jumping in the ocean of phenomenology, or swimming with dolphins. *Transformative Phenomenology* fuses horizons with art, somatics, and other types of reflexive practices. "Phenomenology is not merely transformational; it is conducive to further transformation" (Lori). The students and alumni have heard the sound of the hidden waterfall—the call of phenomenology—they have entered its realm and have transformed others while being transformed. The continuous transformations keep creating ripples inside of selves and their spheres of influence, but also in the community of *Transformative Phenomenology* and towards larger communities.

Touching
Radical
Adventurous
Near
Self-reflective   Participatory
First-person   Heart-filled
Opening   Engaging
Rising to surface   Necessary
Mind-bending   Original
Affirmative   Mindful
Truth   Exciting
Individual   Nurturing
Valued   Of one's own
Experiential   Loving
                    Organic
                    Grounded
                    YES!

"Transformative Phenomenology" Words by Carol E

Fielding phenomenologists (Part 3 contributors)

Epilogue: The Future of Phenomenological Inquiry at Fielding

> *grateful for the invitation to connect more deeply*
> *with the texture of experience...*
> *both a coming-home and an opening to in-dwelling mystery.*
> *what changes when we return to less-mediated experience?*
> *an ineffable sense of greater ease, permeating everything...*
> *a bit more clarity in the lens, and the whole world*
> *appears more vividly.*

Rosa, Fielding student

The legacy Valerie Bentz and David Rehorick established at Fielding has been living in the lives and work of students and graduates, their fields of practices, and social convenings. Its community-of-practice has been active. However, the future retirement of Valerie Bentz inserts uncertainty into the trajectory of phenomenology at Fielding. The establishment of the Valerie Bentz Endowment Fund for Mindful Inquiry and Transformative Phenomenology was launched in 2017 by a group of alumni to support scholarship in the arena of phenomenology and mindful inquiry practice. The continued development of the SPCL community-of-practice is a key activity to ensure that David and Valerie's legacy of *Transformative Phenomenology* will be sustained and evolved by Fielding "Silver Age" alumni, students, and like-minded colleagues around the world.

References

Barber, M. (2017). Foreword. In D. Rehorick & V. Bentz (Eds.), *Expressions of phenomenological research: Consciousness and lifeworld studies* (pp. 6-11). Santa Barbara, CA: Fielding University Press.

Bentz, V. (2002). From playing child to aging mentor: The role of "Human Studies" in my development as a scholar. *Human Studies, 25*(4), 499-506.

Bentz, V. (2014). *Flesh and mind: The time travels of Dr. Victoria Von Dietz*. North Charleston, SC: CreateSpace Independent Publishing Platform.

Bentz, V., Rehorick, D., Marlatt, J., Nishii, A., & Estrada, C. (2018). *Somatic phenomenology as an antidote to technological deathworlds.* Paper presented at Knowledge, Nescience, and the (New) Media Conference: 4th International Alfred Schutz Circle for Phenomenology and Interpretive Sociology, Konstanz, Germany. Accepted for publication in Schutzian Research: A Yearbook of Worldly Phenomenology and Qualitative Social Science.

Bentz, V., Rehorick, D., Marlatt, J., Nishii, A., & Estrada, C. (in press). Somatic phenomenology as an antidote to technological deathworlds. *Schutzian Research.*

Bentz, V., & Shapiro, J. (1998). *Mindful inquiry in social research.* Thousand Oaks, CA: SAGE Publications.

Bentz, V. M. (2003). The body's memory, the body's wisdom. In M. Itkonen & G. Backhaus (Eds.), *Lived images: Meditations in experience, life-world and I-hood* (pp. 158-186). Iyvaskyla, Finland: University of Iyvaskyla Press.

Bentz, V. M. (2016). Knowing as being: Somatic phenomenology as contemplative practice. In V. M. Bentz & V. M. B. Giorgino (Eds.), *Contemplative social research: Caring for self, being, and lifeworld* (pp. 50-79). Santa Barbara, CA: Fielding University Press.

Bentz, V. M., & Giorgino, V.M.B. (Eds.). (2016). *Contemplative social research: Caring for self, being, and lifeworld.* Santa Barbara, CA: Fielding University Press.

Embree, L., & Barber, M. D. (Eds.). (2017). *The Golden Age of Phenomenology at the New School for Social Research (1954-1973)* (1st ed. Vol. 50). Athens: Ohio University Press.

Hanna, T. (1988). *Somatics: Reawakening the mind's control of movement, flexibility, and health.* Cambridge, MA: Da Capo Press.

Melville, K. (2016). *A passion for adult learning: How the Fielding model is transforming doctoral education.* Santa Barbara, CA: Fielding University Press.

Natanson, M. (1973). *Edmund Husserl: Philosopher of infinite tasks.* Evanston, IL: Northwestern University Press.

Psathas, G. (2008). Foreword. In D. A. Rehorick & V. M. Bentz (Eds.), *Transformative phenomenology: Changing ourselves, lifeworlds, and professional practice* (pp. xv-xviii). Lanham, MD: Lexington Books.

Rehorick, D., & Bentz, V. M. (2017a). The emergence of transformative phenomenology: Two decades of teaching and learning at

Fielding. In D. Rehorick & V. M. Bentz (Eds.), *Expressions of phenomenological research: Consciousness and lifeworld studies* (pp. 18-44). Santa Barbara, CA: Fielding University Press.

Rehorick, D., & Bentz, V. M. (Eds.). (2017b). *Expressions of phenomenological research: Consciousness and lifeworld studies.* Santa Barbara, CA: Fielding University Press.

Rehorick, D., & Rehorick, S. (2016). The leregogy of curriculum design: Teaching and learning as relational endeavours. In A. Tajino, T. Stewart, & D. Dalsky (Eds.), *Team teaching and team learning in the language classroom: Collaboration for innovation in ELT* (pp. 43-63). London: Routledge.

Rehorick, D. A. (1986). Shaking the foundations of lifeworld: A phenomenological account of an earthquake experience. *Human Studies, 9,* 379-391.

Rehorick, D. A. (2002). I/"Human Studies". *Human Studies, 25*(4), 467-471.

Rehorick, D. A., & Bentz, V. M. (2008a). Transformative phenomenology: A scholarly scaffold for practitioners. In D. Rehorick & V. M. Bentz (Eds.), *Transformative phenomenology: Changing ourselves, lifeworlds, and professional practice* (pp. 3-31). Lanham, MD: Lexington Books.

Rehorick, D. A., & Bentz, V. M. (Eds.). (2008b). *Transformative phenomenology: Changing ourselves, lifeworlds, and professional practice.* Lanham, MD: Lexington Books.

Rehorick, D. A., & Bentz, V. M. (2012). Re-envisioning Schutz: Retrospective reflections & prospective hopes. *Annual Meetings of the Society for Phenomenology and the Human Sciences (SPHS).*

Rehorick, D. A., & Taylor, G. (1995). Thoughtful incoherence: First encounters with the phenomenological-hermeneutical domain. *Human Studies: A Journal for Philosophy and Social Sciences, 18*(4), 389-414.

Tesch, R. (1980). Phenomenology and transformative research: What they are and how to do them. In J. Handlon & D. Stomff (Eds.), *Fielding Occasional Papers.* Santa Barbara, CA: The Fielding Institute.

About the Authors

Valerie Malhotra Bentz, MSSW, PhD, is Professor of Human and Organization Development, Fielding Graduate University, where she served as Associate Dean for Research. Her current interests include somatics, phenomenology, social theory, consciousness development, and Vedantic theories of knowledge. Her books include *Contemplative social research: Caring for self, being, and lifeworld*, with Vincenzo M. B. Giogino; *Transformative phenomenology: Changing ourselves, lifeworlds and professional practice*, with David Rehorick; *Mindful inquiry in social research*, with Jeremy Shapiro, and *Becoming mature: Childhood ghosts and spirits in adult life*. She also authored a philosophical novel, *Flesh and mind: The time travels of Dr. Victoria Von Dietz*. She is a Fellow in Contemplative Practice of the American Association of Learned Societies. Valerie was editor of *Phenomenology and the Human Sciences* (1994–98). She has served as president and board member of the Clinical Sociology Association, the Sociological Practice Association, and the Society for Phenomenology and the Human Sciences. She founded and co-directed an action research team and center in Mizoram, India. Valerie was co-founder of the Creative Longevity and Wisdom program at Fielding. She is the Director of the Doctoral Concentration in Somatics, Phenomenology, and Communicative Leadership (SPCL). She has 20 years' experience as a psychotherapist, and is a certified yoga teacher and certified massage therapist. She is a member of the board of the Carpinteria Valley Association, an environmental activist group. She also plays bassoon and piano.

Barton Buechner, PhD, is a faculty member of the Adler University Masters in Psychology with Emphasis in Military Psychology (MAMP) program, and co-instructs the Communicative Leadership and Embodied Awareness seminar course with Dr. Valerie Bentz at the University of the Virgin Islands (UVI). He is a Navy veteran with 30 years of military service, graduating in 1978 from the United States Naval Academy in

Annapolis, Maryland and in 1997 from the College of Command and Staff at the Naval War College, Newport, Rhode Island. He also holds a Master of Science degree in Organization Development from Case Western Reserve University, and a doctorate in Human Development at Fielding Graduate University. He is the co-editor with Dr. Miguel Guilarte of the monograph "Veteran and Family Reintegration: Identity, Healing and Reconciliation" (2016) Fielding University Press, and serves as a Board member of the Coordinated Management of Meaning (CMM) Institute for Personal and Social Evolution.

Carol Estrada, MA, is a doctoral student at Fielding Graduate University. Currently, she holds two master's degrees in Human Development; one from Fielding and one from Pacific Oaks College. Professionally she works as an educational specialist, tutor, and coach with pre-K through high school students, many of whom have learning disabilities or other special needs. Her private practice educational work revolves around providing developmentally appropriate interventions with the goal of having the students achieve success academically, socially, and in life. Her doctoral work takes her into the psychosocial world of young adults with terminal cancer. She is active in the Fielding Somatics, Phenomenology, and Communicative Leadership community-of-practice. Carol lives in Northern Utah with her two dogs.

James Leonard Marlatt, PhD, is a dual careerist and practices as both a certified executive coach, leadership and team development consultant, and as a mineral exploration management consultant. He is a Fielding HOD alumnus and holds an MBA from Athabasca University, and a geological engineering degree from Queen's University at Kingston. As the director of global mineral exploration for an international mining company Jim helped facilitate research in applied earth science through industry-academia collaborative research programs and has co-authored scientific publications. Jim is a technical consultant to the International

Atomic Energy Agency, serving as a mission expert, speaker, educator, and author. He is active in supporting the development of the Fielding Somatics, Phenomenology and Communicative Leadership community-of-practice. As a Fielding scholar-practitioner he leverages insights from applied social phenomenology to assist with the development of willing individuals, teams, organizations through his coaching practice. Jim lives in British Columbia with his wife Margaret and has a passion for nature photography. Contact: jmarlatt@email.fielding.edu

Ayumi Nishii, PhD, is an organizational development consultant, enjoys playing the role of catalyst to *connect, collaborate, and create* with people, and works in the fields of organizational development, leadership training, and human resources in Japan and the United States. She explored the meaning of servant leadership with her hermeneutic phenomenological dissertation, *Servanthood as Love, Relationships, and Power: A Heideggerian Hermeneutic Study on the Experiences of Servant-Leaders* (2017). The areas of her interests include servant leadership, dialogue, and Heideggerian philosophy. She was born and grew up in Japan and currently lives in San Francisco with her husband, Jon. She holds a master's degree in Organization Management and Development and a doctorate in Human and Organizational Systems from Fielding Graduate University. Contact address: anishii@email.fielding.edu

David Allan Rehorick, PhD, is Professor Emeritus at the University of New Brunswick (UNB), Canada where he taught from 1974 to 2007. He is also Professor Emeritus at the Fielding Graduate University, serving as Research Consulting Faculty (1995–2006), then full-time faculty (2007–2012). His research, publications, and editorial contributions encompass the domains of phenomenology and interpretive studies, educational praxis and theory, sociological theory, population studies, the healthcare sciences, and the creative arts. He has served on six editorial boards of academic journals, including Review Editor of *Human Studies: A Journal* *for Philosophy and the Social Sciences.* As a developer in higher education, David was appointed Founding Faculty and Fellow in Comparative Culture at The Miyazaki International College in Japan (1994–97). He was also founder of Renaissance College, the first undergraduate leadership studies program in Canada, and became the first Director of International Internships (2001–04). He is an award-winning educator, with an appointment as "University Teaching Scholar" at UNB (2005–08). He received the Association of Atlantic Universities Instructional Leadership Award (1995) and the Allan P. Stuart Memorial Award for Excellence in Teaching (1984). His special areas of teaching embraced qualitative and phenomenological research approaches, interpersonal relations, human development and consciousness, cross-cultural studies, the sociology of culture, of music, and of Eastern religions. David lives in Vancouver, Canada, where he studies jazz piano, with particular emphasis on the creative art of composition. Contact: rehorickunb@gmail.com

CHAPTER 20

BETHEL SYSTEMS INTENSIVE: ALUMNI AND FACULTY REFLECTIONS ON SYSTEMIC LEARNING ABOUT SYSTEMS

Frederick Steier, PhD
Fielding Graduate University

In a recent interview with *The Edge*, when asked for her thoughts on what it means to be a system thinker, Mary Catherine Bateson stated:

> At the moment, I'm asking myself how people think about complex wholes like the ecology of the planet, or the climate, or large populations of human beings that have evolved for many years in separate locations and are now re-integrating. To think about these things, I find that you need something like systems theory.

Bateson's statement illustrates what we had in mind when trying to design a residential learning experience that would feature learning systems – a systems intensive.

The Planning of a Systems Intensive

In the fall of 2000, Charlie Seashore and I talked about how to design a residential learning experience that would feature systems thinking and practice. We asked ourselves how we might invite students to learn about systems, which was a core knowledge area at Fielding, in ways that would bring together the conceptual ideas of systems with the practical wisdom that was at the heart of systems approaches, including a focus on group process. With Charlie's home in Bethel, Maine as a possible site for meeting, and the attraction of the National Training Lab right next door, the Bethel Systems Intensive was born. This would not be the first intensive at Fielding, so we had other Fielding residential experiences to build on, but we thought we might be able to do something innovative that might bring the multiple levels of systems into play. This included understanding ourselves as a learning system as we learned about systems. The different backgrounds in systems that Charlie and I had also afforded an opportunity to bring the kind of binocular vision, allowing for multiple perspectives and variety, to our setting.

The framing question for our invitation for the intensive was: How can we evoke systemic understanding in action by immersing in collaborative experiences and bringing that understanding to systems that matter to each of us? We chose to do it in February, realizing that the likelihood of snow, although it might make travel to and from Bethel more difficult, might also enhance the desire for a "cultural island" that Kurt Lewin had in mind in helping select Bethel as the NTL site.

A key systems issue that was in the foreground for us was how systems balance structure and flexibility. This was a bit tricky for Charlie and me, as both of us tended to lean much more heavily on the flexibility side of things, which we realized might be seen as chaos by some. We had hopes for the intensive to become an annual event, and the idea of the Bethel Systems Intensive as a living system, which would itself co-evolve with the participants and the community, was an integral part of our plan. In other words, we tried to bring whole systems design principles, with their emphasis on flexibility, to the design of the systems intensive.

In our flexible plan, we tried to feature several aspects of systems. One was the idea of encouraging participants to look both inward and outward. For this, we chose to form groups where the participants might collaboratively explore situations in which they were engaged that mattered to them, and where they saw some opportunity for systems change. We had them do this initially online prior to the session, but organized much of the first days of the intensive around these small groups' exploration of each other's cases. We would also have the faculty rotate among the groups as each case situation was explored. Another way was to form different groups that might explore how the community in which our intensive was taking place—Bethel in this case—was experienced by the locals, to develop an understanding of the local ecosystem from a local perspective. Bringing these together at the end we hoped would also afford exploring ourselves as a learning system.

With a site such as Bethel, with its rich history, we hoped to also explore systems approaches to the creation of placeness—so looking outward in that sense. To complement that, we were able to engage a friend of Charlie's, Janet Willey, a local movement therapist, to open each morning with a highly (some might have thought too highly) exercise-based and yet contemplative "body as system" session. Bringing these together, we were able to highlight a relational focus on self and other (where other might be a person, or a plant) as a key to systemic understanding.

Knowing that, apart from National Sessions, most of the participants, if they knew each other at all, knew each other's "online" self, we also chose to always ask ourselves: "What are we doing here while we are in the same physical space that we could not do online?" The "body as system" opener each morning was done in this vein. At the same time, the communication and relational systems aspect also featured in having a lobster dinner (it was Maine, after all, although we also made it lobster and veggie) that featured an opportunity for sharing expertise in how to eat a lobster for those who were somewhat uncertain about the task.

The Players and the Co-evolving Play

The Bethel Systems Intensive actually started off rather small, with eight participants the first year, but grew steadily over the years, even reaching 31 members one year. This growth also meant that we had to expand our faculty to allow for our being present as guides or facilitators of group process for the case situations. With our initial expansion, in addition to Charlie and me, we had Thierry Pauchant, a Fielding faculty member from Montreal. We were also lucky to have the presence of Edie

Seashore, Charlie's wife and Organization Development leader whose well-known NTL background and gracious action knowledge of group process was a gift to all of us. Later, we also added Jane Jorgenson, a Professor of Communication (my wife, so yes, there were two couples on the faculty, making for some interesting emergent conversations about family systems). Jane's area of work/family/life relationships also fit in nicely with the student interests. In addition, we had Janet Willey, the local movement therapist, as part of our faculty.

The structure, although it had to evolve with the expanding size of the intensive, was rather simple. Students were given readings to do in advance of the session and also asked to write a case situation in which they were involved, and that mattered deeply to them, where they felt knowledge of systems might be helpful. These could involve organizational, community, family, or national/international systems. The students posted these in advance and were placed in small groups to discuss the situations, with the idea that a significant part of the session would be organized about the case situation meetings.

We opened with a check-in (of course—this was a Fielding tradition!) and then some discussion of systems principles. We then moved into the small groups, with faculty rotating across the groups, acting as group guides (but not teaching). This occupied much of the second day. The third day was devoted to learning about the community as a system, and here Edie and Charlie's knowledge of people in the community was essential. New small groups were formed, with each going on-site with a member of a community place. These were different over the years, and ranged from the local historical society to a local farm to an Outward Bound group. After meeting with their local guides around issues that were at play for the community from their perspective, the groups returned to our "home" to prepare a report that would be given to our group as a whole, which had now expanded to include the community participants. This afforded a delightful community system reflection—and led to a lobster dinner. The final day was devoted to exploring ourselves as a learning system, returning to also reflect on the systems principles we were now using as our guides for action. A check-out then served as a closing.

The place itself was a key player in all of this. We used the Bingham House, Charlie and Edie's home, as a meeting base until we grew too large—which actually happened fairly early in the process. We were then able to use the Gehring House, the home of NTL, as our meeting base. For many students the evocation of meaning from the place and its history was a significant aspect of the intensive. It was significant that each place had wonderful small spaces, evoking Chris Alexander's *A Pattern Language* that afforded the warmth of small group meetings (although heating varied – it was, after all, February in Maine).

After 2009, when Charlie and Edie had sold Bingham House, and Gehring House was no longer available, we realized we had to move the base of our Bethel Systems Intensive. We were lucky to have the possibility of the newly designed center of two Fielding alums, Alex and David Bennet, and their Mountain Quest Institute. With its location in Frost, West Virginia, it would retain the snowy feel of Bethel in February, and we were able to hold on to the tradition that we had created in Bethel, albeit in a new location, and with new hosts.

The Experiences, on Reflection

A key principle of systems is that of the primacy of mutual relationships, of understanding how *inter*connections and *inter*dependencies are the core of how systemic organization. The Bethel Systems Intensives, including those held at Mountain Quest Institute after we moved the location from Maine, were among the most transformative learning experiences of my professional career. But what made them transformative for me, holding to the mutuality of systems, was how they were transformative for the students, including many who are now alumni and alumnae, and the effect of their transformative aspects on me. Rather than my writing about them, here are some snapshots of experiences in their voices. We can think of each of the following reflections as bringing forth different systemic features of the experience of the Bethel Systems Intensive, in their eyes. Each is presented with the name of the reflector and their "Bethel Year." I have taken the liberty of linking some key systems ideas to their reflections, and perhaps it is the bringing together of experiences and concepts that is what the intensive was about—itself a key systems idea of the second order.

Keeping to space limitations, quotes offered below are taken from larger quotes from each participant, while still retaining their contextual basis.

The Bethel Systems as Understanding Self and Others in Relationship
Mary Nash, Bethel 2003

I was a very new doctoral student, about five months into the program. Living with Charlie, Edie, Fred, and the other students for several days was a bonus to the transformative experience that was the intensive. The profound insights, the relationships that were forged and continue to this day, and learning from Charlie and Fred what it means to be a master in use of self, were all wonderfully unexpected outcomes, along with the intensive immersive learning experience in systems theory and thinking. The confidence participating in this program gave me, as a relatively young, female, introversion-preferring scholar-practitioner was immeasurably valuable. The design of the program—prework based in real life and reading scholarly theoretical work, combined with the immersive experience and the follow-up application and reflection paper were a very effective model, and one I use frequently in developing courses, leadership development programs, and executive coaching engagement. I appreciate this opportunity to reflect on this program, nearly 16 years later.

A key idea of second order systems—applying systems to itself—involves seeing where we are in the systems we are observing: observing SYSTEMS and OBSERVING systems. How to engage that focus on self, while holding to the reflexive aspect of seeing what that focus on self enables in others became a key learning, as it also opened up to the empathic understanding of others and other views of the "same" system.

Mary notes the importance of bringing that understanding to the importance of "use of self" as a systems practitioner, which was a key but challenging aspect of the entire series of Bethel systems intensives. It is important to note that Mary later wrote with Charlie Seashore on this very topic.

Wayfinding and Self-organizing
Terence Chung, 2010 Mountain Quest

The Mountain Quest experience was memorable for me. On the first day, I joined the classmates' car pool driven from the city to the Mountain Quest, although we got lost on the way. Once I realized how the huge snowstorm affected us, these questions worried me, "Will my flight be cancelled? How can one leave the site without a car?" All of our classmates were busy discussing and arranging alternative routes to "evacuate" from the site. As I had no experience in changing a flight schedule, I asked my classmates help me to talk to the airlines for the arrangements. I got a ride to the same airport with a small group. I did not notice whether we had an emerging leader to lead the process. The whole group of people was so self-organizing, so efficient and effective in helping each other make decisions and arrange routes to "evacuate."

Terence's first experience of snow (he is from Hong Kong) also pointed to the recognition that learning in the systems intensive included collaborative travelling to get there. For many, this wayfinding became a key feature of systems learning. Another systems idea revealed here is the importance of flexibility in systems design. In fact, the snowstorm that Terence mentions forced us to change our last day to shift to figuring out how everyone might get home, as all of the airports within five hours were closed or closing. Leadership emerged in the group, as a key principle of self-organizing systems became quite real.

Serious Play and Relationship Sustaining
Gary Wagenheim, 2003 Bethel

As a ski instructor and lover of winter, it was fitting to me that the systems intensive, hosted by Charlie Seashore and Fred Steier, took place in snowy Bethel Maine. The warm Bingham House was a comfortable setting to study my personal changing system.

Our systems experience started a month earlier in Santa Barbara when Charlie and Fred hosted a meeting during Winter Session "loosely" organizing the event. They explained the basic concepts of systems thinking, assigned readings, and outlined the schedule. Students self-organized, making travel arrangements, forming student teams, and preparing a personal case for the learning experience. Charlie and Fred created a unique, playful, and supportive system to study systems.

The systems learning was powerful; the relationships developed in [re]creating my own system even more powerful and important. The systems workshop did not start our friendships but it certainly amplified the intensity.

Here Gary emphasizes the key systems ideas of balancing process, including the process of relationship formation, with content. Allowing for a focus on process becomes a hallmark of a systems approach. Bringing play into the mix also opens space for the kind of creative confidence that is a hallmark of systems practice—play in both the sense of flexibility and trying things out, as well in the sense of good humor.

Caring Systems, Emergence, and Appreciation of Becoming
Carrie Spell-Hansson, Bethel 2004

The workshop was designed to provide us with an opportunity to experience "systems." As unplanned situations developed, such as one student becoming ill and requiring hospitalization, we discussed the implications in terms of how this impacted the system. This allowed us to see how theory is manifested in "real world" situations. One of the major learnings I took away from Bethel was developing the ability to be the observer of (my)self and the importance of bringing my awareness to how I connect to my environment and the systems that I am an integral part of. In addition, I became mindful of the importance of connecting to a system prior to any attempts to effect change within the system.

Carrie's note points to a key feature of whole systems design—that is, allowing for emergent happenings to become part of systems learning and not just labeled as an unrelated disruption that has to be dealt with and then dismissed. What happened was that one of the participants became ill and had to be taken to a medical facility. Concern shifted to caring for the individual, and recognition of the deep systems learning that was involved in our collectively doing so. Of course we could not plan for such an event, and would not want such an event to happen, but when it did happen, foregrounding how we responded as a caring system became a key, if unplanned, feature of that year.

The Interconnection of People, Place, and Context
Keith Ray, Bethel 2005

The day we arrived in Portland, Maine to attend the Systems Intensive there was a light snow falling. As we approached, the snowfall became heavier. That night we received over a foot of snow. When we awoke the next morning, the snow had transformed the landscape into a surreal New England winter postcard-like scene. We seemed trapped in a little snow bubble—a system in a system. Most of us really didn't know what was going to happen during the intensive. The process of the intensive was a nice balance of planned and emergent, with enough structure to have some understanding of what was happening but also enough uncertainty, complexity, and novelty to keep me engaged and curious. The place was beautiful. As an OD practitioner, being in the NTL house with all its history was fascinating to me. The snow added to both the beauty and a feeling as if there was a boundary around our group. This feeling was paradoxically anxiety-provoking and comforting. We could not leave if we wanted to, but then we were also in a beautiful white blanket. The boundary allowed for, or encouraged, creativity.

I did not know most of the people attending before the event though I am still in contact with several of them. It was not an exceptionally diverse group by Fielding standards, and yet several systemic issues around race, class, and age emerged during our conversations. What it means to be "outside" and "inside" a group moved front and center as we talked about what being "from away" meant. I gained new perspectives on identity through that experience.

In a way, we were a semi-artificial system that was examining systems from the inside-out. One belief that I forged during that experience and the reflections afterward, is that we can learn much by taking our experience seriously. Rather than talking about systems, we learned as a system.

Keith's reflection beautifully points to the importance of an eco-systemic appreciation of events. This includes not only the recognition of the importance of place, context, and people, evoking Kurt Lewin's idea of behavior being a function of person and environment, but of the interrelationship of all three.

Balancing Chaos and Structure
Gayla Napier: Bethel, 2008

We arrived in several feet of snow and were welcomed into a warm, caring environment steeped in academic history. Most of us had read the mountain of books and papers assigned in preparation for the weekend. From my initial preoccupation with things as they are (for example, what is the schedule, and how will I navigate my relationship to others?) towards a more reflexive concept of things as I perceive them, describe them, and act upon them. We became a system-in-action! The uncanny correlation between chaos and structure was the perfect learning environment for thinking about systems. Fielding's tradition of practice through experiential learning intensives provides the proving grounds and experimental laboratories for working out ways of acting into the world.

Gayla's reflection points to the very tension Charlie and I discussed throughout—how to recognize that any system needs to find ways to balance structure and chaos. A big challenge for bringing that tension into play involved making that tension clear as it applied to the very organization of our intensive, enabling us to take advantage of opportunities that arose as learning vehicles, while still holding to the basic structure of the intensive, much like the sociotechnical systems criterion of having minimal critical specifications that allow for flexibility of learning. How to create reflective space for holding an appreciation of this balance during the session itself becomes a critical question.

Innovation and Ritual
Keith Earley, 2011 Mountain Quest

Of course, there's a Charlie Seashore story to tell. At the beginning of the intensive, we began with a check in. Charlie pointed to a clock—one of those clocks the face of which separates and rejoins when it strikes on the hour. The requirement was that whenever the clock sounded we had to stop what we were doing to get up and move, shake, or dance. Initially this was viewed as a fun, Charlie-ism. It turned out to be brilliant because when the group's energy waned, or if there was a challenging matter a small group was discussing, getting up to move became an intervention. It was a moment to stop, shift, and reflect. It was Charlie at his brilliant best. I had a great experience at Mountain Quest, and to keep the memories close I bought a clock that plays music on the hour. When it does, I am reminded of my Intensive experience and of Charlie Seashore.

Keith points to a key idea of social systems that is also at the heart of social capital, which is how we create ways of being together that bind us as a group, with a focus on relationships. How we enact rituals that have deep meaning for those inside the family, perhaps in celebration of holidays or occasions that matter to us, becomes our local mode for the relational focus. But how might we do this for a group that is meeting for the first time in a way that takes advantage of what otherwise might be seen as a disruption? How might we innovate to enact a ritual that then becomes a key feature of our group as a system? This balance of ritual and tradition, and innovation to enact a ritual, became a key focus of collaborative learning. And bringing fun into the mix provided a deepening of that bond.

Keith's reflection is actually from the last Bethel Systems Intensive as, sadly, Charlie was too ill for us to hold one that had been planned for 2012. This makes the clock ritual, and Keith's keeping it alive, all the more poignant, as an example of the sustainability of systems innovation.

Some Patterns That Connect the Reflections

There are several ideas that connect the reflections offered here. One central one is the importance of understanding that learning about systems is a process of learning with. Systems knowing is a process of knowing with. The relationships with others—colleagues, co-students, community participants, our environment—are what allow systems ideas to take root and accrue meaning. At the same time, our learning systems are not independent of our learning process. Another idea is the importance of place—of learning how to turn a space that we pass through every day without noticing into a place that has meaning for us. A third is the recognition of the importance of how to hold on to variety in the face of adapting to new and unplanned circumstances, and how to create reflective space to see that as an important feature of whole systems design, including design of a systems intensive.

There was one occasion, not mentioned in the reflections that stood out for me. One year, a student changed her case from the one actually presented in advance to a different one. She stated that, without knowing the group, she presented a case that she felt was "safe." After being with the group, she chose to present a much more difficult situation, but one that held much deeper meaning for her. Her explanation for the change was that she felt trust in the group. This led to a conversation about how to evoke that trust, and how the systems intensive, not as an abstract idea, but as co-constructed by all of the participants, created that climate of trust. We realized how trust is integral to any social system. While we cannot assume that it is present, we can create a mutual feedback system to check to see if it is there. Perhaps this unplanned lesson is a key to any systems intensive, and to any system.

A final pattern is the importance of forming a group that is willing to play together. Charlie and Edie, and then Thierry, Janet and Jane, all helped, together with all of the Bethel Systems alumni and alumnae, to make this a transformative experience, not only for each individual but for all of us as a systemic whole.

About the Author

Frederick Steier, PhD, is a professor in the School of Leadership Studies at Fielding Graduate University. His work focuses on systemic approaches to social/ecological systems, with attention to learning, communication, and design. He has directed participatory action research programs in a wide variety of settings, ranging from government institutions, including NASA, to science centers, such as the Museum of Science and Industry (MOSI), in Tampa, Florida, where he was also Scientist-in-Residence. He is the editor of the volumes *Gregory Bateson: Essays for an ecology of ideas* (2005), and *Research and Reflexivity* (1991), and is a Past-President of the American Society for Cybernetics. He has been on the faculty of the University of South Florida (where he was also Director of Interdisciplinary Studies Programs), Old Dominion University (where he was also Director of the Center for Cybernetic Studies in Complex Systems), the University of Oslo (Norway), and the University of Pennsylvania. He has also had the honor of being King Olav V Fellow with the American-Scandinavian Foundation. Dr. Steier received his doctorate in Social Systems Sciences from the Wharton School of the University of Pennsylvania in 1983.

CHAPTER 21

45 YEARS OF SINCERITY

Four Arrows, aka Don Trent Jacobs, PhD, EdD
Fielding Graduate University

I have served as a professor at Fielding for over 15 years, more than a third of its existence. Although a number of my colleagues have been here from the beginning, this is the longest I've ever stayed in one career position. In contemplating the reasons for my continuing on for so long in contrast to the other jobs, "sincerity" came to mind as the main reason. Dictionary.com defines this word as "freedom from deceit, hypocrisy, or duplicity; probity in intention or in communicating; earnestness." With this definition in mind, Fielding may be the only employer whose sincerity has either matched or sustained my own. We share a passion to inspire individuals and organizations to reach their highest potential on behalf of both present and future generations. To celebrate Fielding's 45th birthday, I thought it would be interesting to briefly look back at my previous jobs and compare them to Fielding in terms of "sincerity." I start with the first one after I graduated from college in 1968.

U.S. Marine Corps officer (three years)

My own sincerity was mixed at the beginning between wanting to serve my country, my egotistical goals relating to the advertised image of the "Marine," and honoring my father's 27 missions in a B-24 during WWII. Halfway through my tour of duty, I realized that neither I nor the Corps represented sincerity when I awakened to the wrongness of the Vietnam War. I knew the USMC was violating most of the terms of our definition of sincerity if we consider its vision to stand ready to promote peace and stability in the world. In comparison, few could rightfully doubt

Fielding's sincere commitment to its vision for "creating a more just and sustainable world."

Bank Auditor (two years)

Although the bank I worked for surely was committed to its purpose of maximizing efficiency and protecting its assets, one might have a hard time seeing probity (strong moral principles) as a part of the institutional soul of any bank. Moreover, my own goals were insincere in relationship to the job description. I took the position, using my B.S. in Economics, to pay off my sailboat so I could sail from San Francisco to the Virgin Islands. Fielding, however, has always stuck to its strong moral principles. Although in times of financial risk, most universities understandably consider putting financial goals above principles, Fielding has remained steadfast to its higher purpose. This in turn has inspired my own commitment to remain. Perhaps it has also why Fielding keeps renewing my contract in spite of my oft-outspoken criticism of Western-oriented educational systems.

High School Teacher (three years)

Although I sincerely wanted to help young people learn in ways that would help them live their lives to their highest positive potentiality, admittedly my choice to become a teacher had more to do with having summers off for sailing, kayaking, horse riding, and other adventures. Perhaps my priorities might have been more balanced, however, if the school seemed to be sincere in its goals for creating a collaborative environment on behalf of a greater purpose, such as what I feel at Fielding. Such a feeling does not prevent one from enjoying life outside the job, but rather enhances it while allowing one to look forward to returning to the work.

Firefighter (14 years)

My time at this job comes closest to the number of years I have spent with Fielding. There was never any doubt about the commitment of the

Fire Department and my fellow firefighters to the saving of those citizens whose lives and property we protected. There was a singular hypocrisy, however, that caused me to be at battle with the County of Marin, owing to my efforts to implement the message of a book I wrote for the National Fire Protection Association about the need for physical fitness programs in the fire service. Heart attacks made the profession rank number one in mortality among all professions in the U.S. Not until long after I left did the department finally adopt the in-house fitness programs I sought. There was a lack of sincerity related to the disconnect between concern for firefighter fitness and the public we were paid to support. I was challenged vehemently by city administration in spite of the then-Board of Supervisors member, Barbara Boxer, being on my side. The good news is that long after I quit, the NFPA put forth nationwide mandatory fitness standards and my department has extensive fitness facilities at each station. Although some of my ideas at Fielding have also met and continue to meet with strong resistance here and there or take a long time to be implemented, ultimately the mutual respect for our collective goals has always superseded, giving me and others the freedom to continue arguing for our positions respectfully.

Director of Residential School for Adjudicated Youth (2.5 years)

When I took over the "Youth Ranch," I replaced a very punitive model with an Indigenous-based positive peer culture based on the work of Larry Brendtro, Martin Brokenleg, and Steve Bockern (2012). I also got rid of all the soft-drink and candy machines and, in association with our school psychologist and physician, took most children off their Ritalin. Additionally, we started fitness programs and assigned youth the responsibility of taking care of a horse, a pig, or a cow (depending on which we thought best suited a personality). By the second year we reduced physical takedowns required to be reported to the state from 122 per quarter to only 14. A strong Mormon community that surrounded the ranch, however, worried that my less restrictive approach would put their families at risk from the students at our staff-secured facility. They had political influence enough to get me fired. To the contrary, if ever there was an educational institution that I know would continue to support an Indigenous perspective, it is Fielding. In fact, Fielding's sincere commitment to Indigenous students and traditional Indigenous values is so exceptional, in some ways it is stronger than it was at a tribal college where I served as Dean of Education.

Dean of Education at a Tribal College (four years)

Living and working on an Indian reservation was a very special time for me. In spite of the poverty, domestic violence, alcoholism, and injustice; the generosity, humor, courage, and dedication to future generations that is still alive there was remarkable. While I was there, however, the college's top administrator thought that the best education for its students was Western education that would prepare them for the white man's world. Although the administrator believed in his position, the position itself supported only half of the institution's vision statement, which targeted both the preparing of students to live in the multicultural and the cultivation of their own cultural values and traditional pathways. Fielding, with whatever bumps in the road it has had, maintains full respect for its vision and commitment to creating "a more just and sustainable world." This is why so many students, staff, faculty, and administrators stay on, including me. As for its willingness to help its Native students preserve their traditional ways, this brings us to the main reason I came to Fielding.

Tenured Associate Professor at a State University (three years)

My final position before coming to Fielding was in the Teacher Education College at a large state university run by a conservative Board of Regents. This university had a number of Apache, Hopi, and Navajo students with whom I worked and supported. Unfortunately, my anti-Iraq War protestations as co-founder of the local VFP chapter and my continued advocacy on behalf of the Indigenous population of the state did not stand well with some administrators, faculty, and students. In spite the university's center for peace education awarding me its "Moral Courage Award" for my activism, the tension and lack of support I continually felt as related to my work on behalf of the Indigenous students and their communities caused me to quit my tenured position and apply for my first three-year contract with Fielding, where the commitment to helping its Native students preserve their language and traditional culture was and is remarkable.

Conclusion

In the Indigenous way, telling stories about personal experiences is a powerful form of truth-telling. Stories often encourage resilience and resurgence. They are respected more and more in Academe as a form of research. They can express the highest source of wisdom—that which comes from honest reflection on lived experience. It seems, without planning on doing so, this article has turned into the telling of my story. In trying to explain why Fielding Graduate University is truly "sincere," I contrasted it with my previous experiences. I hope that in the company of the other narratives in this volume it contributes honestly to the well-deserved celebration of Fielding's 45th anniversary. For the sake of future generations, I hope this institution and its sincerity will be around for many more years.

References

Brendtro, L. Brokenleg, M., Bockern, S. (2012). *Reclaiming youth at risk: Our hope for the future.* Bloomington, IN: Solution Tree Publishing.

About the Author

Four Arrows (*Wahinkpe Topa*), a.k.a. Don Trent Jacobs, has a PhD in Health Psychology and an EdD in Curriculum and Instruction (with a Cognate in Indigenous Worldview). He has authored 21 books on topics related to wellness, education, and Indigenous worldview that have been endorsed by such notables as Noam Chomsky, Thom Hartmann, Greg

Cajete, Sam Keen, Daniel Wildcat, and Jon Pilger. He is the author of over 30 invited book chapters and nearly 100 articles, including a dozen or more peer-reviewed ones. AERO selected him as one of 27 "visionaries in education" and his text *Teaching Truly: A Curriculum to Indigenize Mainstream Education* was selected by the Chicago Wisdom Project as one of the top 20 progressive education books of all time. He was first alternate on the 1996 Olympic Equestrian Endurance Team and placed fourth in the world at the 40th annual Old Time Piano World Championship.

CHAPTER 22

REFLECTIONS ON MY LIFE AS AN EDUCATOR

Jason Ohler, PhD
Fielding Graduate University

I am 65, but my lungs are less than half that age. In the spring of 2014, I was diagnosed with idiopathic pulmonary fibrosis–IPF for short. Idiopathic simply means that we have no idea what causes something. So you can have an idiopathic toothache or leg cramp that defies diagnosis. You can also have an idiopathic career or marriage. I'd watch out for that.

Pulmonary fibrosis is a progressive disease that scars over the lungs, choking off the mechanisms the lungs use to absorb and distribute oxygen and exchange it for carbon dioxide. Slowly, those with IPF suffocate from oxygen deprivation and are poisoned by their inability to expel CO_2. By the summer of 2014 I had become a balloon with a slow leak. I was plugged into oxygen 24/7. Simple movements, such as taking a shower or retrieving a pen I'd dropped on the floor, required help.

IPF kills most who get it, slowly and painfully. But at the eleventh hour I received the only reprieve available to me: a double lung transplant. Due to the foresight and generosity of a stranger, as well as groundbreaking technology and a medical team with uncanny expertise, I am able to be here with you today. Like all miracles, the entire experience was humbling, recalibrating, and ultimately inspiring.

However, for nearly a year I circled the abyss, pretty much convinced from everything I read that I too was going to die a slow and painful death. I was saying my goodbyes to friends, making peace with old girlfriends, making sure I told those close to me that I loved them, and apologizing for not having told them often and clearly enough in the past. I settled in for the downward slide, to be taken care of by my wife, whose kindness and patience transcended friendship and entered the realm of saintliness. If you would like to read about my inspirations and revelations on the journey from IPF to transplant, go to https://realbeing.me.

During that year, it became increasingly difficult for me to manage simple movement, so I sat, as my muscles atrophied, and I reflected. A lot. I will spare you the more ethereal reflections, except to say that prior to my illness I, like all of you, understood that life was fragile and brief. However, that year I felt it on a cellular level and with a sense of depth and connectedness that extended far beyond my normal reality. Much to my amazement, I decided that I liked the fact that life was so fragile and brief. That's what made it so special.

Yet what's truly important here are my reflections on my life as an educator. Or perhaps a better place to start is to tell you what I didn't think about. I didn't think to myself, "Gosh, I wish I had given students more tests," or gone to more meetings, or followed the educational standards more closely. Those kinds of considerations receded into the background as unnecessary noise. Instead, I found myself hoping I had been as good an educator as Miss Phelps, my first and second grade teacher.

Miss Phelps and little Jason

The year this photo of Miss Phelps and me was taken, as best as I can determine, is 1958. During the 1950s all second-grade teachers looked perpetually 65 years old. As you can see, Miss Phelps did not disappoint in this regard. Notice the white shirt buttoned all the way up to her neck. She put so much commercial grade starch in her shirts that when she hugged me it sounded like cellophane crinkling. During the sweltering heat of a Western New York summer day, she would still wear wool skirts half way down her calves. It was the proper thing to do.

But don't let her austere countenance mislead you. She was a ninja teacher with a glint in her eye, a heart of gold, and tremendous teaching talent. She had everyone fooled. She looked conservative, but when the door closed, she went about the business of student learning with a passion that belied her appearance. She had infiltrated the system. I adored her. All her students adored her. I couldn't wait to get to school.

She was also a great educational technologist. She leveraged students' interests by using all of the technology at her disposal: finger paints; books; 45 RPM records; building blocks; toys; those big fat crayons that came eight in a box—you name it. She used the technology of the day to help students learn as much as they could, as enjoyably as they could.

Most importantly, she was a door opener. Rather than insist that every student pass through a standardized learning door, she looked for a special learning door for each student. Then she delighted in opening it and in helping each student embark on a personalized learning journey.

Above all, she used her special talents like an expert. I will never forget something that happened during a unit she was teaching on dinosaurs. I was having a hard time memorizing dinosaur names, and was becoming frustrated, when she said, "Jason, you like to tell stories. Why don't you name them and tell stories about them?" So that's exactly what I did. Ever since then, two in particular have been with me throughout my life: Stegosaurus Stan and Tyrannosaurus Tom.

There are two takeaways here. First, notice how skillfully Miss Phelps adapted my interests and skills to the lesson of the day. She was a great door opener and a true teacher in this regard. And second, notice how successfully storytelling works in education. Fifty years later, I remember these dinosaurs well. But beyond her skills as an educator, I remember Miss Phelps most for the soulful gleam in her eye she had every day that said, "Come on in, let's do an end run around the system, open some doors, have some fun and learn everything we can." God bless Miss Phelps. Thanks to her and two wonderful parents, I had a Disney childhood.

Mr. Hasselback and his pupil

That year, as I sat huddled around my oxygen machine, I also found myself hoping that I had been as good a teacher as Mr. Hasselback. He's in the picture on the left, and that's me playing bass guitar on the right. I was in tenth grade when Mr. Hasselback opened a very important door for me: the music door.

This was the 1960s. The counterculture was exploding. Music was in a state of revolution, from Joni Mitchell to Jimi Hendrix to Blood Sweat and Tears. It was the time in global history known as Beatlemania. For Gen Xers and beyond, you will have to talk to an old person or consult the oracle YouTube to find out more about Beatlemania. It was absolutely amazing.

The newsreels about Beatlemania were riveting. My buddies and I watched in awe as women at Beatle concerts listened to a minute of music, and then screamed and passed out. The spectacle set our adolescent minds ablaze. We raced off to the local musical instrument store in my parents' Rambler station wagon, bound and determined not to let our lack of talent stop us in our quest to become rock stars. That was back in the day when you didn't need to be good; you just needed to be loud. There was a lot of bad, loud music back then. I'm afraid I contributed to it.

However, I actually had talent. I still have it, although I don't have it as much in my fingers as I do in my ears. Beginning at a young age, I have had the ability to listen to most popular songs and figure them out by plunking around on the piano. I had developed my own system for understanding music, which came quite naturally to me. I think Howard Gardner might call my abilities musical intelligence.

So, it's 1968. I'm in tenth grade. I was in a rock 'n' roll band, as I had been for a number of years, mostly to get girls to like me. But by tenth grade I had really fallen in love with music. I had transformed into a real musician. I didn't really care that much about what being in a band did for my social life anymore. I wanted to play music for a living.

Enter Mr. Hasselback. He was offering a music theory course that I knew, in my bones, would take me to the next step in my musical development. I remember reading the course description and feeling my heart light up. His course was exactly what I needed. However, there was a hitch. A prerequisite for the course stipulated that students had to be able to read music. I couldn't.

But I didn't give up. I went to Mr. Hasselback and I said, "Here's the thing. I can't read music but I think I can hear music." He said, "Okay, what does that mean?" I explained to him that I was able to sit at a piano and figure out songs, and I showed him the system I had developed based on popular music. He looked at me quizzically and then finally said, "Okay, it's a bit unorthodox, but I will give you a listening test to evaluate your understanding of note relationships. If you can pass the listening test, I will let you into my class." I passed the listening test, enrolled in the class, and got one of the best grades that semester.

Thanks to Mr. Hasselback's opening that music door for me, I have written symphonic music, string quartets, edgy electronic music, and jazz. Most of the music that's heard playing in the background before my public presentations is original. I have also played in my share of bands, which have been some of my favorite adventures. I still sit at the piano and play for hours, figuring out music and writing my own. Above all, music is very therapeutic, and much cheaper than seeing a therapist. You can go to https://www.jasonohlerideas.com/music-fiction-ringtones, and listen to my music. You can even download original ringtones I've created. They're free.

The point is that when the system said that I had to be able to read music, Mr. Hasselback said, "I don't care what the system says. I'm going to let this student learn." He used an alternative approach to assessing my abilities that opened a door for me that he didn't have to open. Any administrator in any school district would have supported his right to demand that reading music be required of all students who wanted to take his music theory course. But he didn't demand this of me. As a result of his open-mindedness and commitment to student learning, I have had a life of music. God bless you, Mr. Hasselback, for being a door opener.

Bottom line? There are two.

First, don't wait to get a life threatening illness to think about what is truly important to you, as a parent, an educator, a professional, a human being. Think about it now. Let those reflections guide you now. Live each day as though it were your first, and your last. Act now, in the moment, but with a long view, with the understanding that every action echoes for an eternity.

Second, be a door opener. Remember that you are always a teacher, no matter what you do for a living or wherever you find yourself, whether in a classroom, a boardroom, a dining room, an office environment, or an online community. You teach others directly through your counsel and example, as well as indirectly by how you behave towards them. Teach mindfully. If you are a professional educator, then be an activist educator. Find out your students', employees', or colleagues' passions, and then open doors for them. They will be happier. And so will you. Teachers occupy that sacred interface between students, their imaginations, and the world, and we either listen to our students and open doors for them, or we don't. When we don't, everybody loses, including us.

Most importantly, if you spend your life opening doors then you will enter retirement without misgivings. My father was a teacher for his entire working career, from the day he left the army after World War II until cancer claimed his life in 1972. On his deathbed, he told me that other than not getting to spend more time with his family, he had no regrets. He loved opening doors for students every day of his life. And he told me something I will never forget: Get a job you love and never go to work again. That's what he did. I have lived by that advice and it has served me well. I recommend it to you.

Excerpted from the book *4Four Big Ideas for the Future*, © 2016 Jason Ohler. Reprinted with permission.

About the Author

Jason Ohler is a professor emeritus and President's Distinguished Professor of educational technology and virtual learning. Jason has been telling stories about the future that are rooted in the realities of the past during the entire 35 years he has been involved in the world of innovative education. He is also a lifelong digital humanist who is well known for the passion, insight, and humor that he brings to his presentations, projects, and publications. He has spent his many years in education combining innovation, critical thinking (critical and creative thinking combined), and digital know-how to help renew and reinvent teaching and learning.

He has won numerous awards for his work and is author of many books, articles, and online resources. He is currently teaching digital storytelling and digital ethics at Fielding Graduate University inthe Media Psychology program.

PART III

RESEARCH BY FIELDING SCHOLAR-PRACTITIONERS

CHAPTER 23

IMAGINING LIBERATORY, COMMUNITY-BASED ALTERNATIVES FOR BLACK YOUTH DEVELOPMENT: A CONVERSATION BETWEEN A BLACK FEMINIST MENTOR AND HER COMMUNITY ELDER STUDENT MENTEE

Gail Wilson and K. Melchor Hall, PhD
Fielding Graduate University

Fact then: Somehow, my travels crossed time as well as distance. Another fact: The boy was the focus of my travels—perhaps the cause of them. He had seen me in my living room before I was drawn to him; he couldn't have made that up. But I had seen nothing at all, felt nothing but sickness and disorientation. (Butler, 1979, p. 24)

This quote from Octavia Butler's *Kindred* reminds me of the way the Black feminist scholar-activism and activist scholarship travels across time and place, sometimes being pulled into futures not immediately apparent. It also reminds me of the bewildered feeling that comes from being pulled between worlds out of necessity. Ms. Gail Wilson and I honor the past, present, and future of Black feminist possibilities that have laid the foundation for our current collaboration. In this conversational piece about our journeys at Fielding, we express our commitments to research and praxis at the service of our communities.

– Melchor Hall

Reflections of Dr. Melchor Hall, HOD Core Faculty and Mentor

When I first received the invitation for faculty submissions to Fielding's 45th anniversary monograph, I did not consider writing anything. It seemed a bit presumptuous, having not even completed my second year at Fielding, to contribute to such a manuscript. Then, a second call went out, emphasizing the need for diverse voices, and I thought: If I could find the right co-author, I would offer my vision, as a Black feminist scholar-activist at a predominately white institution, for collaboration with Fielding students. The first person who came to mind as a co-author was my mentee, Ms. Gail Wilson. (It is customary in the African American community to use a title for elders as a sign of respect for the wisdom they embody. Ms. Gail Wilson is both my Fielding mentee and my community elder.) I thought about Ms. Gail because of her professional commitment to the African American community, her range of experiences (including working for a railroad company and counseling youth), and her interests (including youth art initiatives and cutting-edge digital technologies). My work as an educator intends to help students better serve their communities. I do not care about creating academics; my goal is to help people translate scholarly knowledge into information that can advance their community work.

Julia Sudbury and Margo Okazawa-Rey (2016) posed some important questions about the relationship between scholarship and activism:

> What are the radical potentialities of the university as a site occupied by communities of resistance but also shaped by elitism, social inequality, and complicities with state violence? Can good scholarship be politically engaged? Is it really possible to bridge the activism-scholarship dichotomy? What are the political imperatives to attempt this work, and how are these imperatives shaped by our relative power and privilege as academics? How can we mobilize the resources and privilege of our position within academia in service of radical movements? What are the costs of such politically engaged scholarship? What are the costs of not attempting it? (p. 2)

(As I write this quote, I can hear it spoken in the voice of faculty colleague Margo Okazawa-Rey, who mentored me in my first year at Fielding.) Indeed, what are the costs to academics and to communities beyond academia? I believe that academia is too small and too elite to simply be about its self-preservation. Instead, those of us in academia must be thinking about how to leverage the resources of the academy for meaningful change in community with those beyond the (virtual or physical) walls of our institutions.

Similar to Ms. Gail, I have a wide range of professional experiences that include providing technical support on an overnight shift at a helpdesk for a multinational corporation, teaching outdoor, hands-on science lessons to children in an urban arboretum, and developing an afterschool robotics curriculum for students at a school for the deaf, to name a few. Although my doctorate is in international relations, I have degrees in mathematics, computer science, and international communication. For much of my education, I expected to get my doctorate in mathematics or computer science. I stopped after earning a Master of Science in computer science because I found that there was no room in the computer science classroom for innovation that embraced cultural diversity. As an example, I was discouraged from pursuing conversations about developing databases with two last names, in spite of the growing Latinx population in the U.S. In a forthcoming article, I imagine the possibilities of "Technology in a Black Feminist World," as a way to do in an article what I was not able to accomplish in the classroom.

When I consider Ms. Gail's interest in youth development (described below), I want to facilitate her supporting young people who remind me of an earlier version of myself, a version who needed someone to make room for creativity in technology. It is this sort of collaboration between mentor (also community pupil) and mentee (also community elder) that explains why I would come to Fielding to defy more conventional hierarchies of knowledge. Ms. Gail gave me the opportunity to share information about STEAM (science, technology, engineering, arts, and mathematics) curricula, so that we might consider together how community organizations are helping youth to develop alternative futures. It has meant that I can introduce Ms. Gail to the AfroGEEKS project (2007), so that she can be reminded that the marginalization of African Americans in tech does not mean our erasure.

An important aspect of this project is its challenge to dominant assumptions about how black communities actually use and develop strategies for incorporating new information media and communication technologies in their everyday lives. This book also reveals that black communities have been IT innovators as well as enthusiastic consumers of technology products. Where the digital divide debate in the U.S. presumes a direct correlation between technological deprivation and minority or "third world" population groups, our work in this volume demonstrates a much more complex scenario where blackness and technology intersect (p. 1).

It has also meant that I can connect Ms. Gail to the living legacies of Black Afrofuturist projects, embodied by BlackSpace (http://theblackspace.org/) in Durham, North Carolina that challenge the overwhelming whiteness of makerspaces as the newest configuration of STEM innovation. These kinds of collaborations that make (virtual and physical) space for communities of resistance within and beyond the academy are what enliven me as a scholar-practitioner.

Melchor Hall (left) and Gail Wilson (right) in front of a Baltimore makerspace

Reflections of Ms. Gail Wilson, HOD Doctoral Student and Mentee

As a student at Fielding Graduate University, I've been given many opportunities to learn and grow through engaging coursework taught by dedicated faculty. This is an ideal learning environment where I'm challenged and encouraged to think beyond what is known about a topic, which in turn has allowed me to grow and thrive as a student, scholar, and practitioner. I've been given room to examine new approaches to engaging the agency of adolescents and young adults (AYA), which is critical to my research.

I came to Fielding with a singular focus—to help AYA from urban, underserved, African-American communities develop the career skills needed to thrive in an unjust world. The term "underserved" used here describes communities that have high levels of concentrated poverty and neighborhoods that are not economically stable. Given the history of U.S.-based discrimination against African-Americans, there continues to be a lack of equitable resources for healthy growth and development. However, there have always been economically successful (e.g., Black Wall Street) and artistically vibrant (e.g., Harlem) African-American communities. I grew up surrounded by African American doctors, lawyers, and business owners, all of whom gave back to the community. My family reached out to other families. We had and have a legacy of hard work, education, and passing the torch forward. Having seen and lived these experiences, I knew I was called to continue this work.

It wasn't until the classes in "Systems Approaches to Leadership, Organizations, and Society," taught by Tracy Fisher, and "Social and Ecological Justice," taught by Melchor Hall, that I began viewing youth workforce development in new ways. This was the first time I was able to see the intersecting systems—human, ecological, social, and global—and examine their interdependencies. I began asking, "How can my research help level the playing field and reduce inequity and inequalities in youth career development?" Fielding has enabled me to explore workforce development through many different lenses—systems, social justice, and critical theories. While there are many ways to approach urban youth workforce development, it remains a social, ecological, and political issue. Despite the structural and systemic barriers to life and career development, I had a strong vision and new hope for a brighter future for young people starting out on their life journey. As a result, I was determined to take a systems approach to life-career youth workforce development.

It was Melchor who introduced me to the STEAM (science, technology, engineering, art, and mathematics) concept, which led me to my current research topic. As a young person, I had separated these parts of myself—the nerdy science geek and the creative artist. Through many iterations of my dissertation topic, I've been able to locate my research in the STE(A) M context. My goal is to better understand the potential created by the marriage of STEM (science, technology, engineering, and mathematics) and art in the context of community-based STEAM opportunities. I am amazed and excited by the union of STEM and art into what is now called STEAM, and I want to explore and understand it from AYA perspectives.

As a practitioner, I've been inspired by the many truly talented and gifted young people around me. There was the 18-year-old artist who didn't want his job coach to know about his "side hustle" (a T-shirt design biz), but wanted to share his creations with me because I was his counselor and our conversations were confidential. I also think of the young 15-year-old writer who shared his winning middle school essay with me while he concealed it from his workforce training facilitator. Lastly, there was the 19-year-old pianist who put his headphones on me so I could listen to the music that inspired him. These young people showed passion and purpose in the work they created, but their lack of adequate family or personal income prevented them from fully exploring what they loved. These experiences changed my focus from one of "helping them get jobs" to learning how to create a youth workforce development model that integrates and develops the "whole child" and leads to the co-creation of a new life-career story.

Over the course of my time at Fielding, I've learned how valuable it is to understand the influences in the lives of young folks that make them who they are at a particular moment in time. All of what I've learned has been liberating and has enhanced my personal development. I have begun to integrate this new knowledge into my emergent theory for work with African-American AYAs in transition. As I reflect on my ongoing journey to becoming a PhD, I can honestly say that I have grown in knowledge and wisdom. The learning at Fielding has augmented the lens through which I see 21st century youth workforce development, specifically for our AYAs in transition. My hope is that the impact on those who share space with me will be the development of a firm foundation upon which to create a successful life and a better world.

References

Butler, O. E. (1988). *Kindred.* Boston: Beacon Press.

Everett, A., & Wallace, A. J. (Eds.). (2007). *AfroGEEKS: Beyond the Digital Divide.* Santa Barbara: Center for Black Studies Research.

Hall, K.M.Q. (forthcoming). Technology in a Black Feminist World. *Frontiers: A Journal of Women Studies.*

Sudbury, J., & Okazawa-Rey, M. (Eds.). (2016). *Activist Scholarship: Antiracism, Feminism, and Social Change.* London: Routledge.

About the Authors

Melchor Hall, PhD, is currently a Human and Organizational Development faculty member in Fielding Graduate University's School of Leadership. However, her first love was mathematics, which she studied as an undergraduate, before earning a Master's degree in computer science. She has taught math, natural science, and computer science in traditional classrooms. More excitingly, she has taught environmental science in arboretums, water science on rivers and in bays, and supported afterschool engineering and robotics clubs. She continues to be an advocate for out-of-school STEM learning. At Fielding, she enjoys pushing students and faculty to explore new ways to connect virtually.

Gail Wilson is a Human and Organizational Development doctoral student at Fielding Graduate University. Her professional experience includes working as a career counselor and her scholarly interests include youth workforce development. She plans to explore how STEM (science, technology, engineering, and mathematics) + Arts, or STEAM, engagement outside of school contribute to child development and growth. Her greatest joy is hearing young people's stories of challenge, accomplishment, and achievement. The re-introduction to STEM and STEAM learning have rekindled her love for STEM+Arts. Ultimately, she intends to improve and expand opportunities for Baltimore's underserved Black youth.

CHAPTER 24

TRIUMPH OVER IMPLICIT BIAS TOWARDS PERSONS WITH TRISOMY 21: HARDSHIP, HUMAN RIGHTS VIOLATIONS, AND HONING THE PATH TO FLOURISHING[1]

Robin Treptow
Fielding Doctoral Student

Attitudes stir social change, yet social views can harm. This essay describes one family's journey rooted in human rights violations. The goal was to gain mastery over society's negative views of persons with Trisomy 21 (i.e., T21 or Down syndrome). An infant's birth, a mother's striving to unravel *courtesy stigma*, and the dyad's academic and social trials are explored. The story gives insight into *parallel process* alongside a son's crossing into meaningful cognitive challenge. *Implicit bias*, that is, a subtle judgment that operates outside awareness, is key to the storyline. This rewriting of a disability-laden narrative supports social models of T21 phenotypes. It *shifts the paradigm* for what infants at risk for lifelong disability can do (Kuhn, 2012).

Trisomy 21 in the Trenches. I hope I can be forgiven for not "getting" the dreadfulness of *implicit bias* against out groups (Sue et al., 2007). When my eldest son was born with Trisomy 21[2] (i.e., T21 or Down syndrome) nearly two decades ago I was naive. I did not grasp what it meant to have one's human rights violated.

Social Bias's Effects. I knew that what I saw in the delivery room and neonatal intensive care unit (NICU) after his birth (Treptow, 2017a) was *social* stereotyping.[3] Early on I named it as others deciding what would happen to my son[4]—that is, *self-fulfilling prophecy* or *interpersonal expectancy effect* (Rosenthal, 2002; Porter, Stern, & Zak-Place, 2009; Tallandini, Morsan, Gronchi, & Macagno, 2014). I even dubbed Trisomy 21's common name as "Double Scoop." Still, the social forces were strong.

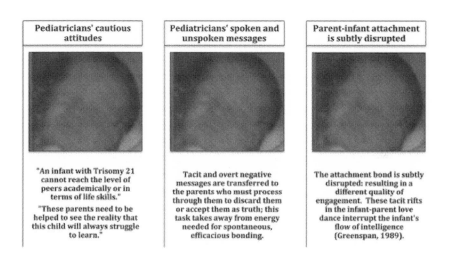

Pediatricians' cautious attitudes	Pediatricians' spoken and unspoken messages	Parent-infant attachment is subtly disrupted
"An infant with Trisomy 21 cannot reach the level of peers academically or in terms of life skills." "These parents need to be helped to see the reality that this child will always struggle to learn."	Tacit and overt negative messages are transferred to the parents who must process through them to discard them or accept them as truth; this task takes away from energy needed for spontaneous, efficacious bonding.	The attachment bond is subtly disrupted: resulting in a different quality of engagement. These tacit rifts in the infant-parent love dance interrupt the infant's flow of intelligence (Greenspan, 1989).

Figure 1. This figure is excerpted from Part A of the author's Fielding Graduate University (Fielding) dissertation and illustrates how implicit bias can get in the way of infants' flow of intelligence by disrupting early parent-infant engagement. (Copyright 2017 held by R. L. Treptow. Used with permission.) Photograph is from the Treptow family library.

Racial-tinged Biases. With shame, I now see those who brave *racial-tinged biases* daily with a new eye. I did not know about *genetic essentialism*, where others decided what my son could or could not do based on how he looked.[5] His observable traits were seen as determined, caused by a third 21st chromosome, shared by others with T21, and natural (Dar-Nimrod & Heine, 2011). I did not know my son would face prejudice rooted in *racism* (Down, 1866) based on how he looked. I had no idea that the physical traits he had might lead others to decide he was less human (Rodríguez, Mateo, Rodríguez-Pérez, & Rodríguez, 2016) or less smart (Enea-Drapeau, Huguet, & Carlier, 2014; Enea-Drapeau, Carlier,

& Huguet, 2017; Marcone, Esposito, & Caputo, 2016)—even while they said they liked him (Enea-Drapeau, Carlier, & Huguet, 2012). I thought *self-fulfilling prophecy* was simple to stop once it was labeled. That is, until I felt the searing pain of *courtesy stigma* (Green, 2003).[6] That pain led me towards *universal learned helplessness* (Abramson, Seligman, & Teasdale, 1978; Donovan & Leavitt, 1985).[7]

A Pathway to Achievement. Hope came our way as my son grew up. I opted to get a degree in Infant and Early Childhood Development (IECD) with Emphases in Mental Health and Developmental Disabilities at Fielding. I wanted to live out Greenspan and Wieder's (2008) emotion-as-driver model of intelligence at the core. It might help my son (all of us) to shed bias's heavy load.

Academia's Demands. Little did I know how tumultuous and terrific my trek for a second PhD would prove to be amid others' *stigma* regarding my son—sparking my developing of a social model for how Trisomy 21 genomes play out as Down syndrome phenotypes (Treptow, 2017; 2018).[8] Struggles to absorb the rules of research and academic rigor nearly always lay just past easy reach. I often felt like giving up. Who needs two doctorates, anyway?

Processing in Parallel. Then it dawned on me (slowly, at first) that I was *living the life of my son*. Excruciating efforts to wrap my mind around statistics, research design, making an argument, and other basic academic skills (e.g., APA style, absorbing reviewers' critiques) were just like his daily work. The rules of English writing, laws of science, algebra story problems, and geometric proofs were no further beyond his pale than good published academic writing lay for me.

Hope—Amid Heartache. This *parallel process*[9] (Heffron, Ivins, & Weston, 2005) where I matched his academic efforts arose strong and steady. I did not plan for my dissertation to look at the social process that ate up much of my (his, our family's) life: *stigma against persons with*

T21. It was the blatant unfairness of the principal at his private school that set it off.

Surviving Bias's Impact. The energy needed to live amid nearly daily human rights' violations was unreal. It prevented one from relaxing—it was too much. My son had been cut out of core classes (e.g., English, science, math), the ones that build neural pathways for college success.[10] We found a free online option. This let us override the *downward spiraling developmental cascade* (Masten & Cicchetti, 2010). He was told he could not play basketball on the school's team,[11] but we quietly helped him just "show up" for practice and the games. See this heart-warming video where a Native American tribe warmly celebrated his diversity.[12] His desire to live out the faith culture kept us going—"to overcome every obstacle to [your] vocation…" But it was tough.

Counteracting Bias. We could have filed a Section 504 civil rights suit. This would have been in accord with Canon Law (i.e., the law of the Roman Catholic Church), too. But we believed it was not the right path, because it would keep our son separate from the peers he needed. These kids his age had virtually no rights violating biases (but see Pace, Shin, & Rasmussen, 2010, for a different perspective on U.S. youths' attitudes towards peers with Trisomy 21). Academic articles revealed the pathway: I must face this issue of *stereotype threat* (Rodríguez et al., 2016) for my son—and for others who share his unique genome (Friberg-Fernros, 2017; Skotko, 2009). I put pen to paper to call out this human rights violation. Borthwick (1996) said it best.[13]

> If one were to add. . . the further stipulations that the group under study was, even now, regarded as *utterly and unquestionably intellectually inferior*, that it has been regarded as *inferior* universally and in all cultures, that individuals in the group are regarded as *inferior* even by their own families and in relation to their own siblings, that

the supports of a common culture are entirely absent, that not only their formal education but their basic instruction had historically been rudimentary or non-existent. . . and that no positive role models for them have ever existed, one would *expect a larger difference still;* and one would be *describing people with Down syndrome"* (emphases added; p. 404).

Scanning the Horizon for More. As I write this essay, I am nearing completion of my dissertation.[14] A Harvard Medical School geneticist will read my findings, an infant mental health guru is my Chair, and a DIR®[15] champion is my Research Faculty member. I look for where our ship will dock as this (bon) voyage sets sail. I hope to spread *resilience* (Masten, 2010) as a *Richard and Yakko Meyers Endowed Human Rights Scholarship* recipient.[16]

References

Abramson, L. Y., Seligman, M.E.P., & Teasdale, J. D. (1978). Learned helplessness in humans: Critique and reformulation. *Journal of Abnormal Psychology, 87*(1), 49-74. http://dx.doi.org.fgul.idm.oclc.org/10.1037/0021-843X.87.1.49

Borthwick, C. (1996). Racism, IQ and Down's syndrome. *Disability & Society, 11*(3), 403-410. doi:10.1080/09687599627688

Carroll, C., Carroll, C., Goloff, N., & Pitt, M. B. (2018). When bad news isn't necessarily bad: Recognizing provider bias when sharing unexpected news. *Pediatrics, 42*(1), 1-5. doi:https://doi.org/10.1542/peds.2018- 0503

Donovan, W. L., & Leavitt, L. A. (1985). Simulating conditions of learned helplessness: The effects of interventions and attributions. *Child Development*, 594-603. doi:10.2307/1129749

Dar-Nimrod, I., & Heine, S. J. (2011). Genetic essentialism: On the deceptive determinism of DNA. *Psychological Bulletin, 137*, 800-818. doi:10.1037/a0021860

Down, J.L.H. (1866). Observations on an ethnic classification of idiots. *London Hospital Reports, 3*, 259-262. doi:10.1038/hdy.1966.69

Enea-Drapeau, C., Carlier, M., & Huguet, P. (2017). Implicit theories concerning the intelligence of individuals with Down syndrome. *PloS ONE, 12*(11), e0188513. doi:10.1016/j.ridd.2014.09.003

Enea-Drapeau, C., Huguet, P., & Carlier, M. (2014). Misleading face-based judgment of cognitive level in intellectual disability: The case of trisomy 21 (Down syndrome). *Research in Developmental Disabilities, 35*(12), 3598-3605. doi:http://dx.doi.org/10.1016/j.ridd.2014.09.003

Enea-Drapeau, C., Carlier, M., & Huguet, P. (2012). Tracking subtle stereotypes of children with Trisomy 21: From facial-feature-based to implicit stereotyping. *PLoS ONE, 7*(4), e34369. doi:10.1371/journal.pone.0034369

FindLaw.com. (2018). *The American with Disabilities Act—Overview.* Retrieved from https://civilrights.findlaw.com/discrimination/the-americans-with-disabilities-act-overview.html

Friberg-Fernros, H. (2017). Clashes of consensus: On the problem of both justifying abortion of fetuses with Down syndrome and rejecting infanticide. *Theoretical Medicine & Bioethics*, 1-18. doi:10.1007/s11017-017-9398-8

Green, S. E. (2003). "What do you mean 'what's wrong with her?'": Stigma and the lives of families of children with disabilities. *Social Science & Medicine, 57*(8), 1361-1374. doi:10.1016/S0277-9536(02)00511-7

Greenspan, S. I., Greenspan, N. T., & Lodish, R. (2010). *The Learning Tree: Overcoming Learning Disabilities from the Ground Up.* Cambridge, MA: De Capo Press.

Greenspan, S. I., & Wieder, S. (2008). The Interdisciplinary Council on Developmental and Learning Disorders diagnostic manual for infants and young children–An overview. *Journal of the Canadian Academy of Child & Adolescent Psychiatry, 17*(2), 76-89.

Heffron, M. C., Ivins, B., & Weston, D. R. (2005). Finding an authentic voice—use of self: Essential learning processes for relationship-based work. *Infants & Young Children, 18*(4), 323-336.

Karmiloff-Smith, A., D'Souza, D., Dekker, T. M., Van Herwegen, J., Xu, F., Rodic, M., & Ansari, D. (2012). Genetic and environmental vulnerabilities in children with neurodevelopmental disorders. *Proceedings of the National Academy of Science of the United States of America, 109*(Supplement 2), 17261-17265. doi:10.1073/pnas.1121087109

Kuhn, T. S. (2012). *The structure of scientific revolutions* (4th Ed.). Chicago, IL: The University of Chicago Press.

Marcone, R., Esposito, S., & Caputo, A. (2016). Beliefs toward social and cognitive competences in people with Down syndrome. *Journal of Intellectual Disability-Diagnosis & Treatment, 4*(1), 44-54. doi:10.6000/2292-2598.2016.04.01.6

Masten, A. S. (2014). *Ordinary Magic: Resilience in Development.* New York, NY: Guilford.

Masten, A. S., & Cicchetti, D. (2010). Developmental cascades. *Developmental Psychopathololology, 22*, 491-495. doi:10.1017/S0954579410000222

McLaughlin, K. A., Sheridan, M. A., & Nelson, C. A. (2017). Neglect as a violation of species-expectant experience: Neurodevelopmental consequences. *Biological Psychiatry, 82*(7), 462-471. doi:10.1016/j.biopsych.2017.02.1096

McLaughlin, K. A., Sheridan, M. A., & Lambert, H. K. (2014). Childhood adversity and neural development: Deprivation and threat as distinct dimensions of early experience. *Neuroscience & Biobehavioral Reviews, 47*, 578-591. doi:10.1016/j.neubiorev.2014.10.012

Mégarbané, A., Ravel, A., Mircher, C., Sturtz, F., Grattau, Y., Rethoré, M. O., & Mobley, W. C. (2009). The 50th anniversary of the discovery of trisomy 21: The past, present, and future of research and treatment of Down syndrome. *Genetics in Medicine, 11*(9), 611-616. doi:10.1097/GIM.0b013e3181b2e34c

OMIM®—Online Mendelian Inheritance in Man. *#190685 Down syndrome; Trisomy 21*. Retrieved from https://www.omim.org/entry/190685

Pace, J. E., Shin, M., & Rasmussen, S. A. (2010). Understanding attitudes toward people with Down syndrome. *American Journal of Medical Genetics Part A, 152*(9), 2185-2192. doi:10.1002/ajmg.a.33595

Porter, J. S., Stern, M., & Zak-Place, L. (2009). Prematurity stereotyping and perceived vulnerability at 5-months: Relations with mothers and their premature and full-term infants at 9-months. *Journal of Reproductive & Infant Psychology, 27*(2), 168-181. doi:10.1080/02646830801918471

Rodríguez, V. B., Mateo, E. A., Rodríguez-Pérez, A., & Rodríguez, N. D. (2016). Do they feel the same as us? The infrahumanization of individuals with Down syndrome. *Psicothema, 28*(3), 311-317. doi:10.7334/psicothema2016.10

Rosenthal, R. (2002). Covert communication in classrooms, clinics, courtrooms, and cubicles. *American Psychologist, 57*(11), 839-849. http://dx.doi.org.fgul.idm.oclc.org/10.1037/0003-066X.57.11.839

Schein, S. S., & Langlois, J. H. (2015). Unattractive infant faces elicit negative affect from adults. *Infant Behavior & Development, 38*, 130-134. doi:10.1016/j.infbeh.2014.12.009

Skotko, B. G. (2009). With new prenatal testing, will babies with Down syndrome slowly disappear? *Archives of Disabilities in Children, 94*(11), 823-826. Retrieved from https://www.researchgate.net/publication/26296718_With_new_prenatal_testing_will_babies_with_Down_syndrome_slowly_disappear

Sue, D. W., Capodilupo, C. M., Torino, G. C., Bucceri, J. M., Holder, A.M.B., Nadal, K. L., & Esquilin, M. (2007). Racial microaggressions in everyday life: Implications for clinical practice. *American Psychologist, 62*, (4), 271-286. doi:10.1037/0003-066X.62.4.271

Tallandini, M. A., Morsan, V., Gronchi, G., & Macagno, F. (2014). Systematic and meta-analytic review: Triggering agents of parental perception of child's vulnerability in instances of preterm birth. *Journal of Pediatric Psychology, 40*(6), 545-553. doi: 10.1093/jpepsy/jsv010

Treptow, R. L. (2017). *Epigenetics and social etiology: Why implicit bias explains Trisomy 21's Down syndrome phenotype better than its extra chromosome.* Manuscript submitted for consideration for publication. It is also Part A of Treptow, R. L. (2018) *Pediatricians' implicit bias towards newborns with Trisomy 21: Merging vignette survey and implicit association test (IAT) methods*, Fielding Graduate University dissertation.

Treptow, R. L. (2018). *Pediatricians' implicit bias towards newborns with Trisomy 21: Merging vignette survey and implicit association test (IAT) methods [Part B].* Fielding Graduate University dissertation.

Weremowicz, S. (2016). Congenital cytogenetic abnormalities. UpToDate®. Retrieved from https://www.uptodate.com/contents/congenital-cytogenetic-abnormalities.

End Notes

---

[1] Richard and Yakko Meyers' *Endowed Human Rights Scholarship Essay.* The scholarship essay was reformatted to meet publication criteria for Fielding's 45th Anniversary Monograph. Some sections were updated with recent literature. Endnotes explain some of the academic terminology.

[2] Trisomy 21 means a group of gene patterns in which chromosome 21 (all or a part of it) appears three times rather than twice in some or all cells of the body (Mégarbané et al., 2009; Weremowicz, 2016). Down syndrome is diagnosed clinically based on signs and symptoms, some of which are visible; such persons have a Trisomy 21 gene pattern (OMIM #190685).

[3] The author had a PhD in clinical psychology with a child-family emphasis at the time of her son's birth, and prior to matriculating to Fielding's IECD program.

[4] Treptow (2018) wrote in her dissertation: "When telling parents about their child having a Trisomy 21 genome, bad news is often presumed. . . and Karmiloff-Smith et al. (2012) theorized that once parents have been told of their child's genetic condition their behavior changes subtly, which slightly alters the baby's responses in relationship interactions." It is hoped that the trend may be shifting as parents challenge earlier ideas of what is possible for their children, and doctors begin to listen (Carroll, Carroll, Goloff, & Pitt, 2018).

[5] Schein and Langlois (2015) found that adults showed very subtle negative reactions to infants (i.e., measurements of facial muscles), based on the infants' perceived attractiveness.

[6] Persons experience *courtesy stigma* when they are physically or emotionally close to others who are treated as less valuable, or even invaluable, based on who they are (Green, 2003).

[7] This is the idea or belief that nothing can be done because all options for change have been exhausted due to one's own past lived experiences, as well as the failed attempts of others to solve the problem. This process might be described as giving up. Its pathway is that (1) objective non-contingency leads to (2) perception of present and past non-contingency; which leads to (3) attribution for present or past non-contingency; and, finally, (4) expectation of future non-contingency; which result in (5) symptoms of helplessness or little effort to change the situation (Abramson, Seligman, & Teasdale, 1978).

[8] "Adopting that social-environmental lens, Treptow (2017) proposed that "implicit biases—resulting in judged inferiority, little social support, and poor education. . . induce Down Syndrome phenotypes. . . further operationalize[ing] Borthwick's idea of a *paradigm shift* wherein the cause of Trisomy 21's prototypical cognitive deficiencies did not reside in the person (i.e., genetic) but resided in the cultural milieu (i.e., environmental)" (emphasis added; p. 8). See Kuhn (2012).

[9] *Parallel process* is a socially interactive practice by which one person influences another person, resulting in interpersonal growth for both individuals. This core infant mental health concept was stressed throughout the author's IECD Fielding degree, especially in reflective practice coursework, where she learned to reflect on her feelings, actions, and thoughts in relationship to others. *Parallel process* can be an antidote to Rosenthal's (2002) *interpersonal expectancy effect* or *self-fulfilling prophecy.*

[10] I think that threat from stereotypes, resulting in exclusion from challenging educational options, holds persons like my son back from reaching their potential. See McLaughlin's early experiences model of cognitive delays (McLaughlin, Sheridan, & Lambert, 2014; McLaughlin, Sheridan, & Nelson, 2017).

[11] I understood that my son met criteria for a disability as defined by the Americans with Disabilities Act (ADA) of 1990. The disability was not because he had Trisomy 21 or could not do things that other youths his age did, but rather because others perceived him to have an "impairment that substantially limit[ed] what the ADA calls a 'major life activity' (FindLaw.com)."

[12] "Watching Kiernan just simply put me at awe and [I] was truly inspired by

his whole Demeanor, character, and love he left on the court for us all to live in. Blessings to you Robin, Kiernan, and to the many people's hearts whom Kiernan has inspired and Touched[.] Respect and love." Retrieved from https://www.facebook.com/100000932225366/videos/1440114609362933/.

[13] "If one were to add. . . the further stipulations that the group under study was, even now, regarded as *utterly and unquestionably intellectually inferior*, that it has been regarded as *inferior* universally and in all cultures, that individuals in the group are regarded as *inferior* even by their own families and in relation to their own siblings, that the supports of a common culture are entirely absent, that not only their formal education but their basic instruction had historically been rudimentary or non-existent. . . and that no positive role models for them have ever existed, one would *expect a larger difference still*; and one would be *describing people with Down syndrome"* (emphases added; Borthwick, 1996, p. 404).

[14] The essay was drafted on 7 October 2017. The Final Oral Review of the author's Fielding dissertation was completed on 11 December 2018, and proofreading and remaining edits were anticipated by 1 February 2019.

[15] The DIR® (Developmental-Individual Differences-Relationship) model was developed by Drs. Stanley Greenspan and Serena Wieder (2008; see also Greenspan, Greenspan, & Lodish, 2010). In their model, higher levels of thinking develop by means of increasingly complex social interaction, beginning in infancy as caregivers' attentiveness encourages an infant's interest in the world.

[16] The author's son with Trisomy 21 has been offered admission to an academically challenging university provisional on his finishing two online classes with a cumulative GPA of 2.0 or greater. Study at this university will keep him on the path towards his dream of becoming a Roman Catholic priest.

About the Author

Robin Lynn Treptow, PhD, has completed the Final Oral Review of her Fielding dissertation, a pilot study looking at pediatricians' implicit bias against infants born with Trisomy 21 and Down syndrome phenotypes. She holds a prior doctorate in clinical psychology from the University of Nebraska-Lincoln (1999), and is Adjunct Professor of Psychology at Divine Mercy University. Dr. Treptow applies Fielding's social justice frame and transformative leadership at a Part C early intervention agency, helping parents and others see optimistic pathways for children who may have early problems. She has published a manuscript on rewriting children's medical narratives, conducted grant-supported research on implicit bias in early intervention workers, and presented about the effects of bias on development in local, regional, national, and international conferences. A sample of her work can be seen at experiment.com. Robin Lynn Treptow is the mother of a son who has Trisomy 21.

CHAPTER 25

"NO RESEARCH WITHOUT ACTION" LESSONS LEARNED FROM ACTION RESEARCH TRAINING WITH DOCTORAL STUDENTS

Jo Ann Prompongsatorn Farrant, Julie Riley, Georgia Rose, Lauren Mizock
Fielding Graduate University

Kurt Lewin, who popularized the action research model, proposed that there should be "no action without research" and "no research without action" (Adelman, 1993, p. 8). Per this motto, the goal of action research is to enhance the value of experimentation by utilizing research outcomes to create social change. Unlike traditional research models, action research involves closer involvement of the participant community in the various stages of the research process. However, many research training programs teach in a positivist model, failing to integrate the participant as a key player in the research cycle, or use research findings to contribute to social change.

The present research project sought to train developing researchers in this social justice-oriented research paradigm by the implementation of research projects by the doctoral students involved through partnering with their local communities. The creation of a school-wide "Social Transformation" grant led to the development of this action research training project with doctoral students from Fielding Graduate University. Our research collective involved collaboration between researchers and participants (faculty, students, and community partners) to identify a community problem, train in the research process, and conduct a research project to create strategies to support community innovation. In this monograph, we will provide an overview of the action research model, present narratives of the doctoral student researchers' experiences, and discuss lessons learned from the project for action research training from the faculty member involved.

Action Research

Action research is defined by its characteristic of producing an outcome that benefits the participants of a study to change a shared social world (Kemmis & McTaggart, 2005). The participants are involved throughout the research process by influencing the design, as well as providing input on the goals of a project. The ultimate intention of this methodology is to contribute to social change within a particular participant community. With its origins in activism, one popularly practiced form is participatory action research (PAR). PAR is distinctive in its inclusion of research participants as owners of the project and a focus on sourcing community knowledge to analyze a social problem (Kemmis & McTaggart, 2005).

The origins of action research can be traced back to social psychologist Kurt Lewin in the 1940s (Kemmis & McTaggart, 2005; Skinner, 2017). Although there are earlier studies using action research approaches in community settings at the turn of the 20th century, it is Lewin that catalyzed the action research movement (Kemmis & McTaggart, 2005). Lewin, a firm believer in applied research, sought to democratize processes to alleviate social problems, while firmly believing that "research that produces nothing but books will not suffice" (Lewin, 1946, p. 35). According to Kemmis and McTaggart (2005), action research in Britain was of a practical nature, while Australia called for a critical and emancipatory method. People such as Paulo Freire in South America and Myles Horton in North America applied the action research methodology to develop adult education and literacy programs (Kemmis & McTaggart, 2005).

Central to the methodological framework of the present study is the feminist action research model. Feminist action research is a conceptual methodology that is grounded in the exploration and pursuit of social justice (Reid, 2004). Reid described feminist action research as a promising, yet underdeveloped framework for approaching women's health and agendas of social justice through research. According to Coghlan and Brydon-Miller (2014) feminist movements and feminist action research critically examine knowledge and "truths." Feminist action researchers and activists seek to uncover the ways in which dominant forms of knowledge systematically justify the subordination of underprivileged groups. They have suggested that unless knowledge is produced in a participative manner—that is, in collaboration with participants—then the research is neither valid (as it will inevitably be irrelevant or even detrimental to those concerned) nor ethically acceptable. This philosophy aligns with feminist epistemologies that advocate integrative approaches to knowledge production. Clearly, feminist action research shares principles with action research theory as a whole, and was central to our research protocol.

Research Reflexivity

Feminist, action, and qualitative research approaches often focus on the sociocultural factors in research and examine issues of power in the dynamic created between those doing the research and those being researched (Etherington, 2004; Rose, 1997). This focus is achieved through reflexivity, which has been described as the "qualitative researchers' engagement of continuous examination and explanation of how they have influenced a research project" (Dowling, 2008, p. 3). Despite the belief in objectivity and being neutral that is characteristic of more positivistic research methods, reflexivity is an active process involving balancing self-awareness with the cyclical questioning of what is known and how it is known (Finlay, 2002). Researchers orient themselves to what they bring to a research project by way of their values, personal and professional identities, and social status (Berger, 2015; Reed, Miller, Nnawulezi, & Valenti, 2012). These factors are understood to readily influence the questions being asked, methods being used, interpersonal context created between researchers and participants, and the resulting interpretations or conclusions (Berger, 2015; England, 1994; Etherington, 2004; Finlay,

2002; Rose, 1997). Researcher reflexivity is especially relevant to this presentation of an action research project, given that action research aims to be a collaborative, interactive, and equitable process with a community group (Skinner, 2017).

The following section will integrate the process of reflexivity to reflect on the research experiences of the three doctoral students who were involved in this action research project. Each student attended monthly meetings to support their identification of a local community that might benefit from an action research project, to carry out the study, and to explore their experiences with the project in research narratives. The first action research project included collaborating with a mediation center to develop a survey capturing the learning outcomes. The second project entailed supporting a foster care/adoption nonprofit looking to creative ways to inform new families within its service range about family communication and attachment. The third project involved facilitating a process group at a residential home for young women in state care and exploring the challenges to living in a transitional living facility. The following vignettes provide details of these projects, as well as the students' reflections on their collaborations with communities using the action research model.

Project Experiences
Jo Ann, Human Development doctoral student
I collaborated with a meditation center through its Transformative Action program for my research project. Transformative Action is a yearlong program whose aim is to introduce and deepen practices of mindfulness in social justice activists. The overall intention is to create a space for individual transformation so that the participants will bring the learning to their communities and help sustain and transform social justice movements. This program is unique in that the cohort members are a majority of people of color and LGBTQI who openly discuss issues of race, gender, class, and economics within the context of contemplative practices. The participants commit to a deep investment in their personal transformation,

which involves a letting go of behaviors that cause personal suffering and engaging in new practices that contribute to emotional liberation.

With regard to reflexive explorations of my position and role, I identify as a cisgender woman. I am a second-generation Asian American from a working-class background. I am a white-collar professional with an executive position at a nonprofit. I am married to a white man who also comes from a working-class background. Both my husband and I are privileged by the status of our positional level at work. As a participant and apprentice teacher of the Transformative Action program, I am positioned as an insider within the community and inherently hold a position of power as a member of the teaching team and as a researcher. To manage my privilege and power as a researcher, I found myself engaging in active listening to give space to the participants I worked with in order to not take on an expert role, nor assume I understood everyone's experiences.

I consulted with the lead teacher in the Transformative Action program to develop a research idea that would be helpful to the community, and together we decided that an evaluation of the program would be a valuable contribution of my research skills. Collaborating with the 30 members of the fifth Transformative Action cohort, we held three meetings to develop a survey to capture the learning outcomes of the program. The group agreed on nine survey questions, which are outlined below.

1. How well were your expectations met in the Transformative Action program?

2. In what types of settings have you introduced mindfulness practices where they didn't exist before?

3. How challenging has it been to introduce mindfulness practices to others?

4. What are your success stories? Remember, success can happen with 1:1 interactions or within very small groups.

5. What types of exercises/practices are you using to engage your communities? Please be specific.

6. In what concrete ways does your activism benefit from your

mindfulness practices?

7. What have you noticed about your personal or professional life that, in your opinion: a) contradicts mindfulness? b) reflects mindfulness?

8. Name the organization/s impacted by your Transformative Action work. Please include a brief description of the organizational mission.

9. Is there anything else you would like to share?

The research process was not without hurdles. Due to a lack of capacity in gathering the email addresses for the survey, we pushed the launch to a later date well beyond the original plans. Also, during the development of the nine-question survey, I encountered two other evaluation processes that were already launched by the teaching team. Due to a lack of coordination as participants in the program and the teaching team, we missed the opportunity to combine efforts on the evaluations.

Additionally, while the lead teacher of the program and my fellow cohort members were very amenable to the idea of the development of a survey, I noticed that my status as a researcher inherently placed me in a position of expertise during my interactions in spite of my reflexive attempts to redistribute this power dynamic. I often heard the lead teacher say, "You know best; you are the researcher." To counterbalance this power dynamic, I continually assured the teacher and my cohort members that the purpose of this research project was to provide an opportunity to serve this community and not the other way around.

Ultimately, I learned a number of lessons from this research process. For one, in spite of attempts to share power with participants in the action research model, they may bring assumptions about the status of the researcher that may affect collaboration and require ongoing monitoring to maintain equity in the relationship. I also learned that the initial goal of an action project could change shape over time. For example, we originally planned to co-develop and launch a program evaluation survey. However, the development of the survey appeared to be a chief outcome of the project in itself, as it provided an opportunity for the community to be heard and to be involved in asking the questions that they believed were important. This reinforced a central tenet of action research—that the research process rather than the outcome may be the most important contribution of the study to social change.

Julie, Clinical Psychology doctoral student

For this project, I collaborated with a nonprofit adoption/foster care organization in Houston, Texas. All of children and families served had been involved with the Child Protective Services (CPS) in some capacity. Within the past year, the organization also began supporting post-permanency families, which are families who have permanent managing conservatorship of a child(ren) who was in the custody of the Texas Department of Family and Protective Services (TDFPS). Case managers within the organization noted that working with the post-permanency families was different than their work with adoptive families. Though exploring the differences and unique needs of families formed through permanent managing conservatorship versus adoption is an area worthy of more in-depth qualitative and quantitative exploration, there were more immediate and tangible, as well as more feasible, ways to support the organization's work with post-permanency families.

Reflexively speaking, I identify as a cisgender, white female. I was born into a middle class family with two parents who worked full time. I grew up in the same house throughout childhood and never had to move or change school environments. For all significant purposes, my childhood was stable. In regard to the research with my local community agency, it was important that I recognized myself as an outsider. I am not adopted; I was raised by my biological parents. I was never removed from my parents' care, nor did I ever have to live separated from my biological parents at any point in my childhood. I am also positioned as someone who has worked with adoptees in individual therapy, family therapy, and support groups. With post-permanency families as the focus of my project, it was important for me to recognize my personal experiences and expectations of family, parents, caretakers, and childhood in order for me to remain mindful of everything that was entering into this project with me.

Following collaborative efforts between case managers at the agency and me, the mutually determined project involved two parts: supporting a multi-family art event hosted by the agency; and developing a brief feedback survey to collect some basic data regarding the event and families' general interests. The agency wanted to utilize my background in art therapy and family therapy by having me lead a discussion regarding using creativity to support the emotional needs of children and to foster connection and communication within the family. The brief feedback surveys allowed for direct family feedback and were separately designed for younger children, adolescents/teens, and parents. All surveys were developed in collaboration with the adoption organization, using language appropriate to the target age groups. The children and adolescent/teen surveys included drawing as well as writing prompts. All surveys evaluated participant satisfaction with the multi-family event, identified what activities would be of interest in the future, and the current challenges/frustrations for self and/or family. Parent surveys also assessed for barriers to participate in activities and services provided by the organization.

The handout I created as a foundation for the discussion was distributed to each parent that attended and given to the organization to distribute to other families as needed. From an observational stance, the discussion regarding art therapy and using creative means to connect with children facilitated dialogue not only from speaker (me) to parents, and parents to speaker, but between families. A total of 10 parent surveys, nine child surveys, and eight adolescent/teen surveys were returned. Data from the feedback surveys were collected, compiled, and utilized by the agency in planning and preparation for future events, targeting the needs and interests of participants. Various concrete themes emerged, including the need for more physical, active, game-related opportunities in the future (from children and adolescents/teens), more activities for family togetherness (from parents, children, and adolescents/teens), as well as the barriers to program engagement in terms of travel and disruptive behaviors/dysregulation (from parents). It is important to note that all participants provided less concrete feedback for the adoption and foster care agency—that is, the need to offer a sense of patience and love toward the families being served.

There were a number of lessons from my action research experience. This project introduced me to the process of going into an agency and asking, "How and where can I be of service?" and "What can I do?" rather than assuming a stance as an expert or investigator within this action research process. Though I struggled with what the "research" needed to look like, once I suspended traditional notions of research and stepped into the needs and dynamics of the organization, my experience led to a productive exchange and an evolving relationship with the community agency. The collaborative relationship between the researcher and participant afforded by the action research model allowed us to find opportunities for continued collaboration even after this project concluded.

Georgia, Infant and Early Childhood Development doctoral student
It amazes me how difficult it was to put into words a statement of how I see myself as part of the process of researcher reflexivity. As an Afro-Caribbean Jamaican woman, I reside in a culture where who I am is very much who so many of the inhabitants are. This may best explain my difficulties here. Through the years my mother would pave her own road and, like many Jamaican women of that time, became a domestic helper for wealthy city families. My mother and father had a romantic tryst that would result in my conception. Unfortunately, they came from different worlds—my mother from a blue collar, low-income black family, my father from a privileged mixed-race family. These were two contradicting worlds that had no room for a middle ground, much like the mix of a plantation where slaves would bear the illegitimate children of powerful

white men. For many years my paternity remained the best kept secret. I was the apple of my mother's eye, undoubted in her love. My father—privileged, travelled, and learned—did not want a stigma on his reputation.

Being an "outside" child meant that I was denied many of the entitlements that children born to married parents enjoyed. My mother, in her attempts to compensate, was a fierce mother. She supported and built and scaffolded beyond needed. She instilled a strength in me like no other. Her commitment to her children and determination not to sacrifice us engendered a loyalty so fierce to her and her ideals within me. The power that her choices fused in me protected me from making the choices my mother felt compelled to make. My family is populated by strong female personalities that demand strength in all its members.

The "scandal" of my life remains a secret, depending on the environment that I am in, out of respect for my mother. This reality shaped much of my own worldview. Sociologists argue that there exists no middle class in Jamaica. We have an upper class, dominated by white expatriates (a small percentage), a working class, dominated by educated professionals and paraprofessionals (the majority), and a lower class, dominated by semi-skilled and unskilled laborers (a significant portion). Many women survive by becoming the objects of wealthy men's affections. As a young female, I made it my intention not to choose such a path, but to carve a life built on my own successes. This has not been easy, as the disparity between social groups is marked and the access to resources is limited. Success or an "easy" life could be achieved by choosing a suitor. I would rather struggle.

Many of the young ladies who are residents in state care have stories no different than my own—"illegitimate" children or children with unknown paternity. However, many lacked a mother to fight for them. My desire to work with these young women was born out of my own desire to empower young women to see the alternatives in life.

Hence, I decided to work with young women in foster care as part of my action research project in my community in Jamaica. Children 18 years and younger who are deemed in need of care and protection receive oversight by the Child Protection and Family Services Agency. The Agency is a quasi-governmental organization that provides supervision, governance, and staffing for eight public homes and 40 private facilities. I reached out to one of these homes to conduct my action research project.

My Father's House is a transitional living facility that accepts young women who are on the path to exit from state care. The residents are enrolled in academic programs or are gainfully employed. I met with staff and youth at the home to discuss how I might be helpful in carrying out my action research project with this community. The women were interested in drawing from my training in mental health to gain support around a number of issues they encounter.

Six of the 12 residents joined me for a support group session. The young women shared the following concerns they faced with living in a transitional home:Feeling confused by the bridge between adolescence and adulthood

- Feeling unprepared for exit from state care

- Feeling denied their basic rights and imprisoned by the rules and regulations of the facility

- Feeling robbed of an authentic adolescent experience

- Feeling confused by the desire to be "free" and the desire to remain "provided for"

- Feeling the lack of staff trust in them and opportunities for social engagement

- Feelings isolation and sadness

- Feeling the need for greater social support

The experience was humbling and somber. The fact that these young women remained in the artificial environment of a group home, void of a maternal figure to protect, shape, and guide them, was ever-present and particularly poignant for me. We were left with several questions from our support group: How do we facilitate an environment that provides safeguards, rules, and boundaries without violating the rights of young women in transitional living? How can the women become prepared psychologically for the transition of "exit"? What does long-term social support look like?

To address these questions we were left with as a group, I created a link between the young women and a psychology club of undergraduate students from a local university who agreed to serve as peer mentors and role models for the young women. I hope to continue my connection to this community and use my additional research skills to evaluate the effectiveness of this new program. In sum, I learned from this project that research could take less traditional forms than data collection but could be a therapeutic experience for participants, involving continued collaboration, and one that bridges connections across communities.

Conclusion and Training Implications

The action research training project involved three student researchers learning a new research method together and collaborating in its application within their local communities. Though each project was independently organized and carried out by the student researchers, the communication and support from the larger group provided the foundation to learn the method, and a space to foster discussion and collectively address challenges the researchers faced. The larger group also functioned as a platform to share outcomes and process the interactional nature of the action research method. We engaged in self-study as a group to understand the challenges and strengths of our project, leading to a number of lessons learned for action research training in this section.

One of our biggest challenges was attrition. We started with a larger group of students (six) and faculty (two), and lost women of color in both groups. We were left with concerns with racial-ethnic disparities in retention and the holistic stability and sustainability of the group due to economic, health, academic, and caretaker demands. The stipend awarded to help support student involvement did not fully prevent loss of members. We reflected on the privilege associated with being able to prioritize research in doctoral training and teaching, representing a barrier to social justice-oriented research at multiples stages of an academic career.

In a group that underwent this much change in membership and activity, we found the Tuckman model of the developmental sequence of small groups (forming, storming, norming, performing, [transforming], adjourning) to be particularly helpful to understanding our dynamics. We understood our difficulty in the forming stage due to changes in membership, leading to "storming" or unrest within the group that eventually settled to allow "norming"—establishment of norms in our operating to help us move forward. Other training programs in action research might also find this model helpful.

Another hurdle that was overcome was carrying out the projects themselves—the "performing" stage. The students spoke to a feeling of pressure to fix and/or rescue and save their communities. They also had assumptions from their doctoral training that research should be dissertation-size in scope. The students found that the emphasis in the project on making the research feasible and pragmatic in breadth and time frame was particularly helpful in ensuring research productivity.

The research cycle in action research was also a good fit with the students' instincts as social justice practitioners. They wanted to maximize the impact of the relationships they worked to form with their communities. They identified additional research projects they could partner in with their evolving involvement with the community, fulfilling the transforming stage.

Lastly, our group found readings and conversations in researcher reflexivity during our final meetings to be useful to understanding our group process and resolving our earlier challenges. This practice could also be valuable to other social justice-oriented research training protocols. We were reminded that in order to be effective in our work with communities we needed to reflect on issues of power and social barriers that we face as researchers, that our own research community could not be divided from the broader social context and deserved the same focus and efforts towards social transformation.

References

Adelman, C. (1993). Kurt Lewin and the origins of action research. *Educational Action Research, 1(*1), 7-24.

Berger, R. (2015). Now I see it, now I don't: Researcher's position and reflexivity in qualitative research. *Qualitative Research, 15*(2), 219-234.

Coghlan, D., & Brydon-Miller, M. (Eds.). (2014). *The SAGE encyclopedia of action research*. Los Angeles, CA: SAGE.

Dowling, M. (2015). Reflexivity. *The SAGE encyclopedia of qualitative research methods* (pp. 3-4). Thousand Oaks: SAGE.

England, K.V.L. (1994). Getting personal: Reflexivity, positionality, and feminist research. *The Professional Geographer, 46*(1), 80-89.

Etherington, K. (2004). Research methods: Reflexivities—roots, meanings, dilemmas. *Counseling and Psychotherapy Research, 4*(2), 46-47.

Finlay, L. (2002). "Outing" the researcher: The provenance, process, and practice of reflexivity. *Qualitative Health Research, 12*(4), 531-545.

Kemmis, S., & McTaggart, R. (2005). Participatory action research: Communicative action and the public sphere. In N. K. Denzin & Y. S. Lincoln (Eds.), *The SAGE handbook of qualitative research* (pp. 559-603). Thousand Oaks, CA: SAGE Publications Ltd.

Lewin, K. (1946). Action research and minority problems. *Journal of Social Issues, 2*(4), 34-46.

Reed, S., Miller, R. L., Nnawulezi, N., & Valenti, M. (2012). Outing ourselves: Uncomfortable reflexivity and community-based research. *Journal of Community Psychology, 40*(1), 11-26.

Reid, C. (2004). Advancing women's social justice agendas: A feminist action research framework. *International Journal of Qualitative Methods, 3*(3), Article 1.

Rose, G. (1997). Situating knowledges: Positionality, reflexivities and other tactics. *Progress in Human Geography, 21*(3), 305-320.

Skinner, H. (2017). Action Research. In K. Kubacki & S. Rundle-Thiele (Eds). *Formative research in social marketing* (pp. 11-31). Singapore: Springer.

About the Authors

Lauren Mizock, PhD, is the Director of the Social Justice and Diversity concentration and core faculty in the Clinical Psychology PhD Program at Fielding Graduate University. She is also in private practice as a licensed psychologist in San Francisco. Dr. Mizock is Chair of the Motherhood Committee and Co-Chair of the Task Force for Women with Serious Mental Illness in the Society for the Psychology of Women of the American Psychological Association (APA), and a Program Developer for the Center for Psychiatric Rehabilitation at Boston University. Areas of expertise include multicultural competence in research and clinical work, transgender and gender diverse populations, and individuals with serious mental illness.

Jo Ann Prompongsatorn is a doctoral candidate in Human Development with a concentration in Inclusive Leadership for Social Justice at Fielding Graduate University. Jo Ann is also the Deputy Director of Organizational Development at the Oakland-based nonprofit, TransForm. She leads organizational systems change to cultivate a workplace culture that embeds equity, diversity, and inclusion as a core priority. As a trained medical qigong therapy practitioner and life coach, Jo Ann incorporates healing practices into her group and one-on-one work to assist social justice activists, advocates, and change-makers in cultivating self-awareness to create transformational change.

Julie Riley, MS, is a doctoral candidate in Clinical Psychology at Fielding Graduate University with a concentration in Social Justice and Diversity. She is involved in qualitative research projects focused on social justice, reflexivity, and community action. Julie earned her Master of Science in Creative Arts Therapy from Nazareth College of Rochester. Areas of interest include complex trauma, adoption and attachment, medically fragile populations, creative approaches in therapy, and blending practice and advocacy. Her dissertation will address the emotional dimensions of mitochondrial disease in young adulthood with a focus on coping theory and narrative medicine.

Georgia Rose, MS, is a doctoral candidate in Infant and Early Childhood Development. She has been providing service in child and adolescent mental health for over 14 years in the Western Region and in 2015 was recognized by the Special Education Unit of the Ministry of Education for "unrelenting and untiring service to special education." She sits on the Board of the Peace management Initiative of St. James, is a consultant on the Ethics Review Board for Kidney Transplants in Western Jamaica and also the Bariatric Surgery Team. Ms. Rose is also the Co-Chair for the St. James Red Cross, and has conducted numerous psychosocial support trainings across the Caribbean on behalf of the International Federation of the Red Cross, Disaster Mental Health Unit, with a focus on the impact of trauma on children and adolescents. She is a lecturer in undergraduate psychology and has presented on numerous topics related to child and adolescent mental health.

CHAPTER 26

REFLEXIVITY AND REFLECTIONS ON PERSONAL TRANSFORMATIONS IN RESEARCH TRAINING

Lauren Mizock, PhD, Alayne Ormerod, PhD, Julie Riley, Erica A. Sotilleo, T. Dawson Woodrum, and Nelly Yuen

Fielding Graduate University

Qualitative research is often conducted by a team of researchers who work together to analyze interview data. Each researcher's perspective provides a potential lens through which the interviewee narratives are interpreted. The final interpretive lens is honed by the researcher's interactions with the participant narratives as well as each other. We will expose this interpretive process in the present monograph, which will include an exploration of the research experiences of a qualitative research team. This team is composed of doctoral students who have worked with faculty in a clinical psychology PhD program to analyze data from a qualitative study focused on employment discrimination and coping among transgender and gender diverse (TGD) individuals. The research project led to experiences of personal transformations in the research team as a process of their qualitative investigation into this population. We will provide an overview of the literature on reflexivity in research, present the narratives of the doctoral students in the research team, and final lessons from research training from the faculty involved.

Reflexivity

Reflexivity is a process associated with qualitative methodology that recognizes that knowledge is actively constructed through subjective and intersubjective experiencing (Etheringon, 2004; Finlay, 2002). Reflexivity involves "a critical, self-aware evaluation of the impact of the researcher on the research and vice versa" (Hofmann & Barker, 2017, p. 140). Reflection and reflexivity are sometimes used interchangeably (Finlay, 2002; Hoffman & Barker, 2017). However, reflexivity is a more involved process by which the researcher(s) openly address subjective responses, intersubjective dynamics, and the research process through a continual process of self-awareness and questioning of what is known and how it is known (Finlay, 2002).

Due to the constructive meaning-making process between the researcher and the participant, there is value in the examination of the researchers' reflexivity regarding their actions and decisions, which contributes to the research process as well as the product (Charmaz, 2014). Some of the researchers' influence in the research process may be known, whereas some aspects are unknown to the researchers. Through reflexivity, the researchers are able to become aware and acknowledge the subjectivity as well as their involvement in the gathering and construction, as well as interpretation of data.

From the feminist methodological perspective, reflexivity is often advocated as a strategy for situating knowledge and functions to counter the false sense of neutrality and universality often associated with academic knowledge (Rose, 1997). Feminist scholarship attends to the marginal members of society by actively and intentionally considering oppression and social power dynamics (Caretta & Riano, 2016; England, 1994; Etherington, 2004). This paradigm stresses equality within the research relationship and transparency on behalf of the researcher (Etherington, 2004). Etherington (2004) indicated that transparency regarding the values and beliefs influencing research lowers the barriers between researcher and the researched.

With the lowered sense of division between research and the researched, positionality becomes an important dynamic within reflexivity. *Positionality* entails understanding one's position in relation to the research as based on class, gender, and race (England, 1994). By examining positionality and biography, the reflexive process allows for "self-critical sympathetic introspection and the self-conscious analytical scrutiny of the self as researcher" (England, 1994, p. 244) that elevates reflexivity beyond mere self-awareness and personal reflection.

While some have characterized reflexivity as nothing more than glorified navel-gazing (Finlay, 2002; Ploder & Stadlbauer, 2016), when used with intention reflexivity can contribute to rigor in qualitative research. Research is ultimately a human endeavor, which leaves research subject to bias and influence that cannot be completely controlled or eliminated. Qualitative approaches recognize this, and hermeneutically address the researcher in relation to the research by continuously engaging and questioning contextual factors, intersubjectivity, and positionality throughout the research process. At the present time, reflexivity does not have a counterpart in quantitative research. In the present monograph, we will examine each researcher's reflection and personal transformation from participation in a research study on an underserved population, transgender and gender diverse (TGD) individuals. In other words, these individual narratives are mini reflexive journals. According to Morse (2015), maintaining a reflexive journal is an important practice in qualitative research for assuring all of the principal components of rigor: validity (internal and external); generalizability; reliability; and objectivity. Forero et al. (2018) noted that reflexive journaling should be used to capture researchers' perspectives about data interpretation. Standing alone, these reflexive vignettes provide a window into how each researcher's prior experience and assumptions influenced data interpretation. Together, they help complete the interpretive picture and contribute to demonstrating study rigor by making the "what, why, and how" of the results more transparent. Tuval-Mashiach (2017) suggests this type of transparency exercise gives research consumers a deeper understanding of study results and that it should be adopted as a best practice.

The Research Project and Role of Reflexivity

Transgender and gender diverse (TGD) individuals face stigma from the public as well as in the workplace. This stigma elevates the rates of unemployment and financial hardship. However, TGD people demonstrate several resilience and protective factors to overcome experiences with transphobia. Our research projects sought to better understand the different experiences of transphobia among TGD workers (Mizock, Riley, et al., 2018) and better identify the specific strategies that transgender individuals use to deal with transphobia at work (Mizock, Woodrum, et al., 2017). Our research team was comprised of two professors (one of whom was involved in the original data collection) and four doctoral-level graduate students. The data included previously collected interviews from 45 TGD participants. The first project targeting themes of employment stigma revealed the following themes: *lack of social support*; *workplace gender policing*; *personal safety threats*; *acquisition and advancement barriers*; *intersectional discrimination*; *intuited stigma*; and *lack of inclusive policy*. The second analysis examining the data for strategies of coping with employment stigma revealed themes about: *gender presentation strategies*; *gender detachment*; *relationship navigating*; *resource utilization*; *job performance strategies*; *maladaptive coping strategies*; *structural strategies*; and *power acquisition strategies*.

While grounded theory methodology was initially used to develop themes from the qualitative interview data, the purpose of this monograph is to reflexively examine the researchers' experiences of interpersonal connection to the participant narratives and each other to reveal the intersubjective nature of the research process. The interpersonal reactions of each researcher will be identified through the reflexive procedure of personal narrative. This analysis can be viewed as an essential secondary data source (Goldstein, 2016) toward understanding the context from which the previous analyses developed. Hence, one is able to better understand the researchers' positions and the subjectivity that were at play in the aforementioned research projects.

Researcher Narratives

Reflecting on the process used to produce qualitative research outcomes can materialize in various forms. In this section, we will present each researcher's personal narrative reflecting on their experiences with reviewing research participant interview responses and the interpersonal dynamics of participating in the combined research projects. These reflections include each researcher's subjective response to each other as well as the participant narratives during the research process. This created independent and unique qualitative data in and of themselves. One gem that emerged from this exercise is the experiential aspect of being affectively engaged in the data and each other, as well as a shared experience of being personally/professionally influenced beyond the overall research project itself.

The intersubjective connections between the researchers and the research participants' narratives are an opportunity instead of a problem to be controlled or eliminated (Goldstein, 2016). Therefore, through reflection, each researcher identified connection, tension, and/or feeling anxiety with the narratives and each other. These observations offer a more contextualized understanding of the interpretations discussed in Mizock, Riley, et al. (2018) and Mizock, Woodrum, et al. (2017). The reflexive process captured in the researchers' narratives provides an essential dimension to the entire data analysis that provides the reader with a deeper understanding of both the strengths and limitations of the research results.

T. Dawson Woodrum, doctoral student

Before joining our research practicum project, I struggled with the decision about picking a topic so close to home for me. It was only a few years before that I had openly transitioned as an executive at a large global corporation. I feared I might read too much into statements or overinterpret them. I took a leap of faith that faculty and my fellow practicum students would keep me in check should I be guilty of overstepping boundaries.

I didn't know whether other transgender and gender diverse (TGD) students would be in the practicum so I felt it was important to represent, as much as I could, a balanced perspective of TGD-related workplace concerns. I also had a brief moment of hesitation as to whether there might be students in the practicum who hold particularly conservative views about gender or are otherwise morally opposed to transition.

Early in the process, I was invited to work with the group to raise our awareness of TGD-related terminology and basic transition-related concerns. Looking back, I would now describe this as "experiential acceptance"—a kind of acceptance that goes beyond being invited to participate and includes the kind of active engagement that pulls people into discussions they might otherwise avoid out of fear they might say something wrong or offensive.

The qualitative methodology in our project drove important discussions within our group about how binary and cisgender privilege can insulate us from stigma. I learned from our experience that the qualitative method itself raises awareness and can provide an environment conducive to the development of allies in the profession. For example, after working on this project, one of my fellow practicum students invited me to provide a Transgender Awareness training presentation at her clinical practicum site.

My experience with this study raised my concern for clients who may be struggling with gender-related issues but remain invisible in systems that are not equipped to address their needs. Based on this experience, I have decided to model inclusiveness by listing my gender pronouns in my email signature line and stating them when introducing myself in person.

Julie Riley, doctoral student

I am a white, cisgender female. When reading the interviews from the TGD participants in this study, I found myself relating to various experiences disclosed within the interviews, such as violation and mistrust, insecurity, and perseverance in spite of others blocking the way. I also found myself relating to the experiences of "hiding in plain sight." However, I also understood where I might relate to aspects of these experiences due to my positionality (England, 1994; Rose, 1997) as a woman in a male-centered society interacting within misogynistic professional/social climates. Also, as a non-Christian living and working within a predominantly Christian community in Texas, I benefit greatly from the privilege of fitting the socially-expected gender dichotomy and my conflict with Christianity is not immediately/visibly known. My privilege has afforded me the ability to traverse social surroundings with minimal outward conflict. Despite the affective states I connected to within the participant experiences, I found the lack of sameness important to explicitly recognize. I learned that I may be able to *relate*, but I will never *know* (in the embodied sense) the participants' experiences. I found relating to situations resulted in intense affective responses, but I reflexively countered by distinguishing that *relating to* does not mean my experiences are *the same*. Intentionally acknowledging my outsider status (Finlay, 2002) in regard to my emotional reactions left me invested in the participants' words and experiences rather than any felt similarities.

As a result of participating in this research experience, my professional perspective has expanded in regard to the nature of the research topics themselves, the complexities clinicians should be prepared to navigate with TGD clients, and the need for safe spaces. This "expanded perspective" seems so logical when I consider it, and it wasn't that I didn't believe these things needed focus/attention before. However, I did not *actively* think about them, which is the subtle pervasiveness of privilege. My awareness of how broader society (cultural norms, societal expectations, media, policies, and politics) actively targets and attempts to delegitimize TGD lives increased by way of participating in this practicum, because participants' worlds became more tangible through my reading of their narratives. I began to see and hear more clearly both the subtle and not so subtle attacks that were present in my surrounding community. As I paid more attention to broader society as it paralleled with this research experience, my cisgender privilege became more tangible. While I may not have agreed with or intentionally aligned with the narrow and harmful

TGD characterizations in the larger social context, I was more often quiet than not in the face of these injustices. The passivity my privilege allotted me was initially uncomfortable to fully own; however, this awareness has been a necessary and welcomed outcome of this work.

Nelly Yuen, doctoral student

Growing up in Hong Kong, I had the physical appearance of a Chinese person with British citizenship, but one of my first languages was Tagalog because my primary caretaker was Filipino. I naively assumed the existence of diversity was synonymous with the presence of equality in my culture. When my family moved to the United States, I suddenly lost privilege I unknowingly held as part of the dominant group in Hong Kong. As I negotiated my new identity in a new culture, I became fascinated with many psychological concepts, including the construction of identity and social power hierarchies.

As we began this research project regarding the stigma and coping strategies of transgender individuals in the workplace, I became incredibly anxious and disheartened as I read the personal testimonies of participants who vulnerably shared their painful experiences. While I have always believed that I would champion equality and acceptance, I realized the prejudice, pain, as well as isolation I experienced as a racial minority had led to personal avoidance around the topics regarding social justice. I had passively become accustomed to survival by staying invisible and pivoting around injustice. The strength and courage of our participants empowered me to not only confront my own pain, but to actively create a compassionate and safe space in my community.

Not only have I learned the necessary terminology and gained entry knowledge regarding the experiences of transgender individuals, but perhaps the most unexpected part of the learning experience has been the healing that has occurred in my personal life. I am regaining a voice I did not know I had lost. I recall a particularly pivotal clinical training opportunity that facilitated this type of growth. As part of an assessment team, I assisted in the assessment of an elderly client who was suspected of dementia or psychosis by family members. Upon clinical interview, it became clear that the client's behaviors and thoughts were deeply misperceived. The client came to the realization that she had recently begun to examine her gender identity, which explained the changes in her personal life and relationships. This experience taught me the importance of appropriately asking a seemingly simple question, "What is your preferred pronoun?" Since the privilege of being able to advocate for her needs with the treatment team and family members, I have been slowly developing the confidence to initiate discussion, address microaggression, and vocalize prejudice that occurs professionally or in my personal life.

As I continue to discover how I can use my new voice with boldness and effectiveness to advocate for myself as well as others, I am grateful that this experience has ignited a passion in me to move away from avoidance into activism.

Erica A. Sotilleo, doctoral student

One recurring question others have asked is, "What made you join that research practicum?" To answer this question, I initially joined this research team because years prior, while in school, I met an individual I will call "Jill." Jill was a transgender individual who transitioned from male-to-female. Jill and I first bonded as we talked about what she referred to as *passing*. As a woman of color, I identified with the term "passing,' because African American women were *passing* when they had a light skin complexion.

Before getting started on our research project, I was not aware of the value of *qualitative research methods* and *reflexivity*. The team discussed the way that *intersectionality* has grown around activism and social justice in the field of psychology. Intersectionality "refers to the notion that an individual embodies multiple social identities, some of which may be oppressed or privileged, that intersect to uniquely shape one's experience" (Mizock & Page, 2016). Our research team members discovered many new ways of thinking and being; we just removed the scales from our eyes in different ways.

While research paired with individualized grassroots efforts is priceless, this project has taught me that advocacy does not need to be a lonely road; it is even more powerful through a team effort. Themes that evolved from our research are friendship, listening, empathy, connections, passing, fear, value, awareness, education, *anti-oppression education*, transformation, finding your voice, and maximized advocacy.

This experience is not value-free. After participating in this research project, I am a different person—a better person and a better clinician because my compassion evolved from awareness to self-awareness, and from education to specific verbal actions supporting advocacy for the rights of transgender individuals. Our research increases efforts in antioppression education in clinical programs such as Fielding Graduate University. While part of my worldview includes peace, it now includes maximized activism towards social improvement for transgender individuals.

Lauren Mizock, faculty

I was a new faculty member in the Clinical Psychology PhD program when I was approached by my colleague, Dr. Alayne Ormerod, to bring my experience in TGD research and practice to her research practicum. We began reading together about TGD people and transphobia, and decided to work with my qualitative data on TGD employment discrimination. To counterbalance our study of employment discrimination, we studied the coping strategies and resilience of our participants. By the end of our data analysis process, we had enough findings for two manuscripts, which we published separately and presented at several conferences. I was proud of our productivity and felt satisfied with the outcomes of our work. But it wasn't until our panel presentation at a national conference session at our university that I came to realize the impact our research project had had on our group and that there was more work to explore. Dr. Ormerod and I exchanged shocked expressions as we watched multiple students in our panel shed tears as they spoke about their reactions to the discrimination faced by the transgender participants in our study—people whom our students had never met but whose stories had retained their power in the interviews we read.

We decided to pursue this publication of the researchers' experiences in a project on reflexivity. As faculty, we wanted to share a few lessons learned from the research experience, and a primary and concrete lesson in research training had to do with organization. It worked well to break the qualitative analysis process into stages of meetings with related readings and discussion. These meetings took the following form: (1) meetings; literature review; (3) grounded theory methodology process; (4) review of interview data; (5) thematic analysis; and (6) identification of two to three representative research excerpts for each theme. In another set of meetings, we developed our publication, reviewing each student's assigned write-up as a group. These meetings took the following order: (7) literature review and method sections; and (8) themes in the results section. As faculty, we wrote the discussion section and revised the rest of the manuscript. We did this for each of the two manuscripts, and divided up our conference proposals similarly to disseminate our findings to the field. Since then, I have used this model in other research practica, attesting to the applicability of this organizational approach to other research training projects.

I also learned less concrete lessons from our work together. Bringing a "publish or perish" drive to our work as an early career academic, I was focused on getting our writing in print in order to add lines to our students' CVs. While I saw our journal reviewers' feedback as my "private battle" to pursue, Dr. Ormerod encouraged me to share the feedback with the group for their learning purposes. It was easy for me to forget how valuable sharing in each stage of the research process could be for research trainees.

Another lesson was in the impact of our participants' stories. Having collected data from our qualitative interviews several years ago, I had forgotten the power of their lived experience. My participants had shared their pain with me because they wanted their challenges to help others. I was moved to see that their stories had maintained their strength on the page. Our empathic students had let those words move them and inspire their commitment to social justice research.

Finally, I was reminded of a lesson I had learned when I was as a graduate student, that research was not just about rotely collecting data but could be a therapeutic space for participants to have their stories heard. Now I learned that this lesson extended a bit further; our participants' stories could also transform us as researchers.

Alayne Ormerod, faculty

Research practicum in the Clinical Psychology program at Fielding Graduate University is a requirement for doctoral students, and members of the clinical faculty offer a variety of research training experiences each year. This particular practicum grew from a class discussion on sexual and gendered violence, where students requested a research practicum on the experiences of TGD individuals and/or LGBTQ issues. My research areas include sexual violence and sexual and racial/ethnic harassment and discrimination in schools, the workplace, and the military, and I had been thinking about developing a quantitative measure to reflect the experiences of LBGTQ adolescents in school. The lab filled quickly with nearly a dozen students, but their interests were somewhat different from my own and from each other, and at times I felt pulled in nearly as many directions. Most members of the practicum had little research or other experience with TGD individuals so we worked to become knowledgeable in the area and, importantly, to discuss members' responses to the material. In essence, we began the process of reflexivity with the material and each other. There were several pivotal moments in the practicum, one of which was a presentation by a member on "Trans 101" that helped to create space for lab members to ask questions, make mistakes, and explore their own reactions to new territory.

Around this time, some of the lab members moved on and Dr. Mizock, an expert on trans issues, was hired by Fielding. I immediately invited her to join the lab; she graciously agreed and, unbeknownst to me at the time, brought data. At first I wondered how this might work, given that the data were qualitative and focused on adult workplace experiences, but it quickly became apparent that we were about to embark on a partnership with four highly engaged students that would yield research training, professional and personal development, and various research products. As this practicum came to a close it was satisfying to reflect on the ways in which engagement with the research process, the participants' stories, and each other had influenced team members. Of the many lessons from this research practicum, one is about the power of research to generate more than knowledge. Our process facilitated compassion for our participants' experiences and our own, it energized individuals to adopt new social justice practices, and it created space to explore and question what we do and do not know. The practicum brought us into contact with participants' stories of discrimination, persistence, transformation and, in many cases, stories about thriving in spite of great odds. As described in some of the student narratives, the participants' stories informed how we understand our own stories. Also as described above, the participants' stories may have lasting effects on how we understand and relate to others in the future. I hope with this monograph and our other publications that our participants' stories will influence others' research, practice, social engagement, and perhaps personal development.

References

Benedetti, F., Carlino, E., & Piedimonte, A. (2016). Increasing uncertainty in CNS clinical trials: the role of placebo, nocebo, and Hawthorne effects. *The Lancet Neurology, 15*(7), 736-747. https://doi. org/10.1016/S1474-4422(16)00066-1

Caretta, M. A., & Riano, Y. (2016). Feminist participatory methodologies in geography; Creating spaces of inclusion. *Qualitative Research, 16*(3), 258-266.

Charmaz, K. (2000). *Grounded theory: Objectivist and constructivist methods*. In N.K. Denzin & Y. S. Lincoln (Eds), *Handbook of Qualitative Research* (2nd ed.). Thousand Oaks, CA: SAGE.

Charmaz, K. (2014). *Constructing grounded theory* (2nd ed.). Thousand Oaks, CA: SAGE.

England, K.V.L. (1994). Getting personal: Reflexivity, positionality, and feminist research. *The Professional Geographer, 46*(1), 80-89.

Etherington, K. (2004). Research methods: Reflexivities—roots, meanings, dilemmas. *Counseling and Psychotherapy Research, 4*(2), 46-47.

Finlay, L. (2002). "Outing" the researcher: The provenance, process, and practice of reflexivity. *Qualitative Health Research, 12*(4), 531-545.

Forero, R., Nahidi, S., De Costa, J., Mohsin, M., Fitzgerald, G., Gibson, N., Aboagye-Sarfo, P. (2018). Application of four-dimension criteria to assess rigour of qualitative research in emergency medicine. *BMC Health Services Research, 18*(1). https://doi.org/10.1186/s12913-018-2915-2

Goldstein, S. E. (2016, 2017). Reflexivity in narrative research: Accessing meaning through the participant-researcher relationship. Qualita*tive Psychology, 4*(2), 149-164. doi:10.1037/qup0000035

Harvey, J. (2013). Footprints in the field: Researcher identity in social research. *Methodological Innovations Online, 8*(1), 86-98.

Hoffmann, M., & Barker, C. (2017). On researching a health condition that the researcher has also experienced. *Qualitative Psychology, 4*(2), 139-148.

Kaptchuk, T. J. (2001). The double-blind, randomized, placebo-controlled trial: Gold standard or golden calf? *Journal of Clinical Epidemiology, 9*, 541-549.

Mizock, L., & Page, K. V. (2016). Evaluating the ally role: Contributions, limitations, and the activist position in Counseling and Psychology. *Journal for Social Action in Counseling and Psychology, 8*(1), 17-33.

Mizock, L., Riley, J., Yuen, N., Woodrum, T. D., Sotilleo, E. A., & Ormerod, A. J. (2018). Transphobia in the workplace: A qualitative study of employment stigma. *Stigma and Health, 3*(3), 275-282. http://dx.doi.org/10.1037/sah0000098

Mizock, L., Woodrum, T. D., Riley, J., Sotilleo, E. A., Yuen, N., & Ormerod, A. J. (2017). Coping with transphobia in employment: Strategies used by transgender and gender-diverse people in the United States. *International Journal of Transgenderism, 18*(3), 282-294. doi:10.1080/15532739.2017.1304313

Morse, J. M. (2015). Critical analysis of strategies for determining rigor in qualitative inquiry. *Qualitative Health Research, 25*(9), 1212-1222. https://doi.org/10.1177/1049732315588501

Paradis, E., & Sutkin, G. (2017). Beyond a good story: from Hawthorne Effect to reactivity in health professions education research. *Medical Education, 51*(1), 31-39. https://doi.org/10.1111/medu.13122

Ploder, A. & Stadlbauer, J. (2016). Strong reflexivity and its critics; Responses to autoethnography in the German-speaking cultural and social sciences. *Qualitative Inquiry, 22*(9), 753-765.

Rose, G. (1997). Situating knowledges: Positionality, reflexivities and other tactics. *Progress in Human Geography, 21*(3), 305-320.

Tuval-Mashiach, R. (2017). Raising the curtain: The importance of transparency in qualitative research. *Qualitative Psychology, 4*(2), 126-138. https://doi.org/10.1037/qup0000062

About the Authors

Lauren Mizock, PhD, is the Director of the Social Justice and Diversity concentration and a core faculty member in the Clinical Psychology PhD Program at Fielding Graduate University. Dr. Mizock is also in private practice as a licensed psychologist in San Francisco. She is Chair of the Motherhood Committee and Co-Chair of the Task Force for Women with Serious Mental Illness in the Society for the Psychology of

Women of the American Psychological Association (APA). Dr. Mizock is a Program Developer for the Center for Psychiatric Rehabilitation at Boston University. Areas of expertise include multicultural competence in research and clinical work, transgender and gender diverse populations, and individuals with serious mental illness.

Alayne (Mimi) Ormerod, PhD, is the Director of Research Practicum Training and a core faculty member in the Clinical Psychology PhD program at Fielding Graduate University. Dr. Ormerod is the 2018 Chair for the American Psychological Association (APA) Committee on Women in Psychology. She has held multiple leadership positions in APA Division 35, the Society for the Psychology of Women, and is past associate editor of the *Psychology of Women Quarterly*. An expert on sexual harassment in the workplace, she has consulted to the Department of Defense on their survey program to assess sexual and racial/ethnic harassment and discrimination in the military. Her areas of professional interest include workplace issues and sexual and gendered violence. Dr. Ormerod's current scholarship focuses on sexual harassment and discrimination in schools, the workplace, and the military, and sexual assault in the military.

Julie Riley, MS, is a doctoral candidate in Clinical Psychology at Fielding Graduate University with a concentration in Social Justice and Diversity. She is involved in qualitative research projects focused on social justice, reflexivity, and community action. Julie earned her Master of Science in Creative Arts Therapy from Nazareth College of Rochester. Areas of interest include complex trauma, adoption and attachment, medically fragile populations, creative approaches in therapy, and blending practice and advocacy. Her dissertation will address the emotional dimensions of mitochondrial disease in young adulthood with a focus on coping theory and narrative medicine.

Erica A. Sotilleo, MS, MA, is a doctoral candidate in Clinical Psychology at Fielding Graduate University. Ms. Sotilleo has served in various clinical, supervisory and doctoral teaching roles. She is an adjunct professor of psychology at the university level for undergraduate students and an editor for the Rose Cross Journal. Ms. Sotilleo has conducted research on domestic violence, co-authored papers in the areas of transphobia in the workplace and coping with transphobia in employment, and authored a book on the area of social skills interventions for children diagnosed with neurodevelopmental disorders. Her current clinical psychotherapy lifework focuses on people diagnosed with HIV/AIDS, post-traumatic stress disorder (PTSD), and major depression disorder (MDD).

T. Dawson Woodrum, MA, JD, is a doctoral candidate in Clinical Psychology at Fielding Graduate University and an Adjunct Professor of Psychology at Piedmont College in Demorest Georgia. He is the 2018 recipient of the Dr. Sherry L. Hatcher Honorary Scholarship (2018), awarded to outstanding students in clinical psychology at Fielding Graduate University whose research takes a creative and potentially impactful approach to addressing important problems in the field. His dissertation will address the relationship between demoralization, community connectedness, and well-being in transgender and gender diverse individuals.

Nelly Yuen, MA, is a doctoral candidate in Clinical Psychology at Fielding Graduate University with concentrations in Neuropsychology and Social Justice. Nelly has been practicing as a Licensed Professional Counselor with a special interest in combining insight-oriented and cognitive-behavioral therapy. Nelly is involved in both qualitative and quantitative research on topics such as the creativity of culturally diverse parents and the benefits of long-term psychotherapy from a client's perspective. Her dissertation will address the various factors that are associated with adolescent inpatient psychiatric hospitalization length as well as subsequent outpatient treatment compliance. Following her internship, Nelly hopes to continue her work with diverse populations, including clients with serious mental illness and clients who do not traditionally have financial means to attain mental health care.

CHAPTER 27

THE INFLUENCE OF IMMIGRANT VETERANS ON A CLINICAL PSYCHOLOGY DOCTORAL STUDENT'S RESEARCH AND PRACTICE

Shantay Mines
Fielding Graduate University

I had never before considered conducting research on an immigrant population. I applied for a PhD in Clinical Psychology to augment the skills I had learned from an EdS in Marriage and Family Therapy to serve active duty military and veterans individually and as couples and families. My focus with this population was treating PTSD and sub-threshold PTSD using a systems approach. I only planned to expand my clinical focus to include neuropsychological assessment, research, and treatment. Research related to immigrants was not on my radar, given my previous research and clinical experience and interests.

My clinical psychology research practicum provided an unexpected introduction to researching immigrant veterans, using an archival database, and considering the mental health needs of immigrants related to military service. The research generated from this practicum was groundbreaking in several important ways. Research related to the mental health of veterans in the United States is well-established, and research related to immigrants joining the military in the country they immigrated to is fair, but my research in this practicum is the first empirical investigation of depression in immigrants who served in the military in their country of origin before immigrating to the United States.

Current research related to military veterans and depression is focused primarily on personnel that served in Iraq and Afghanistan as part of

OEF/OIF/OND combat campaigns with comorbid Post-Traumatic Stress Disorder (Possemato, Andersen, & Ouimette, 2010). Studies related to immigrants and the military have only been conducted in relationship to those immigrants joining the military in the country they immigrated to and their adjustment and adaptation. A study on the assimilation, cultural adaptation, and identity of immigrants to Israel who joined the Israeli Army found that, while national identity is positively associated with adjustment, ethnic identity had no association with adjustment, and those participants from marginalized or separated groups that reject their new country's culture had poor levels of adaptation (Shalom & Horenczyk, 2004).

This immigrant research was originally intended to investigate the instance of post-traumatic stress disorder (PTSD) among legal immigrants to the United States that were active-duty military in their country of origin and are now veterans. A review of the literature shows an absence of literature in this area. However, in the vast archival national database with a large sample that measured thousands of variables related to demographics, pre-immigration experiences, employment, health care, income, assets, social variables, migration history, the Woodcock Johnson, and Digit Span Assessment, there were no variables that, if combined, would meet the criteria for PTSD.

The use of an archival database presented unique challenges for conducting empirical research. The New Immigrant Survey (NIS) (Princeton, 2008) is a longitudinal, nationally representative Immigration and Naturalization Service (NIS) sample, prospective-retrospective, multi-cohort study of 8,566 legal immigrants to the United States from 20 countries between 2003 and 2004. This archival database has limited ease of use for three significant critical reasons.

First, the NIS has a website that explains the project, with each of the 20 individual questionnaires that make up the survey with questions, responses, and variables codes separate from the website where the data is housed. In order to determine the variables for a specific questionnaire in a section, I had to toggle between the two websites. Second, the NIS data related to each one of the 20 questionnaires was separated for downloading. Third, in order to use variables from different questionnaires it was necessary to download each questionnaire and combine the questionnaires using SPSS.

My research advisors and research assistant encouraged me to consider psychological disorders that were sub-threshold or comorbid with PTSD such as anxiety and depression. A review of the literature variables in the NIS database supported the use of depression-related variables. The current study used the demographics and heath questionnaire sections of the NIS. The demographic section had variables related to age, gender, military service, military service-connected disabilities, etc. The heath section of the NIS questionnaire included individual variables that, when combined, suggested depressive symptoms. Items selected from the health dataset met the criteria for depression. Items were as follows: D88 – "felt sad or depressed," D92 – "lost interest," D93 – "feel more tired," D94 – "loss of appetite," D95 – "have trouble falling asleep," D97 – "have trouble concentrating," D98 – "feel down on self," and D99 – "thinking about death."

Descriptive statistics were conducted to determine the number of military and non-military personnel in the sample (N=824); total number of participants (N=8,566); with years in active service in the military ranging from >1 year to 40 years; and gender of military participants (795 men and 29 women) (Mines, 2018). A G*Power analysis (Faul et.al., 2007) was conducted to determine the minimum sample size (N=220) for a χ^2 Test. A chi-square analysis was conducted to compare veteran immigrants (N=824) to a random sampling of non-veteran immigrants (N=824) on depressive items.

EVER SERVED IN ANY MILITARY and Clinical Depression Crosstabulation

Count

		Clinical Depression		
		No	Yes	Total
EVER SERVED IN ANY MILITARY	Yes	810	14	824
	No	799	25	824
Total		1609	39	1648

An independent chi-square test was performed to examine the relationship between military service and clinical depression. The relationship between these variables was not significant (χ^2 [1, N=1648] =3.18, p =.075). The frequency of clinical depression criteria symptoms was not significantly different between military and non-military participants.

Chi-Square Tests

	Value	df	Asymptotic Significance (2-sided)	Exact Sig. (2-sided)	Exact Sig. (1-sided)
Pearson Chi-Square	3.178ª	1	.075		
Continuity Correction	2.626	1	.105		
Likelihood Ratio	3.220	1	.073		
Fisher's Exact Test				.104	.052
Linear-by-Linear Association	3.176	1	.075		
N of Valid Cases	1648				

Those veterans who served from one to three years in the military reported the highest incidence of depression criteria symptoms. There was no significant difference between the depression symptoms reported by military veterans versus non-military. The majority of participants who were in the military in their country of origin were male, with the majority of service completed in one to three years. Those participants that completed one to three years in the military reported more depression symptoms than those who served four or more years. Those veterans who completed one to three years in the military were found to report more service-connected disabilities than those who served four or more years.

Further research should be conducted to determine the relationship between years of military service and depression among immigrants to the U.S. I will be conducting this research because of this research practicum. The difference between when I started the practicum and the present is that now there is growth. Back then, I was unsure about how and what to conduct research on. Now, I am actually the TA for the research practicum course and I am orienting and teaching other students how to use the NIS database. In the future, I hope to have statistically significant findings and publish the results in a peer-reviewed empirical research journal.

References

Faul, F., Erdfelder, E., Lang, A.-G., & Buchner, A. (2007). G*Power 3: A flexible statistical power analysis program for the social, behavioral, and biomedical sciences. *Behavior Research Methods, 39,* 175-191

Mines, S. (2018). Depression in Military Immigrants Living in the United States. Fielding Graduate University National Summer Session.

Possemato, K., Wade, M., Andersen, J., & Ouimette, P. (2010). The impact of PTSD, depression, and substance use disorders on disease burden and health care utilization among OEF/OIF veterans. *Psychological Trauma: Theory, Research, Practice, and Policy, 2,* 218-223. doi:10.1037/a0019236

Shalom, U. B., & Horenczyk, G. (2004). Cultural identity and adaptation in an assimilative setting: Immigrant soldiers from the former Soviet Union in Israel. *International Journal of Intercultural Relations, 28,* 461-479.

Trustees of Princeton University (2005). NIS- new immigrant survey. Retrieved from https://nis.princeton.edu/

About the Author

Shantay Mines is a clinical psychology doctoral student at Fielding Graduate University, expected to complete his doctorate in May of 2022. He has an Education Specialist (EdS) degree in Marriage and Family Therapy and is currently a Licensed Marriage and Family Therapist (LMFT) in Florida and Montana. Mr. Mines is a Florida Approved Supervisor for Marriage and Family Therapy and Mental Health Counseling interns. He is also a Clinical Fellow with the American Association for Marriage and Family Therapy. He currently works with combat veterans and active duty military for the Department of Veteran Affairs, Orlando Vet Center.

CHAPTER 28

CREATIVE LONGEVITY AND WISDOM: GENERATIVE AGING IN TIMES OF TRANSITION

**Connie Corley, PhD, Valerie Bentz, PhD,
David Blake Willis, PhD, and
Barbara Volger, PhD**
Fielding Graduate University

Generative Aging in Times of Transition

Today's world is demonstrably experiencing a major phenomenon that has received relatively little attention, and yet its implications are enormous for all of us. As societies age in the 21st century, one of the most incredible demographic features, following the example of Japan, is the rapid rise in the number of citizens 60 years of age and older. Not only has the percentage of these citizens changed as a larger part of the society, but many of these individuals have continued working, often in new and creative endeavors following retirement from an earlier career. The wisdom and creativity of this group of people is impressive, conferring a "longevity advantage" that needs to be better understood.

Creative Longevity and Wisdom at Fielding Graduate University was launched in 2004 as an initiative and later as a Doctoral Concentration of the School of Human and Organizational Development (now School of Leadership Studies)—fostering events, conferences, and collected papers (Bentz and Rogers, 2007)—plus recognition of 15 outstanding international scholars and over 30 Student and Alumni Fellows. Through the Concentration and with funding through Fielding's Institute for Social Innovation (ISI), these milestones of scholarship and practice have gained attention, as students, alumni, and faculty have received recognition for their research and practice in Creative Longevity and Wisdom (CLW). Many have presented internationally and published their work (e.g., Corley and Southam, 2018; Corley, Willis, Dobberteen, & von Baeyer, in press). Fielding has also become part of the Age-Friendly University international community through the efforts of members of the Concentration.

In this chapter, we describe the evolution and implementation of various aspects of Creative Longevity and Wisdom as an intentional community within Fielding where students and alumni have furthered their careers and the well-being of people in the second half of life, not only as a Concentration but as a process of acknowledging and engaging outstanding scholar-practitioners within CLW. Fielding Graduate University is an early example of an Age-Friendly University at the leading edge of change.

Evolution of the CLW Initiative

In 2004, Dr. Frank Jankovitz, a local Santa Barbara resident, made a generous donation to Fielding Graduate University to launch the Creative Longevity and Wisdom (CLW) initiative under the direction of Dr. Valerie Bentz, long-time Professor of Human and Organizational Development (HOD). Dr. Jankovitz had contributed much to the well-being of older adults in New York under Mayor Michael Bloomberg, where he spearheaded a creative arts program for older New Yorkers and established a symphony orchestra comprised of musicians advanced in age. Dr. Jankovitz's donation allowed the establishment of a fund to honor an Outstanding CLW Scholar-practitioner each year in the area of positive aging. The initiative involved both the Schools of HOD and Educational Leadership and Change (ELC), which are now together in the School of Leadership Studies. The late Dr. Jerry Nims from the School of Psychology was also engaged at the outset, especially focused on legal services to fight against elder exploitation and abuse. Students and alumni became active and funds to support Fellows and scholarships grew.

Valerie Bentz (L), and Frank Jankowitz (third from right) with CLW Fellows

The evolution of the CLW Concentration was dramatically enhanced by the presence and contributions of a range of leaders in gerontology, creativity, and transformation, especially the following visionaries: Harry "Rick" Moody (hereafter referred to as Rick Moody), who retired as the first head of educational initiatives under AARP and is the author of original and well-regarded textbooks in gerontology; George Vaillant of the Harvard Grant Study, regarded by many as the "gold standard" of longitudinal research; the intrepid Gene Cohen, co-founder of the National Center for Creative Aging, whose humor and emphasis on creativity even at an advanced age provided valuable encouragement to many artists, scholars, and others; and Connie Goldman, one of National Public Radio's key early voices on aging and its multiple dimensions for many years. Their works have been featured in course offerings, with our students having a first-hand opportunity to engage with these leading figures in generative aging. Rick, George, Gene, Connie (as we call them) and other CLW Outstanding Scholar-practitioners noted in the Appendix enthusiastically joined our seminars at Fielding's National Winter Session and Summer Session as well as Knowledge Areas (KAs) for student credit during various academic terms. Their formal lectures invigorated large audiences at Fielding, shining a light on the special potential of this reframing of aging.

In 2010, a proposal for a Doctoral Concentration grew out of the CLW initiative, first titled "Aging, Culture, and Society." The original name of "Creative Longevity and Wisdom" was restored in 2016. Along with the Concentration came Fielding's commitment to be the host organization for three years and a subsequent sponsor of the International Conferences on Positive Aging from 2009-2018. Faculty, students, and alumni have been actively engaged in planning and presenting workshops at these conferences. Rick Moody, a lead organizer of the conference series, became not only a Faculty Fellow at Fielding and one of our first CLW Outstanding Scholar-practitioners, but has since joined us for seminars and PhD Committee work as well, mentoring many members of our academic community. His monthly e-newsletter, *Human Values in Aging*, is now sponsored by CLW and distributed by Fielding.

CLW was part of the Institute for Social Innovation (ISI) at Fielding from the outset. ISI has supported intergenerational Social Transformation Projects spearheaded by CLW students and faculty and related research (see "Important Impacts" below). Beyond its influence within Fielding, the designation of Fielding as an Age-Friendly University expands our focus to this international community.

Creative Longevity and Wisdom as a Concentration

The goal of the Creative Longevity and Wisdom Concentration is to enhance knowledge and practice in areas concerning mid-life and older adults. The Concentration draws on various fields, helping students engage with their life experiences through phenomenological writing and in communities through ethnographic approaches. The study of wisdom development, creativity, and enhancement of longevity enhances that of the participants, as well, so that they in turn can bring this into their research and practice. Our student and alumni fellows as well as faculty members have contributed to multiple areas, including: Positive Aging; Caregiving and Caregivers; Hospice and Final Transitions; Intergenerational Engagement; Wise Aging; Encore Careers; and Social and Ecological Justice worldwide. CLW uniquely situates Fielding in the progressive dialogue around the critical role of elderhood in nurturing/sustaining the well-being of life and livelihood (http://www.fielding.edu/our-programs/doctoral-concentrations/creative-longevity-and-wisdom).

Creative Longevity and Wisdom: Outstanding Scholar-practitioners and Their Works

Since 2005, 15 leaders have been recipients of the Creative Longevity and Wisdom Outstanding Scholar-practitioner award. Ranging from visionaries and theorists in aging to esteemed elder authors (see Appendix), their contributions have been recognized annually in public forums such as the International Conference on Positive Aging, the International Association of Gerontology and Geriatrics World Congress, and the Open Your Heart in Paradise Retreat (under the auspices of the Love Serve Remember Foundation). Drs. George Vaillant and Rick Moody are among the award recipients who have also been part of workshops such as Crossing Borders (see manuscript by Willis et al., in this monograph) at National Sessions hosted semi-annually by Fielding.

L to R: Dr. Karen Fredriksen-Goldsen, Dr. Connie Corley, Dr. Mie Ohwa, and John Fitzgerald during a workshop on rhythm and music-making at IAGG (2016, http://www.fielding.edu/news/creative-longevity-wisdom-award/.)

CLW Award to Ram Dass in Maui, Hawai'i (2018)

Fielding as an Age-Friendly University

Fielding Graduate University was inducted as a member of the international Age-Friendly University community in 2018, joining over 30 other universities chosen since 2014 that see opportunities for momentum in new arenas. Going forward and in collaboration with other Age-Friendly Universities, we envision identifying ways for older adults to access graduate education economically. We would also like to build on the concept of age-diverse regional clusters, which are the basis of educational offerings in the face-to-face aspect of Fielding's distributed model, to bring together non-matriculated older adult learners in selected geographic areas with our students and alumni.

In this process, opportunities are envisioned to reduce the social isolation and loneliness that characterizes the lives of a growing number of older adults in Western and other cultures. Mutual mentoring across generations is a component that is already part of several Social Transformation Projects that Fielding has supported; thus there is a natural extension here of CLW's work. Further engagement and support of Emeriti Faculty and our CLW Outstanding Scholar-practitioners to be part of regional cluster events and Fielding National Sessions is envisioned. Fielding is also well situated to build on our international presence at professional conferences and workshops (e.g., octogenarian alumna Dr.

Evelyn Beck presented at a sociology conference on community building through Sacred Circle Dance in Krakow, Poland, in 2017).

Creative Longevity and Wisdom: Important Impacts

Through participating in workshops at National Sessions and multi-day Intensives, and engaging in conferences as participants and presenters, students have experienced seminal advances in their goals and careers. For example, Ryan McCarty started the doctoral program in his mid-20s and decided to focus on the Human Development degree with the CLW Concentration to further his interest in working with older adults:

> Through this concentration, I met Dr. Rick Moody, who in conjunction with Dr. Connie Corley, helped me to learn about the Political Economy of Aging and Critical Gerontology. In my interactions with Drs. Moody and Corley, attending and participating in Positive Aging and Certified Senior Advisors conferences, I have met professionals from all walks of life who want to help older adults in various facets including placement and referral, financial planning, real estate, and elder law.

> Talking with Drs. Connie Corley and Rick Moody has helped me to find ways to hone my desire to help older adults and their families. I have explored many different facets of the aging realm and have worked to refine my ideas through my interactions with them as well as the people they recommend for me to meet at the conferences such as Certified Senior Advisors and Positive Aging. All of these discussions have helped to illuminate the problems within the field of gerontology as well as the long-term care industry, which has greatly impacted the direction of my research.

Along with Drs. Corley and Moody, Dr. David Blake Willis
has helped me both in my networking to meet the other
professionals as well as helping me learn the fundamental
concepts and how to present them in research to better
guide my future business and help to improve my various
projects and my dissertation. Without this program and
concentration, I wouldn't be where I am at today: looking
at research and using it to start a business where I am
able to take all my courses and my own research to help
older adults and their families to make decisions for the
best long-term care options possible. (Ryan McCarty,
personal communication, November 2018)

Theresa Southam joined Fielding in the doctoral program in mid-life
"to explore what I might accomplish in my second half of life" and has had
multiple opportunities to learn and advance her interests:

Thanks to my mentor, Dr. Connie Corley, who is also
the CLW lead, in the first 18 months of graduate school
I attended the International Association of Gerontology
and Geriatrics (IAGG) World Congress and co-authored
an article with her (Corley and Southam, 2018). Inspired
by the contacts I made through Dr. Corley, I applied
for a Social Transformation Grant (STG) to start up an
Intergenerational Leadership and Learning Chapter
with my College (Selkirk College in Nelson, British
Columbia) and in my community that has resulted in
four intergenerational projects: international exchange;
educational technology training; community support for
international students; and a climate change initiative.
The grant provided support for an older adult from our
Learning in Retirement group and myself to travel to
Penn State University and be trained by Dr. Matt Kaplan

(who I met at IAGG World Congress) in intergenerational practices.

Dr. David Blake Willis and Dr. Valerie Bentz helped me to conduct original, IRB-approved research on transcendent generativity in older adults that resulted in a presentation to the Fielding Social Innovation and Transformative Phenomenology Conference, in Surrey, British Columbia, and a poster presented at the Fielding Summer Session (which won Honourable Mention). I also presented two posters at the Canadian Association for Gerontology in 2018. My project as a Fellow of the Marie Fielder Center, *We're Not Done Yet: Older Peoples' Experiences with Initiating and Leading Intergenerational Projects*, is another step in my journey, and also involves CLW Fellow and alumna Dr. Barbara Volger. These activities and my coursework have given me an excellent entrée into the arenas of breaking ageist norms and supporting older adults to be leaders in society. (Theresa Southam, personal communication, November, 2018)

Dr. Holly Bardutz, whose dissertation "Examining the Experience and Impact of a Regular Exercise Program on a Group of Canadian Women Over the Age Of 65" (2016) describes how her connection with the concentration has spearheaded numerous developments in her career:

In January 2017, I graduated from Fielding, where I was part of the CLW Concentration. While going through my program, when it was time to choose an External Examiner for my dissertation, I reached out to the founding director of the Brain Centre at the University of British Columbia, Dr. Max Cynader, to ask him if he would be willing to be the External Examiner on my committee. He agreed. (Dr. Cynader is also a Brain Research Chair in Canada.

He is in the Medical Hall of Fame for Brain Research in Canada; he has been inducted into the Order of Canada, and the Order of British Columbia).

It was a wonderful opportunity to have Max on my committee for my PhD and it gets even better! Since meeting him and working with him on my dissertation, he contacted me and asked me if I would like to collaborate with him and other researchers on further research. Of course, I said yes. Now I am the lead researcher with a team of five brain researchers on a project that is looking at whether or not the brain is affected when a person has a heart attack. I am now employed as a full-time brain research associate at the University of Regina in Regina, Saskatchewan, Canada doing cutting-edge research. I have also designed, currently teach, and have copyrighted Brain Health and Fitness Classes as a result of what I learned during my PhD program. These amazing opportunities opened up for me as result of being at Fielding and of being a part of the Creative Longevity and Wisdom Concentration. (Holly Bardutz, personal communication, November, 2018)

Similarly, Dr. Eileen Cleary examined "Older Workers' Experience of Stereotype Threat" (2016), noting the importance of contacts made through the CLW concentration:

While at Fielding, I was afforded the opportunity to not only study the works of some great minds in our field, but I was able to meet them in person. I had this unique opportunity because I was part of the Creativity Longevity and Wisdom concentration in the HOD program, where I met people like George Vaillant, Connie Goldman, and Rick Moody at conferences on aging as well as at Fielding functions. Having that personal connection with these special people and the deep network of those within Fielding expanded my appreciation and understanding of the field.

When it came time to reach outside for an External Examiner for my dissertation, I found my request attended to promptly and I must attribute that to the connection to the CLW concentration. It was hard to contain my excitement when Dr. Erdman Palmore, a prominent figure on Ageism, agreed to be my External Examiner. Today, as a graduate building my practice around the aging workforce, I truly believe these connections will serve me well. (Eileen Cleary, personal communication, November, 2018)

Other opportunities to present work and publish have evolved from the Crossing Borders workshops at National Sessions, and an Intensive that emerged from the *Cruzando Puentes* (Crossing Bridges) Social Transformation Project, which resulted in a symposium of faculty and students presenting at the 2018 Society for Applied Anthropology conference and a publication in the "Resilience: Navigating Challenges of Modern Life" Fielding Monograph (Corley, Willis, Dobberteen, & von Baeyer, 2019).

Since its inception in 2004, Creative Longevity and Wisdom has spawned numerous projects and dissertations. Hence, Fielding has situated the study of adult development broadly and prominently, not only in terms of topics of study but also in fostering transformational learning among members of its own community of adult learners.

Conclusion

Fielding Graduate University's Creative Longevity and Wisdom contributions over more than a decade are a continuation of the "sea change" noted by the late Gene Cohen (Cohen, 2006) that shifted away from a problem-based view of aging, largely rooted in ageism, to seeing growth and development well into the later years of life. While the concepts of positive aging and creative aging may suggest a less than realistic view of later life, conscious aging (Corley & Southam, 2018), which encompasses end-of-life and spiritual dimensions of growing older, is also an arena where CLW has offered space for research, practice, and praxis to thrive.

Whether at workshops at Fielding National Sessions, or in the context of international conferences, creative expression is integrated and nurtured. For example, Dr. Susan Mazer (the first graduate of the Concentration) along with her husband Dallas Smith, are accomplished musicians who have brought their inspiration into Fielding gatherings and, together as business partners, created the groundbreaking Healing HealthCare Systems, bringing uplifting music and images to people (called The C.A.R.E. Channel) in over 1,000 healthcare settings globally.

Dallas Smith and Dr. Susan Mazer Smith

Fielding's contributions to the development and expression of creativity and wisdom, and the cultivation of and impact on longevity, are increasingly recognized through its affiliated students, alumni, faculty, and staff within academic circles and beyond. Through highlighting the works of our CLW Outstanding Scholar-practitioners such as Dr. Mary Catherine Bateson, who proposes Adulthood II, where active wisdom is cultivated and identity reevaluated (Bateson, 2010), Fielding provides a forum for dialog and the engagement of progressive viewpoints. Students thrive from the rich and direct engagement with visionaries in later life exploration and, along with alumni and faculty, bring the voices and visions of potential throughout life to wider audiences.

We close with the wise words of artist and Holocaust survivor Mrs. Erica Leon, born in Hungary in 1921 and featured in numerous presentations and publications (e.g., Corley, 2010a and 2010b) from her memoir, archived at the Los Angeles Museum of the Holocaust:

> I wrote my memories for my grandchildren, Eve and Akos. I want them to remember that there is hope always in life. There is music and nature—in these you will never be disappointed. Life is full of wonderful things along with the tragic ones.
>
> You just have to discover the beauty and love in life. There is no sunshine without shade. And no shade without sunshine. Everything is gray when we don't have both of them.
>
> We cannot enjoy constant happiness. We're only aware of the difference when we compare it with our troubled times. The shell has to suffer to produce the pearl—and so it is with our soul. Suffering makes it valuable.
>
> Many times what seems to be bad turns out to be for our benefit. We just have to wait and see. (Leon, 2002, p. 176)

References

Bardutz, H. A. (2017). *Women, exercise and neurological changes: A qualitative study* (Order No. 10254160). ProQuest Dissertations Publishing, 10254160.

Bateson, M. C. (2010). *Composing a further life: The age of active wisdom*. New York, NY: Knopf.

Bentz, V., & Rogers, K. (Eds.). (2007). *Creative longevity and wisdom: Collected papers*. Santa Barbara: Fielding Graduate University.

Cleary, E. J. (2017). *Older workers' experience of stereotype threat*. Fielding Graduate University, ProQuest Dissertations Publishing, 0258034.

Corley, C., & Southam, T. (2018). Positive aging perspectives and a new paradigm: Foray (4A) into aging. *CSA Journal, 71*(2), 46-50.

Corley, C., Willis, D. B., Dobberteen, D., & von Baeyer, E. (2019). Crossing bridges, building resilience through communitas. *Resilience: Navigating Challenges in Modern Life*. Santa Barbara, CA: Fielding University Press.

Cohen, G. D. (2006). Research on creativity and aging: The positive impact of the arts on health and illness. *Generations, 30*(1), 7-15.

Leon, E. (2002). *Her story in history*. Unpublished memoir, archived at the Los Angeles Museum of the Holocaust.

Appendix

FIELDING GRADUATE UNIVERSITY CREATIVE LONGEVITY AND WISDOM OUTSTANDING SCHOLAR-PRACTITIONER AWARDEES

2018 – **Mirabai Bush and Ram Dass**

2017 – **Karen Fredriksen-Goldsen, MSW, PhD**

2016 – **Elizabeth Isele**

2015 – **Lars Tornstam, PhD**

2014 – **Lawrence Ferlinghetti, PhD**

2013 – **James Birren, PhD**

2012 – **Richard Leider, MA**

2011 – **Mary Catherine Bateson, PhD**

2010 – **Fernando Torres-Gil, PhD**

2009 – **Connie Goldman**

2008 – **Gene Cohen, MD, PhD**

2007 – **Harry "Rick" Moody, PhD**

2006 – **Gisela Labouvie-Vief, PhD**

2005 – **George Vaillant, MD**

About the Authors

Valerie Malhotra Bentz, MSSW, PhD, is Professor of Human and Organization Development, Fielding Graduate University, where she served as Associate Dean for Research. Her current interests include somatics, phenomenology, social theory, consciousness development, and Vedantic theories of knowledge. Her books include *Contemplative social research: Caring for self, being, and lifeworld*, with Vincenzo M. B. Giogino; *Transformative phenomenology: Changing ourselves, lifeworlds and professional practice*, with David Rehorick; *Mindful inquiry in social research*, with Jeremy Shapiro, and *Becoming mature: Childhood ghosts and spirits in adult life*. She also authored a philosophical novel, *Flesh and mind: The time travels of Dr. Victoria Von Dietz*. She is a Fellow in Contemplative Practice of the American Association of Learned Societies. Valerie was editor of *Phenomenology and the Human Sciences* (1994–98). She has served as president and board member of the Clinical Sociology Association, the Sociological Practice Association, and the Society for Phenomenology and the Human Sciences. She founded and co-directed an action research team and center in Mizoram, India. Valerie was co-founder of the Creative Longevity and Wisdom program at Fielding. She is the Director of the Doctoral Concentration in Somatics, Phenomenology, and Communicative Leadership (SPCL). She has 20 years' experience as a psychotherapist, and is a certified yoga teacher and massage therapist. She is a member of the board of the Carpinteria Valley Association, an environmental activist group. She also plays bassoon and piano.

Connie Corley, MSW, MA, PhD, has a long history in the fields of gerontology/geriatrics as a graduate of University of Michigan, Ann Arbor. Dr. Corley leads the doctoral concentration in Creative Longevity and Wisdom in the School of Leadership Studies. She is Professor Emeritus at California State University, Los Angeles. A Fellow of both the Gerontological Society of America and the Academy of Gerontology in Higher Education, Dr. Corley has engaged in multiple programs as a mentor and leader in curriculum development. Work involving creativity in later life (emerging out of a national study of Holocaust survivors, led by Roberta Greene, PI) led to the Experience, Engagement, and Expression model of creativity based on life course experiences. *Cruzando Puentes* ("Crossing Bridges") was launched in 2015 as an intergenerational and intercultural mutual mentoring program in diverse communities of Los Angeles. Dr. Corley co-hosts and produces a radio show (www. ExperienceTalks.org), interviewing people seasoned in life.

Dr. Barbara J. Volger, PhD, is currently living in Florida and is Honorary Faculty in the Psychology department at the University of Liverpool and the University of Roehampton, both in the UK and online. She also mentors several Psychology dissertation students at the University of Liverpool. She is working with the University of South Florida Osher Lifelong Learning program, teaching workshops on the development of myth and mandalas, and is doing research on the experience of creativity in later life based on the Jungian concept of aging. In addition to her work and research she is an avid nature photographer and works with symbols from dreams to create photographs and mandalas. She continues to bring the concept of creative longevity to senior communities in the Tampa Bay area of Florida.

Dr. David Blake Willis, PhD, is Professor of Anthropology and Education at Fielding Graduate University and Professor Emeritus of Anthropology, Soai Buddhist University, Osaka, Japan. He taught and did research at the University of Oxford and was Visiting Professor at the University of Washington and Grinnell College. His interests in anthropology, sustainability, social justice, and immigration come from 38 years of living in traditional cultural systems in Japan and South India. His scholarly work is on transformational leadership and education, human development in transnational contexts, the creolization of cultures, transcultural communities, and Dalit/Gandhian liberation movements in South India. His publications include *World Cultures: The Language Villages (Leading, Learning, and Teaching on the Global Frontier)* with Walter Enloe (2017); *Sustainability Leadership: Integrating Values, Meaning, and Action* with Fred Steier and Paul Stillman (2015); *Reimagining Japanese Education: Borders, Transfers, Circulations, and the Comparative* with Jeremy Rappleye (2011); *Transcultural Japan: At the Borders of Race, Gender, and Identity* with Stephen Murphy-Shigematsu (2007); and *Japanese Education in Transition 2001: Radical Perspectives on Cultural and Political Transformation* with Satoshi Yamamura (2002).

CHAPTER 29

THE STORY OF FIELDING UNIVERSITY PRESS

Jean-Pierre Isbouts, DLitt
Fielding Graduate University

This monograph is dedicated to Fielding's 45th anniversary, a major milestone for an institution that pioneered adult-centered doctoral education in the 1970s. But the year 2019 also marks another important date: the fifth anniversary of Fielding University Press. Over the past five years, the press has published 18 books, authored by its faculty, students, and alumni, as well as scholars throughout the world. Over 60 graduates of Fielding's PhD programs have been able to publish the results of their dissertation research in our peer-reviewed monographs on a variety of subjects, including Clinical Psychology, Media Psychology, Human and Organizational Development, Education, and Infant and Early Childhood Health.

Until recently, however, the idea that a small, specialized institution like Fielding could have its own dedicated press was unfathomable. Traditional forms of print publishing are woefully expensive. For example, this model requires a printer to create offset plates, which is only cost-effective with print runs of at least 2,500 copies or more. And when those copies are printed, they have to be stored at a major distribution center—such as Ingram's—ready to be shipped, by truck, to book stores and libraries across the country, and around the world. Needless to say, the associated costs of transportation, storing, and shelving are steep, not to speak of the carbon footprint involved. This is why university presses have always been associated with large universities that can afford to maintain them, including the provision of a dedicated staff tasked with editorial, production, and publishing functions.

The Birth of the Digital Revolution

As a scholar-practitioner, however, I was fortunate to have witnessed the birth of many technologies that would ultimately upstage the traditional publishing model. In 1981, shortly after completing my doctoral research at Avery (Columbia University, New York) with a work on the American 19th century architectural firm of Carrère & Hastings, I was given a rare opportunity: to produce a documentary about a fellow Dutchman, the artist Vincent Van Gogh. Of course, there was a catch (there always is). This program was to serve as a showpiece for a new technology developed by Philips and Sony: an optical disk known as the laser videodisc. In other words, as its *raison d'être* the design of the program had to exploit the interactive capabilities of the device as much as possible. The term "interactive" was still quite novel then, because other than videogames, there was no video-based technology that allowed users to control the narrative sequence of the story. The world was still ruled by VHS videocassettes.

In response, I designed the disc in five video segments of six minutes each, all devoted to one of Vincent's artistic periods. In between, I programmed a visual catalog of still frames, thus enabling users to step through the key paintings and drawings of the period they'd just seen, using their remote control. In addition, I produced two separate audio channels: channel 1 featured the film's voice-over, while channel 2 played a narrated selection of Vincent's letters to his brother Theo, cued to the featured period. In that way, the viewer could choose between two perspectives: the modern scholarly view of Vincent's art, or the artist's own thoughts, often expressed in intimate detail. And finally, as the film's director I got to work with Leonard Nimoy, who served as the program's host.

The production team of *Vincent Van Gogh Revisited* on location at the asylum of St. Rémy in France in 1981, seated with the film's host and narrator, Leonard Nimoy (I'm still sporting a mustache).

The disc was released in 1982, in both Europe and the United States and, to my surprise, it made an impact. It had multiple pressings, including a release by the prestigious Criterion Collection. Its success sealed my lifelong career goal as a scholar-practitioner: to try to bridge the vast gulf between academic scholarship and modern media—a gulf that continues to this day. During a recent lecture at Harvard, I argued that for modern scholars to be relevant as change agents, we *must* embrace the media that have been the catalyst for so many social changes in our world, and learn to publish on those platforms ourselves.

The *Van Gogh* release enabled me to stay closely involved with new media, including the launch of the interactive CD and CD-ROM. In the late 1980s and early 1990s, both Media Psychology's Garry Hare and I were involved in the development of a large catalog of digital CDs that covered the gamut of human interests, from films to music, from videogames to art, from travel to encyclopedic reference. In 1994, I used that experience to set up my own practice in Los Angeles, and work with leading publishers to tackle the brave new world of digital media.

For example, I worked with Charlton Heston on a CD-ROM series called *Voyage Through the Bible* that seamlessly blended film footage of him on location in Israel with 3-D reconstructions of ancient biblical sites. This led to a project for Hollywood studio Castle Rock Entertainment, where we produced an educational game about Shakespeare's *Hamlet*, using footage from Kenneth Branagh's Academy Award-winning film starring Kate Winslet, Derek Jacobi and Julie Christie. Disney then engaged us to produce a multimedia encyclopedia about Walt Disney, using much of the same technology.

But when it came to traditional print publishers, I was surprised to find that many major houses did not have a clue about digital technology or how it was about to disrupt their business. And yet, the omens were clear to see. Starting in the early 2000s with Napster, streaming music would eventually lay waste to the music CD business. Next, streaming video all but obliterated the DVD rental industry. Publishing was undoubtedly going to be next, after Amazon introduced the Kindle, and Apple launched the iPad; but most major publishers resolutely continued to focus on their traditional business. One of my doctoral students, Hannah Lee, investigated this problem for her dissertation. She found that the reason why the publishing sector remained in denial for so long was because of the strict hierarchical model of its organizations, abetted by countless mergers and acquisitions: new, innovative ideas from junior managers rarely made it up to the C-suite.

Online Publishing

The development of Print on Demand (POD) technology, however, would radically change the way books are produced, published, and sold around the world. A POD system is essentially a book printing plant, collapsed into a single machine. On one end, the technician loads the digital file of the book; and on the other, a finished book rolls out. Of course, it isn't quite as simple as that but, in essence, the technology allows a publisher to produce and distribute a book using the just-in-time model: we don't print a copy unless we know there is a customer who wants it. Therefore, no need for expensive volume runs, storage space, and laborious logistics.

The company that embraced POD technology and then set out to transform the industry is, of course, Amazon. Amazon's idea was to merge this technology with a national (and eventually international) distribution system that allowed a book copy to be printed on demand, and then deliver this copy directly to the customer, without the intervention (and the sales margin) of a retail bookstore. In the case of an electronic book (or e-book) version, the model is even more disruptive. Once a customer places an order over the Internet, the book is delivered instantly to the user's iPad, Samsung, or Kindle device, without the need for any printing or shipping.

The impact of these models on the publishing business has been immense—and, as some have argued, much more devastating than the impact of digital music and digital video on their respective retail sectors. Scores of independent bookstores have gone out of business. One of the largest book chains in the country, Borders, was forced to close its doors as well, while the fate of another major chain—Barnes & Noble—still hangs in the balance.

Disruptive innovation is often hard and painful. It is hard on the owners who lost their family bookstores, just as it was hard on the Blockbuster, Borders, and Virgin franchisees, and the countless other retailers and their employees who were terminated because of the shift from retail to online distribution.

But at the same time, this revolution inspired the birth of a whole new world of publishing. Just over a decade ago, most of the book business was controlled by the so-called "Big Five," large international conglomerates that are themselves often owned by global media companies. Today, thousands of new start-up imprints are flourishing, publishing books on a wide variety of topics that would never have seen the light of day under the old model.

Just as this revolution was taking shape, I was involved in several publishing projects that tested the boundaries of the electronic book (or e-book) experience. For a British publisher, we designed a software extension of the EPUB format (used on all devices except the Kindle) that allowed dynamic text to flow around large images—something the EPUB standard itself did not allow. Working with Apple, we also produced one of the first e-books with embedded video shorts in the text, shot on location in the Near East, based on my book *From Moses to Muhammad: The Shared Origins of the Three Great Faiths.*

The Idea for Fielding University Press

Given all of these new publishing models, I wondered in 2013 whether Fielding would be interested in developing a university press activity of its own. I am the product of a very traditional university, one in which doctoral education is inextricably linked with original research—such as students working with a professor on a publication. And having spent, at that time, some 10 years teaching in Fielding's School of Psychology, I knew the tremendous creativity and depth of the dissertations that our students were capable of writing. I also knew that many of our graduates struggled to get the results of their dissertation published in peer-review journals. In most cases, the problem was not the quality of their findings, but the fact that there were too many PhDs vying for too little space in academic journals.

Serendipitously, this moment coincided with the appointment of one of our own, Dr. Katrina Rogers, as President of Fielding Graduate University. Her arrival brought a wave of fresh ideas to our C-suite, particularly in the wake of the Great Recession that had eroded much of the academic landscape. When I presented the idea for an academic press activity, she immediately saw the opportunity to promote Fielding as a leading center of original research—something that few of our competitors in the distributed learning space can claim. The result was a prototype, a monograph called *Social Change in the Modern Workplace*, edited by Dorothy Agger-Gupta, which brought together the results of six student dissertations. Each graduate was invited to write an academic article that summarized the results of the research. A peer review panel, consisting of Fielding faculty, reviewed each article and gave feedback. The final drafts were then collated in a manuscript, with an introduction by Dorothy. Thanks to the digital development process that we had perfected for our commercial clients, we were able to design, produce, and publish the book in less than three months.

Social Change has served as the template for FUP's publishing process ever since, even though we continue to tweak it in every way possible. For example, while the POD model has made the actual publishing and distribution process much more affordable, we have also implemented many digital changes in the development process itself. Most of our authors think that when their manuscript is finished, the book is done— but actually, that is when much of the work begins. In fact, producing a book is not unlike the production of a film, or the performance of a music ensemble; many different talents need to work together to produce the final result.

The first step is the review of the manuscript by the designated editor, to ensure that the future book meets our standard of academic quality. Once it has passed this process, the manuscript is handed off to a professional copy editor. "Editing" – the work of an editor—refers to content; copy-editing, on the other hand, refers to the fine detail of checking spelling, syntax, and grammar. Copy-editing is a laborious process, which is why we must schedule a copy editing "slot" well in advance. Sometimes, the copy editor has questions about a passage, which are then routed back to the author. Once a copy editor delivers the text, the manuscript is "locked." No changes are allowed from this point, unless they involve major errors that would damage the integrity of the text.

The locked manuscript is next handed to an InDesign artist. This individual is responsible for converting the text, usually formatted as an 8x10-inch document in Word, into beautifully flowing layouts that are sized 6x9 inches—the standard format in the U.S. for softcover trade books. This process requires great artistry to ensure that headers, paragraph breaks, figures, and images are all properly sited on the page, even though their position has changed due to the transition from 8x10 to 6x9. The very page that you are reading right now, for example, was created in Adobe InDesign. Unfortunately, InDesign is a very unforgiving program, so any changes to the text at this point are very time-consuming and therefore expensive. That is why it is so important that the editor and copy-editor check the text carefully before it is put into production.

In the olden days, the layout process produced a huge stack of printed pages, known as *galleys*, which were then routed to the editor for review. Fortunately, today the InDesign artist can simply produce a PDF, which I then use to check the text—page by page—to ensure that no artifacts or errors were introduced in the process. I usually find a number of problems, both large and small, which I report back to the InDesign artist in an email. Once these changes are implemented, a new PDF is produced, and so the cycle continues until we are all satisfied that the digital "image" of the book is flawless.

In the meantime, I have been working with another artist, who is responsible for cover design. A cover is hugely important, for it literally "sells" the concept of the book in a visual sense. For all of our monographs (i.e., collections of dissertation research) we use a uniform black border design, which allows for a unique image in the center. For our autographs (books published by faculty and scholars worldwide), we design an entirely original cover. Typically, we will go through a number of source images before deciding which ones are most suitable for the book. For our publication of monograph #8, *Veteran and Family Integration*, edited by Bart Buechner and Miguel Guilarte, I was struck by the photo of a young child hugging her father, a returning veteran. We were able to license the photo, and it now graces the cover of the volume—thus perfectly exemplifying the intent of the book.

As both the InDesign and Photoshop artists near the final version of the book, it is time to prepare for publication. Because of our distribution agreement with Amazon, as a publisher we are provided with the tools to

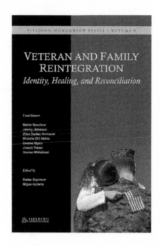

create the page that will eventually appear on the Amazon website. This includes, of course, a description of the book, but it also involves a choice of the BISAC code (the system by which the industry categorizes books) and the ISBN code, by which the Library of Congress and the rest of the publishing world can retrieve information about the book. Because we are an independent publisher, we have access to our own list of ISBN codes. Any additional information that can help users in deciding to purchase the book is also included, such as reviews and "quotes." Quotes are very important in publishing, for they provide an endorsement of sorts—particularly if the quote is from a recognized expert in the field. That is why we always encourage our authors to seek quotes from their scholarly network.

When all the elements are in place, we submit the cover and the PDF galleys to the printer. This is usually a tense moment, because there can always be slight discrepancies—sometimes as much as a tenth of an inch—that can prompt a design to be returned. But after five years, we are getting pretty good at this, so most books are accepted by the printer for processing.

The last step is a proof copy. No book is published until we have a chance to review the actual printed copy and ensure that there are no errors or technical defects of any kind. To do so, we order one copy for us, and one copy for the Provost. This was Gerry Porter, who supervised our press activity until his untimely passing in November of 2018. Today, it is Monique Snowden, our Provost and Senior Vice President, who receives a proof copy of every book that is published. To date, we have rejected three proof copies for a variety of reasons. Most had to do with printing errors; in one case, we rejected the quality of the color image on the cover. Usually, the printer is very amenable to resolving the problem to our satisfaction.

Author Valerie Bentz with FUP editor Jean-Pierre Isbouts at the publication of Valerie's book *Contemplative Social Research*, which contains contributions from 10 scholars around the world.

And then, when all is perfectly in place, we hit the "Publish!" button and the book is published. Its Amazon page will pop up about two or three days later. And our contributors are now published authors.

From the very beginning, Dr. Rogers and I agreed that our press needed to be governed by Open Access principles. Open Access is a movement that took root in the wake of the Great Recession, when Elsevier—which controls over 40% of the world's academic journals—decided to raise its prices. In response, a group of scholars from this country's leading universities staged a protest, and embraced the idea of publishing research through "Open Access" channels. In short, it means that research should be shared at the lowest possible cost, and without any of the usual barriers, such as journal subscriptions. If published by a traditional publisher, for example, our monographs would probably be priced at $79.95—the standard cost of works of original academic research. But instead, our printed books are priced at $19.95, and e-book versions are priced at $9.95. Of course, it is more difficult to break even at such prices, let alone make a profit, but that was never our intent. The mission of Fielding University Press is to share the fruits of its scholarly community on a global scale, maximizing its accessibility for students, scholars, and practitioners worldwide—and thus perpetuating Fielding's reputation as a leading center of original research.

References

Heston, C., & Isbouts, Jean-Pierre. (1998). *Charlton Heston's Hollywood: A History of Post-War American Cinema.* GoodTimes Publishing.

Isbouts, Jean-Pierre (Dir). (1982). *Van Gogh Revisited.* North American Philips and The Criterion Collection.

Isbouts, Jean-Pierre (Dir). (1996). *Charlton Heston's Voyage Through the Bible,* Vols. 1 and 2. GoodTimes and Agamemnon Films.

Isbouts, Jean-Pierre (Dir). (1997). *Hamlet: A Murder Mystery.* Castle Rock Entertainment and EMME.

Isbouts, Jean-Pierre (Dir). (1999). *Walt Disney: An Intimate History of the Man and His Magic.* Disney Interactive.

Isbouts, Jean-Pierre. (2011). *From Moses to Muhammad: The Shared Origins of the Three Great Faiths* (Multimedia e-book). Apple iTunes:https://itunes.apple.com/us/book/from-moses-to-muhammad-enhanced-edition/id409918977?mt=11

Isbouts, Jean-Pierre. (2016). "The Digital Scholar: Embracing New Media in the Pursuit of Scholarly Excellence." *Proceedings of the Fifth 21st Century Academic Forum at Harvard,* Vol. 11, No. 1, pp. 41-47.

Lee, Hannah. (2017). *Adaptation or Extinction: Organizational Change and Digital Disruption of Traditional Trade Book Publishers.* Unpublished dissertation draft.

To see the Fielding University Press catalog, please visit https://www.
fielding.edu/universitypress/.

About the Author

Dr. Jean-Pierre Isbouts is a humanities scholar, *National Geographic*
author, and award-winning filmmaker, specializing in the art and
archaeology of the Mediterranean Basin. A doctoral professor at Fielding
Graduate University in Santa Barbara, California, he gained worldwide
renown with his 2006 book *The Biblical World,* which became an
international bestseller and is now in its fourth printing. This success
led to a series of *National Geographic* books, including the bestsellers *In
the Footsteps of Jesus* (2011), *The Story of Christianity* (2014), and *The
Archaeology of the Bible* (2016). In 2013, Dr. Isbouts authenticated a
canvas discovered in a Swiss vault as Leonardo's first version of the *Mona
Lisa*, predating the Louvre version by at least seven years. In 2016, he
discovered that a copy of the *Last Supper* fresco in Milan, which has hung
in a Belgian monastery for 450 years, was actually painted by Leonardo
and his workshop for the French king Louis XII. These discoveries led to
two TV specials airing on the PBS network, *The Search for the Last Supper*
and *The Search for the Mona Lisa*, which Isbouts hosted and directed.
His most recent publications include *National Geographic's The 50 Most
Influential People in the Bible* (2018) and *The Da Vinci Legacy* (Spring
2019), which reconstructs the amazing arc of how da Vinci, who died as
a virtual recluse in France, became the pop icon and top-selling artist he
is today. As a musicologist, Dr. Isbouts has produced recordings by the
Los Angeles Chamber Orchestra, the Amsterdam Baroque Orchestra, and
other ensembles and soloists.

AFTERWORD

Pam McLean, PhD and CEO
Hudson Institute of Coaching
Katrina S. Rogers, PhD and President
Fielding Graduate University

Our 45th anniversary year offers an opportunity for an institution like Fielding to engage in asking some transformational thinking of our own. It is a time of celebration, self-assessment, reflection, and action, not unlike Mezirow's phases for transformational learning. Fielding has many founders, people who carried the germ of an idea and turned it into a reality: a doctoral institution that soon added master's and certificates with an excellent reputation for graduating clinicians, educators, and organizational leaders. Frederic Hudson, the originator of the concept and our first President, inspired generations of Fielding students with his commitment to empowering their dreams through a transformative education. Creating the educational container based on the concept of adult learning is what Fielding does best, and has done for these many decades.

Pam McLean, Frederic's partner for 37 years, currently leads the Hudson Institute of Coaching, which she and Frederic founded in 1987. The Hudson Institute is well known for providing coaching services to organizations, and for training masterful leadership coaches around the globe. The vision for Hudson parallels that of Fielding, although in Hudson's learning container, leadership coaches frequently already possess advanced degrees. Hudson-trained leadership coaches are immersed in a transformative learning journey that allows them to engage in developmental work with leaders. The Hudson Institute's evolution from the early days of coaching, often termed 'the wild west' to today's mature understanding of all that is required to engage in masterful developmental coaching, mirrors Fielding's own journey of innovation and reinvention. At Hudson, there is an emphasis on developing in coaches the ability to look both inward, to their own internal landscape, as well as outward, to shifts in the human and cultural landscape at large. Like Fielding Graduate University, the Hudson Institute is on the forefront of developing leaders who think in *global* terms about their sense of purpose and their vision for what's possible in today's particularly challenging times. In many ways, these Hudson and Fielding are sisters and kindred spirits both rooted in adult learning principles.

In the modern age, the United States was one of the first countries to invent the idea of public education. The realization that an educated citizenry, or at least a literate one, was essential to the flourishing of democratic traditions has been a constant in our society for many centuries. Fielding Graduate University, born out of one of the many progressive movements in American education, is simply one expression of the diversity of the sector; a diversity that reflects the richness of our varied population and its' needs as well as the variety of the offerings available to the members of our society.

Today, much like our birth year of 1974, higher education finds itself in a period of re-invention. Discussions related to cost, access, and relevance abound, whether in the executive boardrooms of universities, conference agendas of the national associations, or in the trade journals. There are now mega universities with many thousands of students, universities that are entirely online, for profit colleges, for profit and non-profit systems running diverse institutions all across the country, institutions with international partners and owners, and small institutes with focused missions. Mergers and acquisitions, once unheard of in the sector, are becoming much more common. Within all this proliferation is also a period of consolidation as smaller institutions team up to deliver education more cost-effectively, and larger systems cooperate across their missions to share operational costs.

Within this context, Fielding is still doing what it always did—graduate scholar-practitioners in the social sciences ready to take on society's greatest challenges. Now these many years later, Fielding is still the place that focuses exclusively on graduate education for the learner willing to step up, confront the intellectual challenges of a rigorous curriculum, and generate research and knowledge that informs our society and contributes to making a positive social difference in the service of society.

Like the Hudson Institute, Fielding continues to develop nimble leaders and coaches helping to shape new models for learning, leadership and living in our interconnected world with a sense of meaning and a commitment to having a beneficial impact in our work. As we look to the future, Fielding's mission endures. A great society deserves to be supported by a strong educational sector—one that is diverse, inclusive, and succeeds in preparing people for the complexities of the modern age. In this, Fielding does well and will continue to be a contributor, one among many, and one that stands out. Onward to our 50th!

About the Editor

Katrina S. Rogers, PhD, is President of Fielding Graduate University. As faculty, she has taught in her field of global environmental politics and policy, social movements, research, and theory. In the course of her career, Rogers has served in many roles, including executive, board member, and teacher. She led the European campus for Thunderbird School of Global Management in Geneva, Switzerland for a decade, working with international organizations such as the Red Cross, World Trade Organization, United Nations Development Program, and the European Union. She also developed externships for students at several companies, including Renault, Nestle, and EuroDisney (now Disneyland Paris). She holds doctorates in political science and history. In addition to many articles focused on organizational leadership in sustainability, Rogers currently serves on the Boards of Prescott College, the Master's in Sustainability Advisory Group for Northern Arizona University, the Toda Institute for Global Policy & Peace Research, First Nature Ranch, and the Public Dialogue Consortium. She has also worked in conservation as a leader with the Arboretum at Flagstaff and Grand Canyon Trust. She received both a Fulbright scholarship to Germany as well as a Presidential post-doctoral fellowship from the Humboldt Von Humboldt Foundation where she taught environmental politics and history at the University of Konstanz.

Made in the USA
Middletown, DE
01 July 2019